This is a lively and engaging introduction to the contentious topic of Nietzsche's political thought for all students of philosophy, political theory and the history of ideas. Keith Ansell-Pearson traces the development of Nietzsche's thinking on the fate of modern politics from his earliest writings, including the little known essay *The Greek State*, to the mature writings in which he advocates the aristocratic radicalism of 'great politics' in opposition to the 'petty' politics of European nationalism. All the key ideas in Nietzsche's philosophy are discussed, including the will to power, eternal return, and the overman. They are examined as part of Nietzsche's wider philosophy, and also situated in the context of modern political theory. The opening chapters consider how Nietzsche is to be read and deal directly with the question of Nietzsche's appropriation by the Nazis. Nietzsche's major works, *The birth of tragedy*, *Thus spoke Zarathustra*, and *The genealogy of morals* are analysed in detail, and their common themes unravelled. The book concludes with an assessment of Nietzsche's enduring relevance and of the insights afforded by contemporary liberal and feminist readings of his work.

AN INTRODUCTION TO NIETZSCHE
AS POLITICAL THINKER

AN INTRODUCTION TO NIETZSCHE AS POLITICAL THINKER

The perfect nihilist

KEITH ANSELL-PEARSON

Lecturer in Modern European Philosophy, University of Warwick

CAMBRIDGE
UNIVERSITY PRESS

Published by the Press Syndicate of the University of Cambridge
The Pitt Building, Trumpington Street, Cambridge CB2 1RP
40 West 20th Street, New York, NY 10011–4211, USA
10 Stamford Road, Oakleigh, Melbourne 3166, Australia

© Cambridge University Press 1994

First published 1994
Reprinted 1994

Printed in Great Britain by Athenæum Press Ltd, Gateshead, Tyne & Wear.

A catalogue record for this book is available from the British Library

Library of Congress cataloguing in publication data

Ansell-Pearson, Keith, 1960–
An introduction to Nietzsche as political thinker: the perfect
nihilist / Keith Ansell-Pearson.
p. cm.
Includes bibliographical references.
ISBN 0-521-41722-8 (hardback) ISBN 0-521-42721-5 (paperback)
1. Nietzsche, Friedrich Wilhelm, 1844–1900 – Contributions in
political science. 2. Nihilism. I. Title.
JC233.N52A56 1994
320′.01 – dc20 93-5504CIP

ISBN 0 521 41722 8 hardback
ISBN 0 521 42721 5 paperback

I must write, I can't write, I'll write
Lento! my brothers and sisters, Lento!

The noble human being does not sin, the profound poet wants to tell us: though every law, every natural order, even the moral world may perish through his actions, his actions also produce a higher magical circle of effects which found a new world on the ruins of the old one which has been overthrown.

Nietzsche, The Birth of Tragedy (1872)

> Seduced by my kind and style,
> you follow and travel after me?
> Go after your own self faithfully –
> and thus you follow me – slowly! slowly!
>
> Nietzsche, 'Joke, Cunning, and Revenge', from The Gay Science (1882)

Truly speaking, it is not instruction, but provocation, that I can receive from another soul. What he announces, I must find true in me, or reject; and on his word, or as his second, be he who he may, I can accept nothing.

Ralph Waldo Emerson, 'Divinity School Address' (1838)

It is to be understood that war is the common condition, that strife is justice, and that all things come to pass through the compulsion of strife.

Heraclitus

If by keeping the old warm one can provide understanding of the new, one is fit to be a teacher.

Confucius

Contents

Acknowledgements

For inspiration and friendship, heartfelt thanks to Daniel Conway, and David Owen. Thanks to Judith Ayling and Catherine Max at Cambridge University Press for the support and encouragement they offered during the writing of this book, and to Gillian Maude for her inimitable copy-editing. Stephen Houlgate read several drafts of the book and I'm grateful to him for the severity with which he took it to task.

I am grateful to the Economic and Social Research Council for a research grant which enabled me to pursue my studies, including work on this book, at the University of Augsburg in the summer of 1992. For their hospitality on this trip, I wish to thank Günter and Doris Rieger, Susanne Schuster, Alexander Thumfart, and Professor Dr Theo Stammen. I owe a special debt of gratitude to Wilhelm Hofmann, who was truly a gift-giving host.

In chapter six I develop a reading of the *Genealogy of Morals*, which draws on material I first wrote for the editor's Introduction to the new Cambridge University Press edition of that work published in the series 'Texts in the History of Political Thought'. My exposition of the *Genealogy* has benefited from astute comments made by Raymond Geuss during the time the new edition was in preparation. Chapter nine has appeared in slightly different form as an essay in Paul Patton's edited collection, *Nietzsche, Feminism, and Political Theory* (London: Routledge, 1993), and I am grateful to him and to Routledge for giving me permission to use the material here. This material has also benefited from comments made by Christine Battersby, which proved invaluable.

The book is dedicated to the *promise of friendship*.

Notes on the texts and abbreviations

Where I have cited from Nietzsche's writings the references in all cases have been given immediately in the text and not in the notes. References are to sections, not page numbers, unless stated otherwise. I have adopted the practice of slightly modifying the translations for the sake of uniformity or accuracy without explicitly stating so. I have employed the following abbreviations.

AC   *The Anti-Christ*, trans. R. J. Hollingdale, Middlesex, Penguin, 1968.

BGE   *Beyond Good and Evil*, trans. W. Kaufmann, New York, Random House, 1966.

BT   *The Birth of Tragedy*, trans. W. Kaufmann, New York, Random House, 1967.

CW   *The Case of Wagner*, trans. W. Kaufmann, New York, Random House, 1967.

D   *Daybreak*, trans. R. J. Hollingdale, Cambridge, Cambridge University Press, 1982.

DS   *David Strauss, the Confessor and the Writer*, trans. R. J. Hollingdale in *Untimely Meditations (UM)*, Cambridge, Cambridge University Press, 1983.

EH   *Ecce Homo*, trans. R. J. Hollingdale and W. Kaufmann, New York, Random House, 1967.

GS   *The Gay Science*, trans. W. Kaufmann, New York, Random House, 1974.

GSt   *The Greek State*, in volume two of *The Complete Works of Friedrich Nietzsche*, ed. O. Levy, trans. M. A. Mügge, London, T. A. Foulis, 1911.

GW	*The Greek Woman*, in Levy edition, above.
HAH	*Human, All Too Human*, trans. R. J. Hollingdale, Cambridge, Cambridge University Press, 1986.
HC	*Homer's Contest*, in Levy edition above.
HL	*Uses and Disadvantages of History for Life*, trans. R. J. Hollingdale, *UM*, Cambridge, Cambridge University Press, 1983.
KSA	*Friedrich Nietzsche. Sämtliche Werke: Kritische Studienausgabe*, ed. G. Colli and M. Montinari, Berlin/New York, Walter de Gruyter and Deutschertaschenbuchverlag, 1967–77 and 1988.
OGM	*On the Genealogy of Morals*, trans. R. J. Hollingdale and W. Kaufmann, New York, Random House, 1967.
RWB	*Richard Wagner in Bayreuth*, trans. R. J. Hollingdale, *UM*, Cambridge, Cambridge University Press, 1983.
SE	*Schopenhauer as Educator*, trans. R. J. Hollingdale, *UM*, Cambridge, Cambridge University Press, 1983.
TI	*Twilight of the Idols*, trans. R. J. Hollingdale, Middlesex, Penguin, 1968.
WP	*The Will To Power*, trans. W. Kaufmann and R. J. Hollingdale, New York, Random House, 1967.
WS	*The Wanderer and his Shadow*, trans. R. J. Hollingdale, Cambridge, Cambridge University Press, 1986.
Z	*Thus Spoke Zarathustra*, trans. R. J. Hollingdale, Middlesex, Penguin, 1969.

Chronology of Nietzsche's life

1844	15 October: Nietzsche born in Röcken, a Prussian province of Saxony southwest of Leipzig, the son of pastor Karl Ludwig Nietzsche.
1849	30 July: Death of father.
1858	Nietzsche enters the Gymnasium Schulpforta near Naumburg, Germany's renowned Protestant boarding-school.
1864	October: Nietzsche enters the University of Bonn as a student of theology and classical philology.
1865	October: Nietzsche follows his philology lecturer at Bonn, F. W. Ritschl, to Leipzig as a student. He comes across the work of Schopenhauer in a Leipzig secondhand bookshop. Announces to his friends that he is a 'Schopenhauerean'.
1868	8 November: Nietzsche has his first meeting with Richard Wagner in Leipzig.
1869	February: On the recommendation of Ritschl, Nietzsche, who had not yet completed his doctorate, is appointed Extraordinary Professor of Classical Philology at the University of Basle.
	17 May: Nietzsche's first visit to Wagner and Cosima (von Bülow) at Tribschen.
	28 May: Inaugural lecture at Basle on 'Homer and Classical Philology'.

1870	August: Nietzsche volunteers as a nursing orderly in the Franco-Prussian War, but owing to illness returns to Basle after two months.
1871	January: Unsuccessfully applies for the Chair of Philosophy at University of Basle.
	On sick-leave in the Swiss Alps. Becoming increasingly disaffected with his profession as a classical philologist.
	From this year on Nietzsche will be engaged in a constant battle with ill health.
1872	January: Publication of first book, *The Birth of Tragedy Out of the Spirit of Music* (originally entitled 'On Greek Cheerfulness').
	February–March: Lectures to the public in Basle on 'The Future of Our Educational Institutions'.
	22 May: Nietzsche accompanies Wagner on the occasion of the latter's fifty-ninth birthday to the laying of the foundation-stone of the Bayreuth theatre.
1873–1875	*Untimely Meditations.*
1876	August: First Bayreuth festival. Beginnings of estrangement from Wagner.
	September: Leaves Bayreuth in the company of Paul Rée.
	October: The University of Basle grants Nietzsche one year's sick-leave on account of his illness.
1878	First part of *Human, All Too Human* (dedicated to Voltaire).
	3 January: Wagner sends Nietzsche a copy of the recently published text of *Parsifal*.
	May: Nietzsche writes his last letter to Wagner and encloses a copy of *Human, All Too Human: A Book for Free Spirits*. End of friendship with Wagner.
1879	Volume Two, Part one of *Human, All Too Human: Assorted Opinions and Maxims*.

Nietzsche is forced to resign from his Chair at Basle due to ill health.

For the next ten years he leads the life of a solitary wanderer living in hotel rooms and lodgings.

1880   Volume Two, Part two of *Human, All Too Human: The Wanderer and his Shadow.*

1881   *Daybreak. Thoughts on the Prejudices of Morality.*

First Summer in Sils-Maria in the Upper Engadine where he experiences the abysmal thought of the eternal recurrence of the same.

1882   *The Gay Science* (also known as *The Joyful Wisdom*). In aphorism 125 a madman announces the 'death of God'.

March: Paul Rée leaves Nietzsche in Genoa for Rome where he meets Lou Salomé and falls in love with her.

April: Nietzsche goes to Rome and meets Lou Salomé. Within a few days Nietzsche proposes marriage, first via Rée and then in person. Although he is turned down, he is content with the promise of an intellectual *ménage à trois* made up of himself, Rée, and Salomé.

By the end of the year Nietzsche has broken with Rée and Salomé, and feels betrayed by both.

1883   Writes first and second parts of *Thus Spoke Zarathustra: A Book for all and none.*

13 February: Death of Wagner.

1884   Third part of *Zarathustra*, written in Nice.

1885   Publishes fourth and final part of *Zarathustra* in a limited, private edition.

1886   *Beyond Good and Evil. A Prelude to a Philosophy of the Future.*

1887   Discovers Dostoyevsky, chancing on a French translation of *Notes from the Underground.*

10 November: *On the Genealogy of Morals: A Polemic.*

1888	May–August: *The Case of Wagner*; finishes *Dithyrambs of Dionysus* (published 1891). September: *The Anti-Christ* (published 1894). October–November: Composes *Ecce Homo* (publication delayed by Elisabeth Förster-Nietzsche until 1908). December: *Nietzsche contra Wagner* (published 1895).
1889	*Twilight of the Idols* (original title 'The Idleness of A Psychologist'). 3 January: Nietzsche breaks down in the Piazza Carlo in Turin and throws his arms round an old carthorse that is being beaten by its owner. 18 January: Admitted as a mental patient to the psychiatric clinic of the University of Jena. Doctors diagnose 'progressive paralysis'.
1890	Nietzsche's mother takes her son to the family home in Naumburg.
1897	20 April: Death of mother. Nietzsche taken by his sister from Naumburg to Weimar, where she had moved the Nietzsche-Archive in 1894. The morbid Nietzsche-cult begins.
1900	25 August: Nietzsche dies in Weimar. Buried in Röcken next to his father.
1901	Out of the *Nachlass* of the 1880s 500 fragments are published under the title of *The Will to Power*. In 1906 a second edition appears as a series of 1,067 fragments.

Introduction

> Speaking directly, the ultimate possible attitudes toward
> life are irreconcilable, and hence their struggle can never
> be brought to a final conclusion. Thus it is necessary to
> make a decisive choice.
>
> Max Weber, 'Science as a Vocation' (1919)

Nietzsche is an ambiguous and paradoxical thinker whose writings never cease to disturb, provoke, and inspire, even when they challenge one's innermost convictions. He has been a key figure on the intellectual and cultural landscape for over a hundred years, and his thought has to be reckoned with. As Martin Heidegger once put it, everyone who thinks today does so in Nietzsche's light and shadow, whether they are 'for' him or 'against' him. He is important because he was, first and foremost, a philosopher of *life*, not because he is now academically respectable and has all the dubious status of a 'modern master'. Nietzsche's writing deals with the most important questions about what it means to be a human being (he defines man as the *questioning* animal). For Nietzsche, however, this existential questioning about human identity cannot be separated from an understanding of history (especially of morality), of culture, and of politics.

For most of this century Nietzsche's political thought has been a source of confusion and embarrassment. The consensus which held sway for several decades from the end of the Second World War until quite recently, was that Nietzsche was not a political thinker at all, but someone who was mainly concerned with the fate of the solitary, isolated individual far removed from the cares and concerns of the social world. This view was typical of those, such as the renowned Nietzsche translator and biographer, Walter Kaufmann, who tried to rescue Nietzsche's writings from the abuse they had suffered at the hands of Nazi ideologists and propagandists. However, the result was a dehistoricised and depoliticised interpretation which put a closure on a key aspect of Nietzsche's philosophy: his political thinking. Recent years have seen the publication of a number of major studies on the topic of Nietzsche's political thought. As a result, the centrality of Nietzsche to the concerns of human beings living in late modernity, and trying to grapple with the political dilemmas of their existence, is now widely recognised. It remains the case, however, that his overt political thought continues to embarrass some and confuse many. Inquiry into the political dimension of Nietzsche's thought still remains the most contentious and controversial aspect of Nietzsche-studies.

Nietzsche is a thinker preoccupied with the fate of politics in the modern world. One has only to take a glance at his wide-ranging concerns – from his early reflections on the Greek *agon* to his attempt to write a genealogy of morality and his diagnosis of nihilism to characterise the moral malaise and sickness of modern human beings – to realise that Nietzsche is a 'political' thinker first and foremost. I am convinced that there is need for a much more sensitive approach to the topic than has hitherto been adopted.

Nietzsche's political thought is often dismissed and ignored because it fails to conform to liberal and democratic sentiments which have prevailed over the last two hundred years. The moralistic way in which Nietzsche's political thought has been treated hitherto polarises the debate between moral decency (the good liberal) and immoral or amoral power (the bad elitist – Nietzsche). Informing a great deal of the appreciation of Nietzsche is the illiberal supposition that the only way he can speak to us today is on our terms or not at all. We may want to reject Nietzsche's political thinking, deeming its solution to the immense problems facing modern human beings to be inadequate, but that should not mean that we can find no instruction in his work. As in life, so in Nietzsche's work we find both great danger and great promise. Nietzsche himself shows us this.

In the first two chapters, dealing respectively with the question of 'style' in Nietzsche and the issue of his legacy, I offer a general introduction to Nietzsche in which all the salient features of his thought are touched on. Chapters three to seven cover Nietzsche's intellectual trajectory, and show what is of political import in his various writings and principal texts, beginning with his early reflections on the ancient Greeks and closing with his notion of 'great politics'. The next two chapters, chapters eight and nine, look at how Nietzsche's ideas have been appropriated in recent political thought, focusing on issues within contemporary liberalism and feminism. In the final chapter, chapter ten, I offer my personal view of how we ought to take up Nietzsche's legacy and appropriate his thought today. In sum, I offer a picture of Nietzsche as 'the perfect nihilist'.

Every reading of Nietzsche is both a deconstruction and a reconstruction, conditioned by history, time, and place. This book is no exception. It has no pretensions of presenting a definitive and exhaustive treatment of the subject or the topic. Writing on Nietzsche, and interpreting the meaning and significance of his work, is a problematic, if not perilous, exercise. The important thing, I think, is to ensure that the *question of Nietzsche* – of who he is and of who we are to become in reading him – is kept open.

Nowhere in his writings does Nietzsche ever present a systematic account of his political thinking. This is not surprising since his deepest intellectual instincts were 'anti-system'. Nevertheless, his thinking is dominated by two interrelated themes. These are the problems of culture and of history.

From first to last Nietzsche is concerned with what he regards as a permanent conflict between culture and politics: what are the goals of art and culture? Should the organisation of society serve the ends of politics (justice) or those of culture? Which type of polity is best able to promote 'culture' (that is, the cultivation of greatness and true human beings)? Nietzsche's political thinking is based on a complex, and unusual, justification of economic relationships of exploitation and domination (at one point he even defines 'morals' as 'the doctrine of the relations of domination (*Herrschaft*) under which the phenomenon of "life" comes to be', *BGE* 19). Nietzsche believes that the production of human greatness requires that society be established along the lines of a hierarchical social structure (an order of rank – *Rangordnung*). Some form of slavery is, for him, necessary for the creation of culture to take place. In *Beyond Good and Evil* he argues that the creation of ever higher, more complex, and hybrid human types requires there to be distances between human beings, distances which can only be created through certain kinds of social structures and economic relationships. An ever new widening of distances within the soul, making possible the attainment of rarer and higher, more comprehensive, states of being, can only be cultivated through certain social arrangements and a particular form of politics (*BGE* 257). Nietzsche is fully aware of the legitimacy of the demands of politics, but argues, in what he considers to be a 'hard truth', that the cry of compassion cannot be allowed to tear down the walls of culture.

Nietzsche's thinking on the problem of history begins with his first published book *The Birth of Tragedy* in 1872. The problem which preoccupies him is that of how we are to interpret the suffering, pain, cruelty, and horror which characterise world-history. Is it possible to provide history with any meaning and significance? Nietzsche's answer is that we cannot allow ourselves the comfort of a teleological view, of either human history or the universe, which would give them a final goal and purpose. Suffering, cruelty, pain, and 'sin' (sacrilege) are ineradicable features of human existence. What matters is how we comprehend them. Nietzsche urges us to fight for the rebirth of a tragic culture since it is only such a culture which is able to create a space (a *polis*) for the disclosure of human being in all its variegated nature. However, the most important medium for the disclosure of the 'truth' of human being, according to Nietzsche, is not politics, but art. He believed that it is through an appreciation of tragic art that the individual can attain a standpoint *beyond* his narrow personal existence and achieve Dionysian insight. It is art, for Nietzsche, which not only affords us the deepest insights into the human condition, but which also enables human beings to give meaning and significance to the terror and absurdity of existence (art *as* truth). A society established on absolute moral values of good and evil is unable to comprehend the 'general economy of the whole'. Moreover, a society based largely on instrumental and utilitarian values, and determined by power-politics and driven by a 'money-economy', such as Nietzsche found in the modern German state, is incapable of arriving at a proper conception of culture. It is important to appreciate that the 'art' Nietzsche speaks of and esteems is *public* art, that is, art such as Greek tragic drama, which gathers together a people or community and discloses to them the 'truth' of their existence. One could say, therefore, that in this sense the experience afforded by art *is* political. Much depends on how we conceive the word 'political'.

It is often argued that Nietzsche's 'aestheticism' (captured in his formulation that it is only as an aesthetic phenomenon that life and existence can be justified) is inadequate to deal with the problems life calls upon human beings to solve. In the face of the apparent moral nihilism of Nietzsche's so-called 'aestheticism' (by which is meant an attempt to extend the category of the aesthetic to all spheres of life) many find it necessary to advocate an explicit moral (and moralistic) standpoint of good and evil. However, a simple opposition between art and morality cannot be attributed to Nietzsche. Neither is the charge of 'aestheticism' wholly applicable to his thinking. This, I believe, is to misunderstand his thinking on art and morality. As I argue in this book, for Nietzsche we need art not to make us immoral, or to take us beyond the sphere of the ethical, but to enable us to carry on being moral in the face of our recognition of the terror and absurdity of existence. Writing in the context of the emergence of Bismarck's German *Reich*, Nietzsche is severely critical of 'politics' (by which he means *Machtpolitik*) as a way of addressing, or solving, the problem of human existence (*SE* 4). From his early to his last writings Nietzsche's thought is characterised by an opposition between 'Geist' (spirit) and 'Reich'. What humanity needs is not a violent political revolution, but changes in education and in its ways of thinking. It needs to ground 'spirit' in a conception of 'culture'.

In many respects Nietzsche's critique of modern politics has much in common with the political thinking of Alexis de Tocqueville (1805–59) and John Stuart Mill (1806–73). Like Tocqueville, for example, Nietzsche sees hidden dangers in the new political realities opened up by the modern industrial world, modern democracy, and a money-economy. Modernity for both is characterised by social atomism, moral malaise, and the cultivation of private experience and private taste at the expense of public action. This creates a political culture that is lacking in vigour. The danger of this degeneration of politics, in which politics is dominated by the class interests of the modern money-economy and by the instrumental rationality of modern technology, is that it can lead to a situation in which people lose political control over their own destinies and become politically apathetic. At this point the 'state' – the 'cold monster', as Nietzsche liked to refer to it – begins to dominate political life and to cultivate the tyranny of the majority ('public opinion') at the expense of individual liberty and genuine public action (this menace, also clearly seen by Mill, is what Tocqueville referred to as 'soft despotism').

Like Tocqueville, Nietzsche gave a pejorative flavour to liberal individualism. Both saw modern individualism as resulting in a self-centred preoccupation with purely personal ends. For Nietzsche, the danger is that society will lose sight of the importance of culture and allow philistinism to take over. Society becomes made up of a herd of 'last men and women' who are concerned only with 'happiness' (understood in the sense of the satisfaction of material desires) and who cannot conceive of anything higher or nobler beyond (*über*) themselves. These people no longer wish to cultivate themselves, to engage in risks and experiments, but seek only a dull and safe 'bourgeois' existence. As Nietzsche saw things, somewhat presciently, the problem of German society was that it was becoming dominated by purely power-political interests (*Machtpolitik*), and, in its struggle for national identity through statist and militarist policies, would experience the end of culture, making itself ripe for the flourishing of a crude and aggressive nationalism. Throughout his life Nietzsche (the philosopher of will to power!) opposed the principles and aims of *Machtpolitik*. For him an adequate conception of politics is one which sees it as a means to an end; the production of culture and human greatness. Once our conception of politics becomes dominated by the concerns of material power, then, according to Nietzsche, we are unable to provide human social existence with any spiritual or cultural justification. With the notion of the *Übermensch* Nietzsche tries to envisage a human type which is spiritually higher and nobler than the kind of narrow egoism and materialism which he, like Tocqueville, saw as prevailing in modern societies. The revolution that Nietzsche sought was not a political revolution, but an educational and cultural one. He makes this clear in his writings from first to last. How the writings of this most spiritual of thinkers could be employed in the service of German material and military power (the total opposite of what he had in mind) is something I shall examine in chapter two of this book.

What sets Nietzsche apart, however, from the likes of Mill and Tocqueville, is the depth of his insights into the modern moral and spiritual malaise. For Nietzsche, the problem is not just a social or political one which can be solved simply by refining and improving liberal–democratic institutions and practices. He sees Western civilisation caught in the grip of debilitating and demoralising nihilism in which our most fundamental conceptions of the world are no longer tenable and believable. Nihilism is thus a condition which affects the metaphysical and moral languages through which we fabricate an understanding of the world and on which we base our acting in the world. Nietzsche gives examples of concepts such as 'aim', 'unity', 'purpose', 'truth' itself, 'pity', 'justice', and so on, to illustrate the depth of the crisis as he sees it. All of these concepts he believes are in need of a comprehensive self-examination. If God is dead, and if we have lost the traditional metaphysical–moral structure which enabled us to make sense of existence, to give it a meaning and a purpose, how is it possible for us now to interpret the world and to give meaning to our lives? How can we endure such an experience and overcome it? For Nietzsche the event of nihilism affords us the opportunity of rethinking the aims and goals of social existence (of politics): why does society exist? What purposes should it serve? How should it be organised and for what ends? Today it remains as necessary as ever to think through the problem of nihilism and perform Nietzsche's demand for a revaluation of all our values.

There are no easy answers in life, only difficult choices. To comprehend the weight of these choices it is necessary to pose the right kind of questions. This is what Nietzsche helps us to do. We err if we approach his work from some undeserved height of moral superiority. Labelling a thinker of his greatness a 'Fascist' on account of his confusions and excesses – and ignoring his nobility of mind and character, as well as the appositeness of a great deal of his *political* thought – is not a sign of insight, but of moral laziness and intellectual stupidity. We not only do Nietzsche a great disservice in this respect, but ourselves too.

A note on Nietzsche and liberalism

Nietzsche is widely considered to be a thinker who upholds the value of the individual self-realisation against political structures, making his thought compatible with a liberal individualism. However, as this study will seek to show, Nietzsche's thought cannot be assimilated so easily to the political philosophy of liberalism. I will, therefore, identify at the outset the points on which he departs from liberalism.

As a doctrine, and body of thought, 'liberalism' is the product of several centuries of development. Its meaning cannot be encompassed in a single definition. In the *International Encyclopaedia of the Social Sciences* (ed. David L. Sills, Macmillan, 1968, IX, pp. 276–82), some of the central tenets of philosophical liberalism are listed as follows:

1 It values the free expression of individual personality.
2 It believes that human beings have the ability to make that expression valuable to themselves and to society.
3 It upholds those institutions and policies that protect and further free expression and its tolerance.

Liberalism has two primary themes: a dislike of arbitrary authority, and the free expression of individual personality. The term 'liberal' first acquired its modern political connotations from a Spanish party known as the 'Liberales' who supported a version of the French constitution of 1791. However, as a coherent system of political ideals, liberalism originated in England in the seventeenth and eighteenth centuries. Its chief ideals included religious liberties and toleration, constitution-

9

alism (rule of law, separation of powers), and political rights. In Germany there developed two main, and conflicting, schools of liberal thought. The first, derived from Locke, and found in the writings of the educationalist and humanist Karl Wilhelm von Humboldt (1767–1835), sought a constitutional government and a minimal state, and saw the aim of society as one of providing mutual security. The second tradition was statist and wanted the freedom of Germany as a national unity. The German national liberals thought in terms of collective rights rather than individual rights.

Nietzsche's critique of liberalism developed over a period of years, and has three main aspects to it:

(a) that the noble ideals of European liberalism – largely, of creative personality – have been corrupted by nationalism;

(b) that when viewed historically the development of philosophical liberalism has to be seen as inseparable from economic liberalism (*laissez-faire* capitalism). The effect for Nietzsche of the domination of the polity by a money-economy is that the basis for a strong communal, ethical life is undermined, and culture is overtaken by philistinism. The expression, and realisation, of true individuality becomes almost impossible in the modern world. For Nietzsche liberalism emancipates the 'private person' (of bourgeois society), but not the 'true individual'. It lacks a conception of culture;

(c) that liberalism rests on an abstract and ahistorical conception of the individual self and its realisation. What is needed is an examination of the historical and psychological evolution of human agency (which is what he attempts in a *Genealogy of Morals*) in order to demonstrate the existence of different human types and different moralities.

The 'freedom of the individual' (understood as the 'private person') which characterises modernity is an ambiguous achievement, in that, while modern individuals are no longer constrained by hierarchical social ties or religious bonds, the responsibility is entirely upon each individual to create themselves and their own laws (*BGE* 262). The foundations of social relationships have now to be constituted along the lines of the integrity of these 'sovereign individuals', not on the basis of any absolute moral or religious values. For Nietzsche, however, the modern polity lacks a conception of culture and, therefore, an adequate and proper conception of politics. The modern state engages in a 'power-politics', and finds itself dominated by nationalist and militarist concerns and ambitions. It fails to see that politics is simply a means to an end, that of the production of true or great human beings and the perpetual self-overcoming of 'man'.

Nietzsche's individualism is best understood, therefore, as an aristocratic, not a liberal, individualism. As he himself tells us, his philosophy 'aims at an ordering of rank, not an individualistic morality' (*WP* 287). His thinking departs from liberalism in a number of key respects. Unlike liberalism, Nietzsche does not hold that the individual person is inviolable and human life sacrosanct. His thinking on 'man' is anti-humanist (where humanism is taken to mean placing man at the centre of the universe and interpreting its value from a human/moral perspective). *Contra* modern liberalism and feminism, which he sees as leading to a sentimentalist politics, Nietzsche promotes the values and virtues of the *warrior*. And, unlike liberalism, Nietzsche does not base his noble ethical code on a commitment to a notion of equal respect for all persons regarded as moral beings possessing equal sensitivity (these definitions of liberalism are taken from Barbara Goodwin, *Using Political Ideas*, Chichester, John Wiley, 1992, third edition, p. 37). Nietzsche's political thinking challenges the basic sentiments and deepest convictions of liberal societies. For Nietzsche, individuals can only attain 'value' by placing themselves in the service of culture (which for him means the cultivation of great or true human beings), and by representing, in some sense, the ascending forces of 'life'. Perhaps the clearest expression of his view is to be found in a section entitled 'The natural value of egoism' in *Twilight of the Idols*. Here Nietzsche states quite clearly that he regards 'the individual', the 'single one' (*Einzelne*), believed in by people and posited by philosophers, to be an error. He is nothing by himself, not an atom, neither a link in the chain nor something merely inherited from the past. Rather, says Nietzsche, he must be conceived as 'the entire *single* line "man" up to and including himself'.

PART I

The question of Nietzsche

CHAPTER I

A question of style?
An introduction to reading Nietzsche

> The first rule, indeed by itself virtually a sufficient
> condition for good style, is *to have something to say.*
>
> Schopenhauer, *Parerga and Paralipomena* (1851)

In understanding Nietzsche, the *way* in which he writes and
expresses himself (his style) is just as important as paying attention to *what* (the content) he says. This fact raises tremendous
difficulties of interpretation, especially when taking into account
Nietzsche's conception of truth. Here I can only touch on the
complex role a notion of truth plays in Nietzsche's writings,
indicating how it is bound up with his concern with style.[1]

Nietzsche rejected a correspondence theory of truth – the
view that our concepts and judgements give us unalloyed access
to 'reality' – in favour of Kant's view that we impose categories
upon the world in order to make our experience of it intelligible
and calculable. Nietzsche was concerned to reject the claims of
the school of thought known as 'positivism', which holds that
we have access to the facts about the world through sensory
experience and empirical observation. But, for him categories
such as 'cause' and 'effect', 'subject' and 'object', and notions
such as 'rule of law', 'freedom', and 'motive' are to be
understood as 'conventional fictions for the purpose of des-
ignation and communication – *not* for explanation' (*BGE* 21).
The development of human knowledge has to be understood as
the result of a will to power by which the human species
increases its control and mastery over the external world:

Knowledge works as a tool of power... The meaning of 'knowledge':
here, as in the case of 'good' or 'beautiful', the concept is to be re-

garded in a strict and narrow anthropocentric and biological sense. In order for a particular species to maintain itself and increase its power, its conception of reality must comprehend enough of the calculable and constant for it to base a scheme of behaviour on it ... In other words: the measure of the desire for knowledge depends upon the measure to which the will to power grows in a species: a species grasps a certain amount of reality in order to become master of it. (*WP* 480)

The question Nietzsche invites us to consider is to what extent axioms of logic are adequate to reality, or are they simply a means by which we *create* reality (including the concept of 'reality' itself) (*WP* 516). Truth, he holds, is not something to be 'found' or 'discovered', but something 'that must be created and that gives name to a process'; introducing truth, he says, as 'an active determining – not a becoming conscious of something that is in itself firm and determined. It is a word for the "will to power"' (*WP* 552). In response to Kant's epistemological inquiry, 'how are synthetic *a priori* judgements possible?', Nietzsche asks the psychological question, 'why is it necessary for us to believe in such judgements?' (*BGE* 9). His answer is that there is a human need to believe in such judgements, not because they are in fact 'true', but because they increase our feeling of power in the world. A judgement about the world can be false, Nietzsche argues, and nevertheless still be 'life-promoting' and 'species-preserving' (*BGE* 4). What should interest us most, he argues, is not whether our interpretations of the world are 'true' or 'false' (this we can never absolutely know), but whether they cultivate the will to power in the direction of control and strength, or of chaos and weakness. Nietzsche applies the same perspective to moral values and moral judgements. Our analysis of these, he says, should not focus on their putative 'truth-claims', but on the question of whether they reflect rich, strong, and abundant forms of life, or weak, exhausted, and degenerating ones. To think about judgements in this way is to think in terms of a radical 'perspectivism' and from a standpoint that is 'beyond good and evil', for such a mode of thinking recognises the conditionality of human forms of knowledge and is not concerned with absolutes, moral or otherwise.

Nietzsche applies this critique of the unconditional and absolute 'will to truth' (the view that human concepts and categories provide uncomplicated access to reality as it is in-itself) to the notion of the 'subject'. Descartes, for example, sought to establish the grounds of certain truths and knowledge with a notion of the human subject ('"I" think, therefore I am', *ego cogito*, *ergo sum*), conceived as a structure of self-reflection. Nietzsche, however, argues that the existence of this 'subject' is mythological since the existence of the 'I' is simply taken for granted. Because of our faith in grammatical categories, which leads us always to posit the relationship between 'man' and the 'world' in terms of a 'subject' and an 'object', we view the human ego in terms of a substance or cause of all our actions in the world, as the doer of all our deeds. As Nietzsche says, we will not get rid of God so long as we retain a belief in grammar (*TI* 'Reason in Philosophy' 5). Our belief in things, in substance, and in being is the result of grammatical prejudices. Our reliance on nouns and verbs, for example, enables us to master and break down a complex reality, to speak of a 'self' (an ego) which is separate from its actions and to construe entities as fixed and stable. Through the reification of language we forget that 'reality' is made up of processes, and is characterised by constant movement and ceaseless change.

What we call the 'will' is part of the same mythology concealed in language. Nietzsche writes concerning the *naïveté* of 'reason':

> this which believes in will as cause in general; this which believes in the 'ego', in the ego as being, in the ego as substance, and which *projects* its belief in the ego-substance on to all things – only thus does it *create* the concept 'thing'... Being is everywhere thought in, *foisted on*, as cause; it is only from the conception 'ego' that there follows, derivatively, the concept 'being'... At the beginning stands the great fateful error that the will is something which *produces an effect* – that will is a *faculty*... Today we know it is merely a word. (ibid.)

Even though Nietzsche posits the 'will to power' as 'reality', as what the world would be if it could be viewed from inside (*BGE* 36), this does not commit him to believing in the metaphysical existence of a human 'will'. Nietzsche holds, in fact, the radical view that notions of free will, of the subject and the 'soul', are fictions which have been invented by weak and oppressed human groups at various points in history in order to give a sense of substantiality to their lives, as well as an imaginary freedom. Through the invention of a free willing subject the weak could hold the strong responsible for their actions and make them feel guilty about their strength (you are evil to be strong) and, at the same time, glorify their own lack of strength as a condition of inner freedom. One of the results of this process of the invention of the free human subject which acts intentionally is the creation of a moral universe in which notions of blame, guilt, and responsibility predominate our understanding of action in the world. For Nietzsche, by contrast, the most authentic action is that which takes place unconsciously from a free-flowing, abundant health and strength. The appearance of 'consciousness' in the human animal is to be regarded as a sign of decline, not necessarily progression (see *GS* 354). In *The Birth of Tragedy* Nietzsche argues that in the productive human being instinct is a 'creative–affirmative force' while consciousness acts critically and dissuasively; but in the decadent human type instinct itself becomes the critic (*BT* 13). 'To *have* to combat one's instincts', he writes, 'that is the formula for *decadence*: as long as life is *ascending*, happiness and instinct are one' (*TI* 'The Problem of Socrates' 11).

There are two main problems with Nietzsche's radically subversive views on truth and knowledge. Firstly, if we have no access to a reality independent of our categories, and if we can never know what is 'true' and what is 'false' in any real (as opposed to 'symptomatic') sense, how is it possible for Nietzsche to claim that reality *is* 'will to power'? Secondly, how can he avoid the problem of relativism? One of the problems facing Nietzsche's doctrine of perspectivism is that the interpretative pluralism it seems to be promoting – the view which holds that there is no single truth about the world, but only different interpretations which serve the need of ascending and descending forms of life – can easily degenerate into a theoretical anarchism in which all claims to truth are taken to be nothing more than expressions of an assertive will to power possessing equal validity. Unfortunately, an analysis of these problems would take me much further than it is possible to go here, so I simply draw the reader's attention to them. While I see no adequate solution in Nietzsche's writings to the second problem, he does respond to the first one by explicitly declaring the perspectival character of his own view of the world as will to power. If one were to object to Nietzsche's position by pointing out that it, too, is 'only an interpretation', his response would be to say 'so much the better!' (*BGE* 22). Nietzsche's preoccupation with style is an essential part of his perspectival theory of truth and knowledge.

In the preface to the second edition of *The Gay Science* (1887) Nietzsche speaks of philosophy in terms of an 'art of trans-figuration'. In this preface Nietzsche speaks as a 'convalescent'. The goal of life, he suggests, is to transform sickness into good health. The only way in which we can ultimately overcome sickness is by affirming the necessity of pain and suffering as essential ingredients of life. For Nietzsche, philosophy is 'maternal' in that it rests on a unity of body and soul. The work of every philosopher, he holds, represents an unconscious, involuntary memoir of their existence, of who they are (*D* Preface). The true philosopher, for Nietzsche, is one who recognises that his or her thoughts are born out of the pain of experience which, like the experience of giving birth, should be endowed with 'blood, heart, fire, pleasure, passion, agony, conscience, fate, and catastrophe'. 'Life' is about transforming everything that we are, including that which wounds and hurts us, 'into light and flame'. It is only the experience of great pain that affords us the deepest insights into the human lot. Nietzsche points out that this experience does not necessarily make us 'better' human beings, but only 'more profound' ones. From our 'abysses' and 'sicknesses' we are to 'return' to life 'newborn' (*GS* Preface).

Nietzsche described his work as a 'schooling' in suspicion, courage, and audacity. His thinking on life, he said, may be not only a consolation, but also a deception: but this, he suggests, is to speak 'unmorally, extra-morally, "beyond good and evil"'

(*HAH* Preface). His writings, he further confesses, are designed to inspire in people a desire to overturn and revalue all previous values (of good, of evil, of what is just and unjust, etc.). Nietzsche questions whether his experience of life – 'the history of an illness and a recovery' – is his personal experience alone, or whether it has a more universal significance (ibid., section 6). Nietzsche cannot answer this question himself. Towards the end of his sane life he begins to realise that it will be his fate to be 'born posthumously'. His philosophy of 'beyond good and evil' addresses itself to an unknown audience which resides in the future, a future he can only anticipate and prefigure. This is one of the meanings of the *Übermensch* (overman) in his work: those who come after 'man' are also those who will come *after* (in the sense also of 'over', 'across', and 'beyond') Nietzsche.

Nietzsche says that he speaks as a 'Doppelgänger' (*EH* 'Why I Am So Wise', section 1). It is his belief that for over two thousand years occidental humanity has lived under the spell of what he calls 'Christian-moral culture', which rests on a denigration of earthly, sensual, human existence. The product of this culture is man 'the sick animal'. Nietzsche recognises that he, too, is subject to this history and, as a result, is also a 'sick animal' deformed by his inheritance. He construes his personal fate as a philosopher in terms of both an end and a new beginning: a decadent and a newborn. In his autobiography, *Ecce Homo*, realising that his fate shall be a posthumous one, he bears testimony to himself and tells us 'who he is'. What he essentially is, is the 'disciple of the philosophy of Dionysus', a teaching he counterposes to the religion of Christianity (*EH* 'Foreword', section 2). He asks:

Have I been understood? What defines me, what sets me apart from all the rest of mankind is that I have *unmasked* Christian morality... Christian morality – the most malicious form of the will to the lie, the actual Circe of mankind: that which has *ruined* it... Contempt has been taught for the primary instincts of life: that a 'soul', a 'spirit' has been *lyingly invented* in order to destroy the body; that one teaches that there is something unclean in the precondition of life, sexuality; that the evil principle is sought in that which is most profoundly necessary for prosperity, in *strict* selfishness. (*EH* 'Why I Am A Destiny' 7)

He concludes:

The *unmasking* of Christian morality is an event (*ein Ereigniss*) without equal, a real catastrophe. He who exposes it is a *force majeure*, a destiny – he breaks the history of mankind into two parts. One lives *before* him, one lives *after* him. (ibid. 8)

If we know who Nietzsche is, we can decide for ourselves whether we come before him or after him, whether we are for or against him. The overriding aim of Nietzsche's philosophy is to promote autonomy in his readers. It cannot be without significance that he closes the foreword to *Ecce Homo* with an important passage from *Thus Spoke Zarathustra*. Zarathustra descends to humankind, after enduring ten years in solitude, to teach the meaning of God's death. However, what he seeks is neither followers nor disciples, but companions and fellow-creators:

You had not yet sought yourselves when you found me. Thus do all believers; therefore all belief is of so little account.

Now, I bid you lose me and find yourselves; and only *when you have all denied me* will I return to you.

Nietzsche himself believed that he was unreadable by modern human beings, and so he wrote primarily for a future, 'post-modern' (as in post-*man*) audience. In the preface to the *Genealogy of Morals*, for example, he states that what is required in order to read him effectively is for the reader to be 'skilled' in the 'art of interpretation'. What is needed to learn this art is something modern human beings lack, 'rumination'. Elsewhere Nietzsche had written that the worst readers are those who proceed like 'plundering soldiers', taking bits from here and from there. The way to read him attentively and critically is to follow the path of his thinking and understand the tasks he set for himself as a philosopher.

There are tremendous dangers in reading Nietzsche. One can seriously damage one's health in the process. It is also easy to misinterpret him and to read him out of context. Nietzsche laid particular emphasis on his view of the world that there are no 'facts in themselves', but 'only' interpretations of so-called facts (*BGE* 108). What I hope to achieve with this introduction is to give readers a desire to cultivate within themselves the 'art of interpretation' (in order to decipher not only the meaning of Nietzsche's life, but that of their own also), and to produce an interpretation of Nietzsche that is both instructive and provocative, one which is able to comprehend the weight of his challenge. Erich Heller has written that Nietzsche's example is so unique and terrifying that it cannot be imitated; and yet, it is so important it cannot be ignored either.[2]

CHAPTER 2

Nietzsche's legacy

There is no doubt that a 'thou shalt' still speaks to us too, that we too still obey a stern law set over us – and this is the last moral law which can still make itself audible to us ... we *men of conscience* who do not want to return to that which is outlived and decayed, to anything 'unworthy of belief', be it called God, virtue, truth, justice, charity; we do not permit ourselves any bridges-of-lies to ancient ideals; we are hostile to every kind of faith and Christianness existing today; hostile to all romanticism and fatherland-worship.

Nietzsche, 1886 Preface to *Daybreak*

NIETZSCHE AND THE FATE OF GERMAN POLITICS

As the German historian Golo Mann remarked, Bismarck's Germany was founded not on lofty principles of political philosophy, as was the case with the foundation of the American union, but on brutal pragmatism.[1] The foundation of the German Reich was not preceded by profound philosophical deliberations on the nature of man and society, but by wars, annexations, alliances, and a customs parliament set up by blackmail. Bismarck came to power by announcing that he was opposing the politics of 'speeches and resolutions' with a polity of 'iron and blood'.

Nietzsche wrote his books and espoused his Dionysian philosophy during the years of Bismarck's Germany. He was seventeen when Bismarck came to power, and he descended into madness a year before the Iron Chancellor was dismissed from office. His education at Schulpforta was a classical liberal one. The rector of the school was a strong supporter of the revival of liberalism, which he saw as combining the ideal of *Bildung* (denoting a personalised striving for inner growth) and cultural nationalism as formulated by Johann Gottfried Herder (1744–1803).[2] Nietzsche's teachers were classical liberals in the sense that they identified with the traditions of Weimar classicism and epitomised mid-century Prussian nationalism. Nietzsche was also formed by his revolt against his religious upbringing. An earlier generation could define their break with Pietism in terms of an heroic inner struggle. But with the universal retreat of Pietism in the 1850s and 1860s this was no longer possible. Like other mid-century rebels brought up in the Pietist tradition, such as Strindberg and Van Gogh, Nietzsche found it difficult to place his struggle with religion. Having witnessed the collapse of clerical authority in 1848 they came of age in a period of rapid de-Christianisation among Protestants. The failure of religious politics ensured that the crucial issue facing Nietzsche and his contemporaries was that of secularisation. One biographer notes, reflecting on the spiritual anxiety affecting Nietzsche's generation, 'Secularization threatened to leave them displaced and rootless, yet enticed them forward with the alternative of a post-religious identity as the first of the "new men"'.[3] Nietzsche's early development was characterised by a reorientation on both the political and religious fronts.

It was during Bismarck's rise to power, and the dramatic events of the 1860s, that Nietzsche came of age politically. His contemporaries considered themselves to be absolute beginners at the dawn of a new political and cultural era. In the early 1860s Nietzsche's political views were decidedly royalist. Combined with his classical liberal education, his royalism served to foster a respect for the heroes of history, for the nation, for great leaders, and for the classics. The war with Austria in 1866 tested his political views. Several of his friends attended anti-war and anti-Prussian demonstrations, and his first response to the crisis was to support the liberal call for a reconvened German parliament that would avert the menace of war. He considered it 'an audacity on Bismarck's [*sic*] part to create a united

Germany in this manner'.[4] However, once the war was underway, Nietzsche supported the Prussian military machine. At this time he made sense of the great upheavals he was witnessing with the aid of Schopenhauer's pessimistic philosophy. As Prussia emerged victorious, battle after battle, he reflected, 'One can learn much in such times. The earth, which appeared so solid and unmovable, quakes. Masks slip from faces, selfishness flaunts itself. Above all, one notices how weak is the power of ideas.'[5]

Nietzsche was anxious to align himself with the triumphant cause. As a Prussian in occupied Leipzig, he joined a small band of Bismarckian liberals who called for the annexation of Saxony by Prussia. The intellectual leader of the movement calling for annexation was Heinrich von Treitschke who applauded Bismarck's revolution as a 'revolution from above' which had finally resolved the dualism between Prussia and Austria by allowing a new centralised Germany to emerge. Nietzsche was later to make a number of biting criticisms of Treitschke, who was destined to become a celebrated nationalist historian of the new Reich; but at this point in his life he shared his vision of the role of Prussia in Germany. In the summer of 1866, Nietzsche involved himself directly in his first and last political campaign. In order to aid the Prussian cause he became a keen supporter of the Saxon National Liberals and a partisan of their candidate, Stephani, in the local election for the constituent Reichstag of the North German Confederation, an election which turned into a plebiscite on a the new Bismarckian state. The National Liberal Party was 'national' in the sense that it advocated a German empire, and 'liberal' in the sense that its programme contained the classic demands of liberalism, such as a free economy, free trade, and a constitutional state. The campaign was marked by bitterness and recriminations on the sides of all the major parties, as local patriots of the left and right united against the pro-Prussian 'traitors'. The election was a disaster for the liberal cause with Treitschke declaring that, although he did not despair of the future, the time was not yet right for the rule of liberalism. In the next few years Nietzsche's Bismarckianism would express itself in terms of an aloof disdain towards party politics. His main concern in the 1870s was to use the new political climate as the occasion to demand a rebirth of tragic culture and pessimism, inspired by the philosophy of Schopenhauer and the music of Wagner, which he believed would give a new depth to the classical ideals of German education and culture.

The Nietzsche of the 1880s is a very different figure from the youthful one of the 1860s and 1870s. In this period he became an incisive critic of modern German politics; in the words of one German historian, 'there has never been a shrewder critic at any time anywhere'.[6] Nietzsche now saw the German Reich of Bismarck as a state which prided itself on its philistinism, advancing its power-politics through racist, statist, and nationalist policies. He believed that classical liberal values had been corrupted by the nationalist cause, and that culture had been overtaken by a dangerous philistinism.

The reasons for the profound change in Nietzsche's attitude towards the new German Reich have a lot to do with his own intellectual maturity and his realisation that his initial hopes for cultural regeneration in Germany had been idealistic. His growing disaffection with the new German Reich was also connected with the break up of his relationship with Richard Wagner. Wagner himself was an immensely complex figure who began his youthful career as a revolutionary defending the right of men to live according to their own laws. In the 1860s he became the *protégé* and favourite of the king of Bavaria, to whom he gave advice and for whom he wrote essays on German politics and on what is German. Eventually he became reconciled to Bismarck's Reich, and in 1872 began to build his festival theatre at Bayreuth. The theatre was intended to be a temple of German art and a centre of the national community. In the early to mid 1870s Nietzsche had been a close associate and worshipper of the master, and had used his own intellectual talents to support the Wagner cause. Nietzsche placed his early hopes for a rebirth of tragic culture on Wagner's theatre. The theatre had no boxes or circles to represent social differences, and it did not provide mere commercial entertainment, but combined all the arts in a new unity, including poetry and philosophy, music and painting, and religious worship. It was for these reasons that at first Nietzsche saw Wagner's art as offering modern man the possibility of a Dionysian experience of universal oneness and harmony. However, Nietzsche was to grow sick of what he came to perceive as Wagner's romanticism and egomania, and he became perturbed by his virulent anti-Semitism. Nietzsche's break with Wagner is equally a break with the political idealism and cultural romanticism of his youth.

Although Nietzsche became an outspoken critic of the Bismarckian Reich in the 1880s, he had already expressed his distrust of the German sensibility in the early 1870s. He found it, and continued to find it, characterised by coarseness, dullness, and stupidity. In his early writings he is careful to argue that his primary concern is not so much with unification in a narrow political sense, but with the unity of a German spirit and life in a cultural sense. He makes his position clear in the opening page of his first untimely meditation, on David Strauss, where he draws a contrast, amounting to an opposition, between German 'spirit' (*Geist*) and the German 'Reich'. Writing just a few years after the Franco-Prussian war and the constitution of Germany as a modern nation-state, Nietzsche argues that German public opinion forbids careful reflection on what victory for the German people means. A 'grave consequence' of the war which he singles out, is the widespread error committed by public opinion that German culture (*Kultur*) was victorious in the war with France. 'This delusion', he writes, 'is in the highest degree destructive', not because it is a delusion – as he points out delusions and errors can be productive – but because it turns a victory into a defeat, into an 'extirpation *of the German spirit for the benefit of the "German Reich"*' (*DS* 1, p. 3). In Germany 'there no longer exists any clear conception of what culture is' (ibid., p. 5). The things which made possible Germany's victory over France, such as superior generalship, stern discipline, and unity and obedience in the ranks, are not to be confused with culture.

In his mature work Nietzsche describes himself as 'the last anti-political German' precisely in order to distance himself not from politics altogether, but from the petty politics of nationalism and statism which he thought had overtaken Germany. In *Twilight of the Idols* he fears that the cry of '*Deutschland, Deutschland über alles*' signals the end of serious thinking, of philosophy, in German (*TI* 'What the Germans Lack' 1). Moreover, in his autobiography *Ecce Homo*, composed in 1888 a few months before his breakdown, but suppressed by his anti-Semitic sister until 1908, Nietzsche launches a powerful attack on Treitschke. '"German"', he writes, 'has become an argument, *Deutschland, Deutschland über alles* a principle, the Teutons represent the "moral world-order" in history... There is now a historiography that is *reichsdeutsch*; there is even, I fear, an antisemitic one – there is a court historiography and Herr von Treitschke is not ashamed' (*EH* 'The Case of Wagner' 2). 'Nationalism' for Nietzsche represents the 'anti-cultural sickness' *par excellence*.

In *Beyond Good and Evil* Nietzsche calls for a 'great politics' to be instituted in which an elite of philosopher-legislators will guide Europe beyond the petty politics of nationalism and promulgate what it means to be a 'good European'. In spite of the rhetorical excesses of this work, it consistently opposes any politics which encourages racism, and is especially vitriolic in attacking German politicians who use anti-Semitism in order to promote a nationalist politics (see *BGE* 52, 195, 248, 250, 251). The book was recognised at the time as being offensive to Germans since it was seen as resting on 'a glorification of the Jews'.[7] Nietzsche's political thought centres on what it sees as the need for a 'self-overcoming of man'; and, while his anti-humanism may offend the moral sensibilities of good liberals, socialists, and Christians, it never justifies itself along either racist or nationalist lines.

It is somewhat paradoxical that a writer who promoted the cause of Europe as opposed to that of Germany, who lambasted all forms of racism in politics, especially anti-Semitism, should be perceived so widely as an ideological founder of Nazism. In spite of all that has been written about Nietzsche since the Second World War it remains the case that anyone who approaches his work for the first time, especially in the domain of politics, does so with these Nazi connotations. How did this fateful association of Nietzsche with Nazism come about?

The dissemination and reception of Nietzsche's philosophy after his mental collapse in 1889 was very varied. His work did not immediately appeal to the right, as one might expect given its aristocratic pretensions and distaste for socialism. On the contrary, in the two decades following his breakdown, it was taken up with interest and imagination by socialists, anarchists, and feminists, all of whom saw Nietzsche's work as preoccupied with the quest for individual self-realisation. For socialists, Nietzsche's ideas on the creative personality (*Persönlichkeit*) could add a much-needed notion of the 'authentic individual' to socialist doctrine.[8] A number of his contemporaries read him as a multi-faceted figure who had no sympathy for the postures of political radicalism or socialism, but who, at the same time, was no friend of German nationalism and statism. His atheism also served to alienate him from German conservatism. Nietzsche's position was thus complex and explains why his writings could be of such interest and value to a wide range of people. As the German historian Ernst Nolte argues, the name of Nietzsche at this time represented a 'battlefield' (*Schlachtfeld*). His books were essential reading for any educated European, and he was read by many of the most significant men of this period (including, Gustav Landauer, Benito Mussolini, Georg Simmel, Ferdinand Tönnies, Max Weber, Ludwig Klages, Thomas Mann, Stefan George, and Gabriele d'Annunzio).[9]

It was the popularity of Nietzsche's writings gained in Germany during the First World War which made it possible for the Nazis to exploit him as an ideological ally in the inter-war period (German soldiers went to the front, it is reported, with the Bible in one trench-coat pocket and *Thus Spoke Zarathustra* in the other). Nietzsche was enlisted to the Nazi cause in order to provide the movement with philosophical justification and legitimacy. He was by now an internationally celebrated and controversial philosopher, whose ideas could lend intellectual credence and power to their views. Nietzsche's sister, Elisabeth, played a decisive role in the transmogrification of Nietzsche into the philosopher of German militarism and imperialism. She wielded total control over her brother's literary estate, and it has now been conclusively shown that she not only suppressed the publication of certain manuscripts such as *Ecce Homo*, but also tampered with material and forged letters which she claimed to have been written by Nietzsche.[10] Several times she invited Hitler to the Nietzsche archive, and on one occasion presented him with Nietzsche's walking stick (for what purpose remains unclear). It seems to have been her hope that by promoting Nietzsche in this way she would increase her own importance and fame.

With the assistance of Elisabeth, the Nazis turned Nietzsche into one of the most popular and widely read philosophers in Germany and abroad. They made his writings part of their educational training and published inexpensive commentaries, collections, and anthologies. A number of academic and professional German philosophers, including Alfred Baeumler and Alfred Rosenberg, were entrusted with the task of propagating Nietzsche and providing the correct Nazi interpretation of his work. Baeumler, for example, wrote one of the first works on Nietzsche's politics, published in 1931, *Nietzsche as Philosopher and Politician*. The book set out to interpret Nietzsche as the philosopher of the Nordic race. This was done through massive oversimplification and distortion of Nietzsche's ideas. Thus, the attacks on the German people which run throughout Nietzsche's writings were explained as attacks only on the Christian, non-Germanic elements in the German character, while Nietzsche's vituperative attack on the supreme Germanic artist, Wagner, was said to arise out of envy. Other philosophers wrote even cruder interpretations, and one, Heinrich Härtle, produced a popular handbook and manual called *Nietzsche and National Socialism*, in which he celebrates Nietzsche's ideas as the material on which a Nazi philosophy can be constructed.

The Nazis used suspect but highly effective means to make their nazification of Nietzsche successful. The most effective trick they used was to print small anthologies containing the essential 'Nazi sayings' of Nietzsche.[11] These were published under his name, but with no indication that they had been edited. As a result people thought that they were actually reading Nietzsche and not an editor's selection and interpretation. One of these anthologies, for example, entitled *Judaism, Christianity, Germanity* presents bits and pieces, grouped in themes, taken from Nietzsche's published and unpublished notes. The passages on the Jews, as well as the notorious passage on the 'blond beast' from the *Genealogy of Morals*, are taken out of context and encourage a misreading of Nietzsche's argument. In order to present him as *the* Germanic philosopher, the Nazis were forced to censor a great deal of his writings, including his admiration for Latin culture and his attacks on German nationalism. The notion of the 'blond beast', for example, is not a Nazi concept, since it specifically includes the Arabs and the Japanese (*OGM* I, 11). Nietzsche never defined the value of an individual in terms of either biology or race, but always in terms of 'culture'.

An example of how the Nazis misrepresented Nietzsche's thoughts and ideas is provided by the great French thinker and poet Georges Bataille. He cites the example of Richard Oehler, Nietzsche's cousin and a collaborator of Nietzsche's anti-Semitic sister at the archives. In his work *Nietzsche and the Future of Germany* Oehler tried to demonstrate the existence of a deep kinship between Nietzsche's teachings and those espoused in Hitler's *Mein Kampf*. Bataille quotes the following from Oehler's book:

Most important for us is this warning:
'Admit no more Jews! And especially close the doors to the east!'...'That Germany has amply *enough* Jews, that the German stomach, the German blood has trouble (and will still have trouble for a long time) digesting even this quantum of "Jew" – as the Italians, French, and English have done, having a stronger digestive system – that is the clear testimony and language of a general instinct to which one must listen, in accordance with which one must act'.[12]

As Bataille – the foremost defender and exponent of the anti-Fascist Nietzsche – points out, what we have here is not only the case of an impudent hoax, but of 'a crudely and consciously fabricated falsehood'. The citation given by Oehler is taken from section 251 of *Beyond Good and Evil*. When the section is consulted and read properly, one discovers that the opinions being expressed are not those of Nietzsche, but of anti-Semites which he, Nietzsche, has chosen to present in order to mock. Nietzsche says:

I have not met a German yet who was well disposed toward the Jews; and however unconditionally all the cautious and politically minded repudiated real anti-Semitism, even this caution and policy are not directed against the species of this feeling itself but only against its dangerous immoderation, especially against the inspired and shameful expression of this immoderate feeling – about this, one should not deceive oneself. That Germany has amply *enough* Jews, etc.

There then follow the remarks attributed by Oehler to Nietzsche. What is deliberately excluded from Oehler's contorted citation is Nietzsche's recommendation that 'it might be useful and fair to expel the anti-Semite screamers from the country'. What Nietzsche argues for is the assimilation of the Jews, not their 'extermination'.

Even this short account should serve to show that the Nazi appropriation of Nietzsche was crude and highly selective. Can Nietzsche be saved from such massive abuse? One commentator expresses what I believe is the appropriate response to this question when he writes:

Nietzsche's works certainly make me feel uneasy. But my uneasiness is not due to the clumsy abuse of Nietzsche by the Nazis. I can only understand the persistence of the widespread label of Nietzsche as Nazi, if I interpret this name-calling as our defense mechanism, as our strategy, our excuse for not having to deal with Nietzsche. We of course also use another label that seems to excuse us from having to face Nietzsche's works: Nietzsche the madman.[13]

Many eminent writers insist, however, on holding Nietzsche responsible for Nazism and the evils it perpetrated. J. P. Stern has argued that no one came closer to embodying Nietzsche's model of personal authenticity, which consists in creating one's values for oneself, than Adolf Hitler.[14] But what this portrait of Hitler as a self-created person neglects is that for Nietzsche the task of becoming what you are (by, for example, giving *style* to your character – *GS* section 290) is designed to liberate the self from an attitude of resentment, in which a human being can only esteem its sense of selfhood by negating that of others and declaring itself to be 'superior'. This, for Nietzsche, is the embodiment, not of personal authenticity, but of the type of morality he calls a 'slave morality', in which a person or a social group defines others as 'evil' and only define themselves as 'good' after this act of negation. In other words, their characterisation of their identity rests not on self-affirmation, but on the negation of others. Hitler was a man whose whole being was pervaded by feelings of deep-seated resentment and poisonous revenge, and he can hardly be held up as an example of Nietzsche's model of the noble individual.

Another commentator has argued that it is not fantastical to infer that there exists an affinity between Nietzsche's views and Fascism.[15] Perhaps the reason for this proximity of Nietzsche's ideas to a Fascist style of politics is his belief that politics is by definition 'machiavellian' on the grounds that all morality has its basis in immorality and all struggles for justice are carried out by unjust means (*WP* 304).[16] Nietzsche's advocacy of elitism and of cruelty as a means of achieving political ends, as well as his break with the past and his assault on a Christian ethos of compassion, lends itself, it is argued, to a Fascist reading. However, there are many things in Nietzsche which are anathema to a Fascist politics, including his opposition to nationalism, his pan-Europeanism, his commitment to culture over politics, and his attack on the modern bureaucratic state for its stifling of creativity and individuality. As Georges Bataille astutely remarked:

A rejection of classical morality is common to Marxism, Nietzscheanism, and National Socialism. The only essential is the value in whose name life asserts these higher rights. Once this principle of judgement is established, Nietzschean values are seen as opposing racist values within a context of the whole... In Nietzsche's mind everything is subordinated to culture. While in the Third Reich, a reduced culture has only military might as its end.[17]

The real problem with the labelling of Nietzsche as a Fascist, or worse, a Nazi, is that it ignores the fact that Nietzsche's aristocratism seeks to revive an older conception of politics, one which he locates in the Greek *agon*, and which, as we shall see, has striking affinities with the philosophy of action expounded in our own time by Hannah Arendt. Once an affinity like this is appreciated, the absurdity of describing Nietzsche's political thought as 'Fascist', or Nazi, becomes readily apparent.

Nietzsche himself certainly had a premonition that one day his name would be associated with something terrible, as he put it 'with a crisis without equal on earth, the most profound collision of conscience' (*EH* 'Why I Am A Destiny' 1). He also knew that it would be his fate to be 'born posthumously': thus, the question of Nietzsche's responsibility for the evils to which his writings were put lies beyond his control. In this sense we are all born posthumously, since anything we say or write during our lifetime can be misinterpreted and misunderstood after our death. What remains true, however, is that *during* his own lifetime, Nietzsche did not, except for a brief spell in 1866, speak for a political party and, moreover, not once did he encourage his writings and ideas to be used for the cause of German nationalism and racism; on the contrary, he did everything he could to warn his contemporaries of the dangers of the new German Reich.

NIHILISM AND ARISTOCRATISM

Nihilism

Where Marx looked forward to a social revolution in which the economic structure of society would be radically transformed, Nietzsche envisaged a cultural revolution in which our appreciation of language and our conceptions of truth and knowledge would undergo a fundamental transformation. This emphasis on the crucial importance of language does not mean that Nietzsche is guilty of idealism. For him language is a material phenomenon which is rooted in our animal bodily human needs and which has historically evolved. In one of the opening sections of *Human, All Too Human*, for example, he attacks philosophers for lacking a historical sense which results in their inability to grasp the fact that the human animal is a creature which is not an '*aeterna veritas*' but is one which has 'become'; the same applies to the human faculty of cognition. 'Everything', Nietzsche insists, 'has become. There are no *eternal facts*, just as there are no absolute truths'. Consequently, he argues, 'what is needed from now on is *historical philosophizing*, and with it the virtue of modesty' (*HAH* 2).

The human being is a symbolic animal whose understanding of 'reality' is conditioned by the language it uses. Its experience of the world is mediated through language and through the concepts it employs to master reality. A change in concepts means a change in our conceptual understanding of the world. For Nietzsche it is the advent of 'nihilism' which provides the opportunity for a revolution in language and knowledge, involving both a revaluation of old values and the creation of new ones. But what is nihilism? And what are its causes?

Something of the experience of nihilism, and of what it means for human self-understanding, is captured in the following passage from John Gunnell's book *Political Philosophy and Time*:

When modes of thought and action which are informed by a particular orientation or arrangement of symbols come up abruptly against 'anomalies' in experience or problems which cannot be encompassed by existing symbols and forms of understanding, it may require a re-evaluation of the prevailing 'paradigms' or assumptions about reality which govern activity. Social action changes when the images which orient and justify it no longer meet the demands of life and when such demands create new commitments or when the vision of creative individuals confronts operative assumptions and introduces new symbols and forms which subvert existing images.[18]

Nihilism describes a condition in which there is a disjunction between our experience of the world and the conceptual apparatus we have at our disposal, which we have inherited, to interpret it.[19] As such, the experience of a metaphysical–moral crisis, in which our habits and traditions no longer sustain us, is not specific to the modern age, but characterises any epoch in which a fundamental transformation in self-understanding takes place, such as the collapse of the mythical foundations of ancient Greece, for example.

For Nietzsche it is important not to mistake the symptoms or experience of nihilism for its causes. Some of the symptoms he speaks of include: social distress, physiological degeneration, corruption, widespread pessimism, and so on. Our present experience of nihilism is the result of a particular interpretation of the world, and of human existence, which has governed the cultural horizon of occidental humanity for nigh on two thousand years: the 'Christian-moral interpretation' of the world (*WP* 1). Initially it results in a failure of meaning and loss of self-understanding. Nihilism means that 'the highest values devalue themselves' and the question '"why?" finds no answer' (*WP* 2). We move from one extreme experience to another, from believing in absolute religious and moral values to believing in *nothing*. With the collapse of the Christian world-view and its system of universal values, the world now seems devoid of meaning, aim, or purpose. It is for this reason that Nietzsche describes nihilism as a 'pathological transitional stage' (*WP* 13). It is something humanity must experience and pass through.

The causes of nihilism, according to Nietzsche, are deep and manifold. He suggests that the modern experience of nihilism can be understood in terms of a fate or destiny, since it is the logical outcome of the values and ideals which human beings have believed in for several centuries. One of the consequences of humanity's faith in morality is the cultivation of 'truthfulness', of a *will* to truth (think of the Christian confession, for example). Over time this will to truth in Christianity is transmuted into the intellectual conscience which underlies modern scientific inquiry. The result is that the will to truth eventually leads to calling into question the foundations of Christianity (one thinks of the discoveries of Darwin, for example). Science discovers that morality is only a partial perspective on life conditioned by the evolving physiological and psychological needs of the human animal. As a result we find ourselves caught in a tension captured by Nietzsche in the following terms:

Now we discover in ourselves needs implanted by centuries of moral interpretation – needs that now appear to us as needs for untruth; on the other hand, the value for which we endure life seems to hinge on these needs. This antagonism – *not* to esteem what we know, and not to be *allowed* any longer to esteem the lies we should like to tell ourselves – results in a process of dissolution. (*WP* 5)

Nietzsche insists, therefore, that for we moderns the experience of nihilism must have the character of necessity. The values we have hitherto believed in draw their final consequence, and it now becomes necessary to undergo the experience of nihilism in order to find out what value these 'values' really had. Eventually, however, we will require new values (*WP* Preface 4).

The ultimate causes of nihilism lie deep within the history of Western religion and philosophy (what Nietzsche often calls 'metaphysics'). Our religious and philosophical understanding of the world has been built on a resentful attitude towards life. Along with Christianity, for example, both Platonic and Kantian metaphysics have been built on a two-world theory in which one realm of reality – the 'true world' – is esteemed as the real world, and another realm of reality – the 'apparent world' – is devalued as inauthentic and less real, as mere semblance (see *TI* 'How the "Real World" Finally Became A Fable'). In Western metaphysics the 'soul' is elevated at the expense of the 'body', and human beings are encouraged to denigrate earthly, sensual existence and seek redemption from the suffering of life through belief in an after-life. Christianity, for Nietzsche, is ultimately a betrayal of Christ's teaching, of the symbolic meaning and significance of his suffering on the cross. One must accept death, not as a prelude to another life, but as the affirmation of the final end-point of this life (*D* 68; *AC* 34, 37, 39). Nietzsche also reads Schopenhauer's philosophy of pessimism, which rests on the denial of the will to life, and which had greatly influenced him in the formative years of his intellectual training, as but one more expression of the Christian ideal (*GS* 99; *AC* 7).

Despite his stern anti-Christian stance, Nietzsche does not underestimate the cultural importance of Christianity as a religion. Christian morality developed as the 'great antidote to theoretical and practical nihilism' (*WP* 4). In the face of the flux of life and eternal becoming, Christianity granted the human being an absolute value; through its eschatology it imbued the existence of evil in the world with meaning; and it preserved the human animal through the belief that it was possible for 'man' to have knowledge of absolute values, to clearly demarcate good from evil and judge life accordingly, and thus to have adequate knowledge about the most important things (ibid.). Now, however, in the wake of Darwin and modern science, modern human beings believe they are no longer entitled to a belief in another, higher and truer, world. What an inquiry into the origin of morals, of good and evil, discovers is that the original positing of values was nihilistic since it rested on belief in a 'beyond' which transcended contingency, 'becoming', and history (from Plato's theory of forms to Kant's noumenal reality of the thing-in-itself), and which served to denigrate and devalue earthly, mortal, suffering life.

One way of understanding Nietzsche's characterisation of the experience of nihilism as a *psychological* experience of weariness, distrust, apathy, and hopelessness, is by reflecting on some recent events in our own time, such as the collapse of communism in Eastern Europe and its existential impact on committed socialists and Marxists. Nihilism entails an abandonment of the belief that there is a meaning to the process of history (a teleology). Nietzsche writes:

Nihilism then, is the recognition of the long *waste* of strength, the agony of the 'in vain', insecurity, the lack of any opportunity to recover and regain composure – being ashamed in front of oneself, as if one had *deceived* oneself all too long. – This meaning could have been the 'fulfilment' of some highest ethical canon in all events, the moral world order; or the growth of love and harmony in the intercourse of beings; or the gradual approximation of a state of universal happiness; or even the development toward a state of universal annihilation – any goal at least constitutes some meaning. What all these notions have in common is that something is to be *achieved* through the process – and now one realizes that becoming aims at *nothing* and achieves *nothing*. (*WP* 12A)

For Nietzsche we must give up the moral ideal which leads us to believe that history is designed for the purpose of the progress and betterment of the human race.

Nihilism presents major difficulties for Nietzsche's own thinking. It results in a condition in which no proposition is believed to be true (what can 'true' now mean?), and all political structures and political modes of thinking are exposed as lies or myths (Plato's noble myth; Hobbes' fiction of the state of nature; Rousseau's notion of the 'Supreme Being'; modern democracy's belief in the equality of all individuals, and so on).[20] Even the slogan of the modern nihilist – 'nothing is true, everything is permitted' (*OGM* III, 24) – results in a performative contradiction (is it 'true' that 'nothing is true'?). For Nietzsche, all values and ideals go through a process in which they begin life as 'lies', then they become 'convictions', and finally they are called 'virtues' (*HAH* 99). However, in the modern age of nihilism this process has come to a halt and the lie is recognised as a lie, and 'untruth' is recognised to be a condition of life. The question which must arise for Nietzsche's thinking, therefore, is: what is the status of his own Dionysian teaching and doctrines, such as the *Übermensch*, the will to power, and the 'eternal return of the same'? Moreover, what becomes of politics in the wake of our experience of nihilism? I have already dealt with the first problem (as far as Nietzsche is concerned we need to change the way in which we think about this question, and forgo the question of whether something is true or false, and ask whether it is life-enhancing or life-depressing). I want to try and show now that it is the problem of nihilism which accounts for many of the difficulties frequently associated with Nietzsche's conception of politics.

Aristocratism

In section 257 of *Beyond Good and Evil* Nietzsche sets out the basic principles on which his 'aristocratism' rests. He argues that every 'enhancement' (*Erhöhung*) of the human type is the work of a society that believes in an order of rank and differences in value between human beings. It is a society which 'needs slavery in some sense'. The 'continual self-overcoming of man' (which Nietzsche uses as a 'moral formula in a supra-moral sense') requires this order of rank, and the 'pathos of distance' it generates, in order that 'ever higher, more rarer, more remote, further-stretching, more comprehensive states' can be attained. Nietzsche is of the belief that it is only through a class or caste society, in which a ruling group 'looks down' upon subjects as 'instruments', that these various 'states' can be reached.

For Nietzsche the most important question which individuals can ask themselves is how their life can receive 'the highest value' and 'deepest significance'. He replies, only by living in the service of the rarest and most valuable human types, not for the good of the majority (*SE* 5). Such a perspective on the life of the individual leads Nietzsche to expound a clearly defined political *Weltanschauung*, albeit one which may strike us moderns (liberal egalitarians) as deeply illiberal and elitist:

The essential characteristic of a good and healthy aristocracy is that it experiences itself *not* as a function (whether of the monarchy or of the commonwealth) but as their *meaning* and highest justification – that it therefore accepts with a good conscience the sacrifice of untold human beings who, *for its sake*, must be reduced and lowered to incomplete human beings, to slaves, to instruments. Their fundamental faith has to be that society must *not* exist for society's sake but only as the foundation and scaffolding on which a choice type of human being is able to raise itself to its higher task and to a higher state of *being*. (*BGE* 258)

Nietzsche objects to both socialism and liberalism on the grounds that, despite the differences between them, they are no more than attempts at an economic management of society in which culture is devalued and a utilitarian logic governs. Liberalism has no notion of an order of rank, and rests on an abstract individualism which gives rise to a timid conformity in society, while socialism subordinates the goal of culture to that of social justice and gives rise to a society dominated by bureaucracy.

Nietzsche also emphasises constantly that to be a 'master' and to command is a hard task in self-discipline and self-mastery. 'The most spiritual human beings', he writes, 'find their happiness where others would find their destruction', namely, 'in the labyrinth, in severity towards themselves and others, in experimenting' (*AC* 57). A high culture, therefore, has to be conceived along the lines of a pyramid in which each social group is assigned privileges and duties appropriate to its social role. Nietzsche's political theory makes the classic move of resting a theory of the political on a theory of nature:

The order of castes, *order of rank*, only formulates the supreme law of life itself; the separation of the three types is necessary for the preservation of society, for making possible higher and higher types – *inequality* of rights is the condition for the existence of rights at all. A right is a privilege. The privilege of each is determined by the nature of its being. Let us not underestimate the privileges of the *mediocre*. Life becomes harder and harder as it approaches the *heights* – the coldness increases, the responsibility increases. (ibid.)

Thus, for example, Nietzsche argues that 'for the mediocre it is happiness to be mediocre', and that to be a 'public utility, a cog' is for the great majority of people 'a natural vocation'.

The weakness of Nietzsche's aristocratism is that it justifies itself in terms of an untenable naturalism. It is precisely this kind of justification – the noble *lie* disguised as a natural *law* – which is now no longer credible in the modern age of nihilism. The question arises: how can Nietzsche legitimise his political thinking given that we live in an age in which the lie has been revealed as a lie?[21]

Nowhere in his writings does Nietzsche develop a notion of legitimacy to support his theory of politics. His notion of a future humanity, the *Übermensch*, bypasses the question of legitimacy and simply justifies itself in terms of the willed creation of a new human type. Every new advancement of 'man' rests on a new enslavement, so the overcoming of man he now calls for, it is clear, will take place through force and violence (see *GS* 377). However, because of this neglect of the question of legitimacy Nietzsche fails to appreciate that his new aristocratic order, which institutes itself through compulsion and violence, must give rise to permanent class conflict, to a politics of pride and glory, on the one hand, and one of envy and resentment, on the other. In modern political thought the self-constitution of society has been conceived in terms of a notion of social contract in which free and equal human beings agree to come together and form themselves as social beings.[22] Each political theory of the modern period rests on a particular theory of human nature. In Hobbes, the contract results in granting legitimate power (authority) to an absolute sovereign (deduced from a pessimistic theory of human nature in which the state of nature is conceived as a 'war of all against all').[23] In Locke, the contract results in the setting up of a limited, representative government (deduced from an account of the pre-political state of nature in which human beings are not, as in Hobbes, aggressive or egoistic, but in which life is inconvenient owing to the absence of law and settled rules of conduct).[24] In Rousseau it results in the creation of a just, virtuous order in which all are citizens, and in which sovereignty expresses itself as collective autonomy (deduced from an optimistic theory of human nature, what Rousseau calls our 'natural goodness').[25] Nietzsche, by contrast, rejects social contract theory as no more than the reflection of a slave morality which aims to seduce the strong and convert them to the morality of the weak.

The reason why a notion of legitimacy is so important to thinking about politics has been captured well by Stephen K. White. He argues that any political thinking which envisages a radical break with the present must place a notion of legitimacy at the forefront of its concerns in order to provide a procedural bridge to a new politics. If it does not, it falls into the danger of unleashing a new tyranny and a new despotism.[26] Nietzsche, however, simply argues that in order to embark upon a new stage in what he calls 'the Dionysian drama of the destiny of the soul' (equivalent to the 'self-overcoming of man') a new slavery is needed (*GS* 377). Nietzsche's diagnosis of nihilism is important because it reveals to us the context (a crisis of moral values) in which we have to think about politics and problems of political order today. However, his thinking is deficient in that its political programme of a new aristocratic legislation relin-

quishes any concern with legitimising itself except in problematic aesthetic terms of the 'self-overcoming of man'.

Nietzsche's political thinking finds a number of echoes in our
own century in the thought of Hannah Arendt. It is worthwhile
noting the similarities in order to discredit the charge of Fascism
placed against Nietzsche, and to appreciate the distinctive
features of this type of political thinking, as well as some of its
problems.[27] Both Nietzsche and Arendt affirm violence and
slavery as necessary to the establishment of society. For both,
true freedom is that which takes place in the heroic context of
the public arena, and both see the Greek *agon* as the model for
such an arena. Freedom is equated with action, and great or
creative action is 'beyond good and evil' in the sense that it does
not conform to existing rules and norms, but establishes new
ones. The private realm of the household is the realm of social
and material interests, which encourages cowardice and a fear
of the courage that is needed for public action. Freedom is
severe, demanding sacrifice and self-mastery, as well as a
denigration of economic and moral concerns. Both view the
modern liberal state as resting on a devaluation of the political
conceived as a public arena. Liberalism sees the chief goal of
society as one of securing a realm of private freedom – freedom
as non-interference – for individuals.

Common to both is an aristocratic notion of the self in which
there is no separation between doer and deed, between actor
and act. For Nietzsche and Arendt modern thinking has
inherited a Christian-moral conception of the self which posits
an essence (the subject or soul) independent of acting. Arendt
defines this as 'existential' or 'liberal' freedom in which what
matters above all else is the cultivation of *inner* freedom (freedom
conceived as a permanent attribute of the self and as an inner
possession). But, for Nietzsche and Arendt, this is the freedom of
the slave. For them action cannot be tied to utilitarian self-
interest – the freedom of 'bourgeois man' – since this is to
ignore the expressivist, poetic, and aesthetic dimensions of
human action. If Plato and Aristotle subsume the political
under the 'moral' (the contemplative pursuit of the true or the
good), then, for Arendt and Nietzsche, modern political thought

subsumes it under the economic (the pursuit of material satisfaction and well-being). For both, politics – as happened in the case of the Greek *agon* – degenerates when it is placed in the service of economic interests and mere self-preservation.[28]

Perhaps the most distinctive feature of Nietzsche and Arendt's political thinking is that, like Machiavelli's, it seeks to separate politics from morality.[29] Unlike a moralist like Rousseau, for example, who saw the kind of theatrical action they esteem as immoral and hypocritical, they maintain that the essence of politics is not the willing of what is morally 'right' and 'just'; rather, creative action must place itself beyond morality, and is not to be judged by its consequences or by the standards of conventional morality, but by the excellence contained in its performance.[30]

This is a highly aestheticist notion of action and freedom which is not without problems. The main problem is that, by conceiving politics as an aesthetic activity, in which actions are prized not for their moral ambitions or consequences, but simply in terms of their performative and glorious dimensions, action is deprived of substantive moral content. As Bhikhu Parekh has asked in an examination of Arendt, do not great words and deeds require great and noble objectives? As he argues, if economic and moral questions are excluded from politics it becomes difficult to see what issues can inspire human beings to utter great words and perform great deeds.[31] In addition, there is a refusal in Nietzsche and Arendt to see economic issues as part of politics, and to appreciate the necessity of a notion of social justice to avoid the destructive cycle of the reign of vanity and resentment that would characterise the life of their ideal polities. Nevertheless, such a contrast does enable us to appreciate the distinctive nature of Nietzsche's understanding of politics and of free action, as well as the inappropriateness of describing his political thinking as Fascist. Like Arendt, Nietzsche is seeking to retrieve an ancient understanding of the political that is very different to our modern 'bourgeois' understanding. This point has to be grasped if a proper assessment of his political thinking is to take place.

ON THE TRAGI-COMEDY OF EXISTENCE: LIFE AS WILL
TO POWER

Nietzsche was preoccupied with the question concerning the purpose of existence. He poses this question in a very specific context: if God, and all that he stands for, is dead, and if Christian values can no longer provide European civilisation with its ethical and cultural foundations, as he believed, then the question 'immediately comes to us in a terrifying way: *Has existence any meaning at all?*' (*GS* 357).

Nietzsche's response is to encourage modern human beings to cultivate the only attitude he believes can redeem the world in the absence of a centre-point or a God, and restore innocence to the flux of life: a 'tragic pessimism of strength'. What is tragic is the fact that life has to be seen as devoid of final purposes or moral goals. However, for Nietzsche, this should not lead us to despair or to taking revenge on life because of our resentment; rather, we should strive towards a joyous affirmation of reality as it is, and attain an attitude towards life that is beyond the 'good' and 'evil' of absolute and unconditioned moral judgement. Our attitude towards the world is to be born not of weakness or resentment, but out of benevolence and gratitude, of superabundant health, energy, wisdom, and courage.

In this picture of existence, life is seen to be governed by a monstrous and merciless energy of forces which can only be endured if we see it, and ourselves, in terms of an aesthetic spectacle. It is 'only as an *aesthetic phenomenon* that the world and existence are eternally *justified*', Nietzsche declares in *The Birth of Tragedy* (*BT* 5). Or, as he puts it in *Beyond Good and Evil*: 'Around the hero everything turns into a tragedy; around the demi-god into a satyr play; and around God – what? perhaps into "world"?' (*BGE* 150). This passage can be interpreted as follows:[32] the highest human being (the hero) is one who affirms his own life as a sacrifice; the human being who becomes a 'demi-god' is one who yields to life's totality and looks upon its existence as a piece of fate; and finally, a human being becomes 'God' when he is able to identify with the logic, the law, of life

and is absorbed into its totality: he is now a god out of which the
world flows and is born again.

In his autobiography *Ecce Homo*, Nietzsche paints a portrait of
himself as 'the first *tragic philosopher*'. Philosophy for Nietzsche is
'the most spiritual will to power' (*BGE* 9). What should guide
its reflections on the meaning of life is not truth (as we have seen
Nietzsche holds that 'untruth' may be a condition of life) but
'power', that is, the creative abundance of life. The notion of
'life' as 'will to power' is probably the most notorious aspect of
Nietzsche's thinking. It is frequently employed to support the
image of him as the philosopher of German militarism. This
theory of life has many aspects, not all of them coherent. It is
perhaps best seen as Nietzsche's attempt to arrive at a more
adequate and affirmative notion of the forces of life than that
found in Schopenhauer's concept of the 'will to life'. It is worth
noting that in German the word Nietzsche uses for 'power' in
the compound formulation 'will to power', *Macht*, is derived
from the verb *mögen*, meaning to want or desire, and the word
möglich, meaning potential (it is also related to *machen*, meaning
to make or create). For Nietzsche 'power' exists as potentiality,
so that in the term 'will *to* power' the word 'power'
denotes not simply a fixed and unchangeable entity, like
force or strength, but an 'accomplishment' of the will overcoming or overpowering itself. As we shall see, Nietzsche
defines a 'sovereign individual' as someone who is able 'to make
promises' because they have attained or earned the right to do
so (*OGM* II, 2). This definition shows the extent to which he
thinks of sovereign power in terms of an achievement and an
accomplishment.

The 'will' is described by Schopenhauer as the noumenal
form of the body, that is, as the in-itself of existence. Following
Plato and Kant he posits the world in terms of a duality: the
world as 'idea' or 'representation' (*Vorstellung*) is the outer,
physical world, the realm of time, space, and causation; the
world as 'will' is the inner, subjective world beyond space and
time, the eternal substance of all that lives.[33] Every individual
embodies this will to strive to live, which is construed by
Schopenhauer in terms of a blind, aggressive, force with an

insatiable appetite for annihilation and destruction. He follows Hobbes in positing natural life in terms of universal struggle and conflict. It is not surprising that from this view of life Schopenhauer should see a wilful life in terms of permanent suffering, pain, and misery. The only way out of the vicious circle of life (where willing more only leads to more suffering and pain), is through the denial of the will, the refusal to engage in the contest of life. Redemption from the incessant striving of the will to life can be attained momentarily in the will-less contemplation of art and in the state known as 'Nirvana'.

In its essence Schopenhauer's will to life expresses the will as a *lack*. It is on this point that we can perhaps best understand the essential difference between the will to life and the will to power. It is crucially important to appreciate that the 'will to power' is a compound idea in which the 'power' posited in the notion does not simply refer to an object desired (because it is lacking) by a subject (the 'will'). Power denotes the *essence* of willing (that it is 'overpowering'). Against Schopenhauer, and other psychologists of the will, Nietzsche insists that one must not subtract the content from the character of the will (its content, its 'whither'). He argues that what Schopenhauer calls the 'will' is merely an empty word, and that life is simply a special case of the 'will to power'; as a result, it is quite arbitrary to claim that everything which lives strives to enter into this form of will to power (*WP* 692). For Nietzsche 'willing' refers to a process, a becoming without a fixed subject, and is not to be confused with 'desiring' or 'striving'; it is characterised, above all, by 'the affect of commanding'. There is, he argues, no such thing as 'willing', but only a 'willing something'. The relationship between the 'will to' and 'power' in the formulation 'will to power' is a dynamic and active one. As propounded by metaphysicians, however, the 'will', and the phenomenon of 'willing', are pure fictions (*WP* 668).

All driving force, for Nietzsche, is to be understood as 'will to power', where 'power' denotes the whither and whatness of the will. Against not only Schopenhauer, but also Hobbes and Spinoza, he argues that 'self-preservation' does not characterise the object or goal of the forces and energies of life. Every living thing, he holds, does all that it can, not to preserve itself, but to become 'more' (*WP* 688). On this level, will to power refers to the desire every living thing has to grow, expand, and develop (what Nietzsche calls a 'drive for freedom' in the *Genealogy of Morals*). Pleasure and joy are symptoms of the feeling of power which has been attained and through which we reach a consciousness of 'difference'. Life is to be understood as 'specifically a will to the accumulation of force', in which 'nothing wants to preserve itself, but everything is to be added and accumulated' (*WP* 689).

Nietzsche's theory of life rests on a peculiar conception of power which is often misconstrued. We can best appreciate the novelty and uniqueness of Nietzsche's notion of power if we compare it to that found in Hobbes, the other great modern philosopher of power. In Hobbes, 'power' is understood in terms of the means by which a living thing preserves its existence against other beings. 'Power' is thus understood in utilitarian terms as a means to an end; it is a means to 'obtain some future apparent good'.[34] Because of the warlike condition of the state of nature, which Hobbes depicts as the natural condition mankind would find itself in prior to the formation of society and the creation of law and justice, this quest for power is ongoing and perpetual. On one level, Nietzsche agrees with this Hobbesian conception of power.[35] In section 259 of *Beyond Good and Evil*, for example, he describes life in terms of 'appropriation, injury, overpowering of what is strange and weaker, suppression, severity... and, at the least and mildest, exploitation'. However, Nietzsche's thinking on power differs from that of Hobbes in that it does not rest on a utilitarian logic. For Nietzsche, power refers, above all, to a process and an activity, in which the important thing is the expenditure (the squandering even) of force, not an end-state that is to be achieved. He warns us that in thinking about the will to power we should be suspicious of all superfluous teleological principles. A living thing, he argues, desires most of all 'to discharge its strength... self-preservation is only one of the indirect and most frequent *results*' of the will to power (*BGE* 13).

In contrast to the Hobbesian tradition, therefore, Nietzsche thinks of the law of life, not as 'self-preservation', but as 'self-overcoming'. This leads him to an entirely novel conception and justification of power, one which has a dramatic influence on his thinking about morals and politics. It informs both his extra-moral thinking of 'beyond good and evil', which rests on an affirmation of 'the grand economy of the whole', and his conception of politics, which is viewed not as an end in itself, but merely as a means to the production of culture (human greatness through perpetual self-overcoming and the squandering of energies and resources by the creative genius or great individual). By affirming the 'grand economy of the whole' Nietzsche invites us to think about life beyond the standpoint of fixed or absolute moral judgement. We must recognise that everything is a unity and necessity. To think 'over' or 'beyond' oneself is to employ creatively, not morally (where morality denotes a 'restrictive economy of life' as opposed to a 'general' one) the erotic passion, or *pathos*, which is the will to power. It is through the affirmation of the general economy of life that an individual attains a perspective on life which is 'beyond good and evil'. Nietzsche is quite clear that this 'economy' will be found unpalatable by most people:

If a person should regard even the affects of hatred, envy, covetousness, and the lust to rule as conditions of life, as factors which, fundamentally and essentially, must be present in the general economy of life (and must, therefore, be further enhanced if life is to be enhanced) – he will suffer from such a view of things as from seasickness. And yet even this hypothesis is far from being the strangest and the most painful in this immense and almost new domain of dangerous insights; and there are in fact a hundred good reasons why everyone should keep away from it who – *can.* (*BGE* 23)

However, for those 'daring travellers and adventurers' who recognise a profound insight here, such a view of life is an enticement to 'sail right *over* morality' (*über die Moral*) (ibid.)

There are a number of problems in Nietzsche's presentation of his view of life as will to power, not least the problem of its epistemological status as a cosmological theory. But what is clear is that Nietzsche is not proposing that to become a creative human entails the simple unleashing and assertion of instinctual

and primitive energies, in which the human self gives free rein
to its drives. Self-creation is, for Nietzsche, a hard task requiring
severe self-discipline. He admires the fact that Goethe 'disciplined himself into a whole' (*TI*, 'Expeditions of an Untimely
Man', 49). Attaining greatness might involve learning how *not
to will*, not in the sense of a denial of the forces of life, but in the
sense of knowing how to master and control desire by, for
example, deferring a decision: 'All unspirituality, all vulgarity,
is due to the incapacity to resist a stimulus – one *has* to react, one
obeys every impulse' (*TI* 'What the Germans Lack', 6).

Notions of strength and weakness, of health and sickness, are
at the centre of Nietzsche's thinking about life and culture. He
holds that a strong will to power does not need to dominate
others; on the contrary, it is usually weak people who need to
control others and employ power and violence against them.
Only in this way can they gain self-esteem and confidence (a
feeling of power). A strong or noble will to power, as Nietzsche
sees it, relates to others in terms of overflowing abundant,
creative energy, inspiring and transforming others. It has a
generous and joyous spirit or soul. Nevertheless, Nietzsche does
regard the 'exploitation' (*Ausbeutung*) of weaker powers by
stronger ones as a necessary and essential aspect of an
aristocratic social structure. On one level, he seems to be
suggesting that injury and overpowering of others are unconscious effects of a strong will to power; on another, the level
of his overt political thinking, he makes the radical suggestion
that in order for there to be a perpetual self-overcoming of
'man', which guarantees the creation of new and rare human
types, the state, or the 'social structure', has to be built on
relationships of command and obedience. This is necessary, not
only to guarantee the privileges of higher responsibilities and
higher tasks of a noble elite pursuing self-creation (justification
of an economic arrangement for a particular cultural end), but
also because the experiences of mastery and servitude are in
themselves beneficial to life conceived as self-overcoming (*BGE*
257).

Without the 'pathos of distance' created by the difference
between social strata, Nietzsche is suggesting, the noble class

would not feel that sense of rareness and uniqueness which, he believes, is necessary for it to engage in self-creative activity. The performance of heroic deeds, for example, may require feelings which transcend the ordinary, the everyday, and the utilitarian. Nietzsche believes that this kind of activity can only be performed by the few (only a minority will have the courage and appetite for it), and that it requires an order of rank in society to sustain it (*AC* 57): 'Independence is for the very few; it is a privilege of the strong' (*BGE* 29). Exploitation and domination here do not assume a direct form for Nietzsche, but are mediated by social and political institutions. But what is missing from his account of the creative, aristocratic polity is anything to do with what one might call, for want of a better term, 'social justice'. The lack of such a notion in his work could be regarded as one of the chief deficiencies of his political thinking, since it means that the political order he envisages as necessary for the production of genius and culture can only assume an authoritarian form. The legitimacy of this order must remain unquestioned and unchallenged if culture is to develop without regard for the *political* claims of justice (as we shall see, this is exactly what Nietzsche argues in his early, unpublished reflections on the Greek state). This is what one might call, with a certain degree of caution, the 'totalitarian' moment of Nietzsche's political thinking, not unlike the one often attributed to Plato.

Nietzsche's conception of human life, of its tragic and comic aspects, needs to be explored further before it is possible to develop a critical perspective on it. It is important, to begin with, to appreciate the sorts of questions he is most concerned with as a philosopher. These centre not so much on 'what is the world really like?' and 'can we ever have true knowledge of the world?', but rather do our values and forms of knowledge serve to enhance life (conceived as will to power), or do they act to constrain it? Is life 'ascending' or 'descending'? Nietzsche has a 'tragic' perspective on life which he defines as follows:

Saying Yes to life even in its strangest and hardest problems; the will to life rejoicing over its own inexhaustibility even in the very sacrifice of its highest types – that is what I called Dionysian, that is what I understood as the bridge to the psychology of the tragic poet. Not in order to get rid of terror and pity, not in order to purge oneself of a dangerous affect by its vehement discharge…but in order to be oneself the eternal joy of becoming, beyond all terror and pity – that joy which includes even joy in destroying. (*EH* 'The Birth of Tragedy', 3)

Nietzsche attempted to teach this view of life through his doctrine of the eternal return in which the return of life is affirmed in all its terrifying seductive, sublime beauty again and again without subtraction, addition, or selection of any kind. What one affirms in the eternal return is life as 'self-over-coming', that it, life as an eternally self-creating and self-destroying force, and the 'law' of life as passing away, death, change, and destruction, and, as Nietzsche says, this must include: 'saying Yes to opposition and war' (ibid.). This is a tragic view of life because it sees no redemption from the pain and suffering of life, and, moreover, wants none.

As we have seen, Nietzsche's logic or 'economy' of life informs his conception of politics at its deepest levels. Only with an aristocratic culture is it possible to organise the social life of human beings in such a way that it serves the extra-moral, purely aesthetic goal of 'self-overcoming'. The problem of the present age is that creativity is stultified by the experience of nihilism. What is needed is an attempt to 'assassinate two millenia of antinature and desecration of man' by Christianity and to form a 'new party of life' which will attempt the 'greatest of all tasks', the raising of humanity to a 'higher level', which entails 'the relentless destruction of everything that is degenerating and parasitical'. Nietzsche looks forward to a new tragic age in which the highest art of saying yes to life will be reborn when 'humanity has weathered the consciousness of the hardest but most necessary wars *without suffering from it*' (ibid. 4).

A real clue as to how Nietzsche conceived his philosophical intervention in the crisis of values brought about by the advent of nihilism, is to be found in the opening section of *The Gay Science*. It begins with Nietzsche claiming that one of the strongest instincts of the human herd, which can be found operating in both men of benevolence and men of evil, is the instinct to do what is good for the preservation of the human race. We may think it appropriate to divide human beings into good types and evil types. However, when looked at from the perspective of 'large-scale accounting' we discover that such a division is too simple: human, all too human, one might say. 'Even the most harmful man', Nietzsche argues, 'may really be the most useful when it comes to the preservation of the species'. Nietzsche then states what his thinking beyond good and evil amounts to: an affirmation of the total economy of life:

Hatred, the mischievous delight in the misfortune of others, the lust to rob and dominate, and whatever else is called evil belongs to the most amazing economy of the preservation of the species. To be sure, this economy is not afraid of high prices, of squandering, and it is on the whole extremely foolish. Still, it is *proven* that it has preserved our race so far. (*GS* 1)

Nietzsche argues that, in order to bear the tragic nature of the human condition, and to overcome its depressing effects, it is necessary to cultivate the art of laughter, to learn to laugh '*out of the whole truth*'. The 'truth' of history and civilisation, Nietzsche suggests, is that the preservation of the species is everything and the individual nothing. Once we are able to laugh at this truth, he says, then laughter will forge an alliance with wisdom and the 'gay science' will be born. At present, however, we still live in 'the age of moralities and religions'.

The human animal is the peculiar animal, Nietzsche argues in this section, in that it possesses a fundamental need to find a meaning to existence. It cannot be content with just existing, but must locate an aim and a value to life. This fact has meant that human history has been characterised by the emergence of a number of key ethical teachers who have attempted to lead others to enlightenment (Buddha, Jesus, Muhammad, Socrates, etc.). However, what the ethical teachers forget, Nietzsche says, is that, owing to the nature of time, their teaching on the purpose of existence will inevitably become outmoded and be seen as comical. It is clear that he sees himself in this genealogy of teachers. He is attempting to describe the conditions of his *historical moment* as the teacher of the philosophy of the future he

names 'beyond good and evil'. Nietzsche will seduce us into
believing his teaching, he may transform our lives, and he hopes
that he will have a profound impact on history (for good or ill
he cannot tell and, besides, such a judgement is too easy and too
human). But, at the same time, he recognises that his teaching
will one day be seen as inadequate or irrelevant, and that there
will come a day when people no longer find it necessary to read
him. But first there must come the 'moment' of his teaching:

...O, do you understand me, my brothers? Do you understand this
new law of ebb and flood? There is a time for us too! (*GS* 1)

One of the most incisive readings of Nietzsche's tragic
philosophy can be found in a work by his former friend Lou
Salomé. Salomé shows that Nietzsche's rejection of Christianity
and his return to Greek ways of thinking about existence
represent a turn away from ethics towards an aesthetics of
existence.[36] To think beyond the opposition of good and evil
means to recognise that the continuous creativity of life is only
possible through excess and destruction. Nietzsche is not simply
a philosopher of war and destruction, but the advocate of the
infinite creativity of life. For Nietzsche the problem with
adopting a moral standpoint towards life is that it negates the
basic and most powerful conditions of life by failing to affirm the
whole.

One can easily see how Nietzsche's thought links up, for many
people, with a Fascist or authoritarian politics, not because it is
itself avowedly Fascistic, but because it eschews any concern
with justice, and relinquishes any commitment to absolute
moral values, such as the dignity and integrity of each individual
human being. In response, Nietzsche would argue that all
political systems are systems of authority and discipline. The
key point to raise, he would argue, is that concerning the
objective of the political system. Why does society exist? And
what kind or type of human being does it want to cultivate?
Nietzsche would also point out that the teaching which preaches
the dignity of each person and the equality of all human beings
– Christianity – is a religion that is based on an organizational
structure that is deeply hierarchical, authoritarian, and miso-

gynistic. Nietzsche's anti-humanist political thinking does not give equal value to every individual human life, but assesses the value of an individual life in terms of whether it represents an ascending or a descending mode of life. The individual gains value by placing itself in the service of the creation of culture. If individuals cannot attain greatness, they should at least serve it. This is the essence of Nietzsche's aristocratism, as well as the principle on which he bases his unorthodox, illiberal, and anti-Christian notion of justice. 'Justice', Nietzsche declares in a note from the *Nachlass*, is the 'function of a panoramic power (*Macht*) which looks beyond the narrow perspectives of good and evil' in order '*to preserve something that is more than this or that person*' (*KSA* 11, p. 188). In this conception of justice we find expressed both Nietzsche's illiberalism and anti-humanism.[37]

There are contradictory, perhaps even irreconcilable, aspects to Nietzsche's thinking. On the one hand, one finds authoritarian strands in his work, primarily reflected in his views on the state, on men and women, and on the necessity for hierarchy and inequality in the social structure. On the other hand, however, his thinking is characterised by libertarian dimensions which are profoundly liberating; such as, for example, his Dionysian conception of life as perpetual self-overcoming, which implies the necessity of overcoming fixed boundaries, divisions, and orders of rank, his notion of joyful knowledge or science (*Wissenschaft*), and his celebration of laughter (it is interesting to note that in the *Republic* Plato explicitly forbids laughter to the guardian class, that is, the ruling class). In terms of his political thinking Nietzsche very much fits into the classic authoritarian mould. He believes that political order (and order is necessary for the creation of culture) can only be established through discipline, hierarchy, and slavery (at least in some form and however defined). But what strikes one about his 'Dionysian' philosophical thinking is the extent to which it undermines the foundations on which his conception of political order is constructed.

THOMAS MANN AND ALBERT CAMUS ON NIETZSCHE

The link between Nietzsche's teaching and the horrors of the twentieth century is a highly complex one which cannot be treated either glibly or superficially. Two of the best attempts to think through this issue can be found in Thomas Mann and Albert Camus.

For Thomas Mann, Nietzsche is a 'personality of phenomenal cultural plenitude and complexity, summing up all that is essentially European'.[38] For Mann, as for many writers, Nietzsche is essentially an unpolitical thinker ('remote from politics and innocently spiritual', he writes) whose ideas nevertheless prefigure the age of imperialism and, moreover, the Fascist era of the West in which 'we are living and shall continue to live for a long time to come, despite the military victory over fascism'. For Mann, Nietzsche was not a Fascist, but one who saw the menace coming and knew what dangers lay ahead. However, he also argues that the chief failing of Nietzsche's thinking was that it constituted an 'heroical aestheticism' which was powerless to do anything to prevent an evil like the Holocaust. At the same time, Mann points out, it is precisely this 'Dionysian aestheticism' which makes Nietzsche 'the greatest critic and psychologist of morals known to the history of the human mind'.[39] What the case of Nietzsche presents us with, Mann argues, is the irresolvable conflict between the aesthetic and the moral view of the world (Mann equates the latter with socialism). Mann concludes his reflections on a stridently moral note, arguing that the aestheticism, under whose banner the free spirits of the nineteenth century such as Nietzsche rose against bourgeois morals, belongs, in the last analysis, to the bourgeois era itself. What is evident now, Mann writes, in the wake of horrors of the war, is that we need to transcend the aesthetic view of life and step into a moral and social one, for 'an aesthetic philosophy of life is fundamentally incapable of mastering the problems we are called upon to solve'.[40]

A similar perspective is adopted by Albert Camus in his classic study, *The Rebel*. In a chapter entitled 'Absolute Affirmation' Camus construes Nietzsche's work in terms of a peculiar logic of life, a logic of affirmation. Like the work of de Sade, the challenge of Nietzsche's work consists in its undermining of the basis of morality. These thinkers push thought to the point where, quite literally, all hell breaks loose and a godless universe opens up:

When man submits God to moral judgement, he kills Him in his own heart. And then what is the basis of morality? God is denied in the name of justice but can the idea of justice be understood without the idea of God? Have we not arrived at an absurdity?[41]

Nietzsche's great question for Camus is whether one can live while believing in nothing. Nietzsche's answer is yes; yes, provided one accepts the final consequences of nihilism – of the insight into the world and existence which reveals that 'nothing is true, everything is permitted' (*OGM* III, 24) – and if one, emerging into the desert, feels both pain and joy. 'Good' and 'evil' in their absolute, unconditional, or universal forms no longer exist. The task now is to live *beyond*: beyond good and evil in which the creative unity of good and evil results in the affirmation of the creative good. It means that one frees oneself from the necessity of passing judgement on the world, from the anthropomorphic arrogance of human beings. To pass judgement on life is to negate and slander it. This is the antinomy, Nietzsche says: in so far as we believe in morality we condemn life (*WP* 6). For centuries morality has existed supported by the religious foundations and beliefs of Christianity. But now Christianity is declining and approaching its end, and morality reveals itself as a symptom of decadence and declining life. 'We' want to ascend to higher forms of life. Atheism for Nietzsche, therefore, Camus points out, is both radical and constructive. 'Deprived of the divine will', Camus writes, 'the world is equally deprived of unity and finality'.[42] This is not an easy or cosy world to live in. The ones who cannot stand their ground *above* (*über*) the law, must find another law or seek refuge in madness (*D* 14).

To be free is to abandon ends, purposes, goals, and aims. In this way one restores to life the innocence of becoming. Total acceptance of total necessity – that one wants nothing to be different – equals freedom. The logic contained in this affirmation of life without goal or aim leads Camus to write that:

This magnificent consent, born of affluence and fullness of spirit, is the unresolved affirmation of human imperfection and suffering, of evil and murder, of all that is problematic and strange in our existence.[43]

He makes the crucial point: 'Nietzsche wants no redemption'. The joy of self-creation is the joy of annihilation since the individual 'is lost in the destiny of the species and eternal movement of the spheres'.

What, according to Camus, is Nietzsche responsible for exactly? This is a difficult question to answer. Camus' critique of Nietzsche, like Mann's, is made from the moral point of view. 'From the moment that the methodical aspect of Nietzschean thought is neglected', he writes, 'his rebellious logic recognizes no limits', and the killers and mass murderers, in denying the spirit for the letter of this thought, can find their pretext in Nietzsche. For Camus, Nietzsche represents the 'acute manifestation of nihilism's conscience':

From the moment that assent was given to the totality of human experience, the way was open to others who, far from languishing, would gather strength from lies and murder. Nietzsche's responsibility lies in having legitimized, for worthy reasons of method ... the right to dishonour of which Dostoyevsky had already said that if one offered it to people one could always be sure of seeing them rushing at it.[44]

In looking forward to the future reign of the *Übermensch* Nietzsche succumbs to the great temptation found in all radical utopian thought of the modern period: the secularisation of the ideal. This, for Camus, is the source of Nietzsche's great failure. In claiming that Nietzsche's philosophy ultimately rests on religious ambitions (Nietzsche seen as yet another messiah in the long line of ascetic priests), however, Camus overlooks the self-referential aspects of Nietzsche's philosophy, which mock his own authority and draw attention to the personal nature of his principal thoughts and teachings (that the will to power is *his* interpretation of existence; that eternal return represents *his* formula for the highest affirmation of life possible, etc.). As we shall see later, Nietzsche conceives himself, not as another ascetic priest, but as a *comedian* of the ascetic ideal.

Writing in the aftermath of the war, and trying to come to terms with the full scale and nature of the Holocaust, Mann and Camus find it impossible to leave, as Nietzsche invites us to, the 'illusion of moral judgement beneath them' (*TI* 'The Improvers of Mankind', 1). They also found it difficult to read Nietzsche as a comedian, given the profound impact his writings had had on German political culture. Their responses to his challenge, written at a specific historical juncture, raise questions which must be central to any reading of his work. To what extent is it necessary to advocate war and 'evil' in order for the creative forces of life to be cultivated and harnessed? Can one live without moral judgement? If being *over*-human means that moral judgement is transcended, should we not do all we can to become human (all too human)? Is it possible to transcend the human? How does one distinguish between 'ascending' and 'descending' forces of life, let alone define such forces? I shall return to the critical questions thrown up by the readings of Mann and Camus in chapter seven.

The charge of 'aestheticism', which both Mann and Camus level against Nietzsche, needs to be disputed. Nietzsche's problem is that of how to comprehend the 'general economy of the whole'. This is the 'economy' of life in its rich and awesome totality: in addition to pleasure, love, joy, and happiness, we recognise that central to human behaviour – to human being as such – are 'phenomena' like violence, cruelty, pain, murder, suffering, and so on. The significance of the Greeks, for Nietzsche, is that in their tragic art they recognised that there is no clear line to be drawn between 'good and evil' (no simple black and white). It is necessary to recognise, as the Greeks did, that even the 'evil' affects and passions can be productive and have played their part in the preservation of the species (*GS* 1). It is too easy to attribute to Nietzsche a simple and straightforward opposition between art and morality. For Nietzsche art represents a form of 'truth' (perhaps the highest form of truth available to human being) in that it discloses to individuals the sublime nature of their suffering, their pain, their foibles, and their failures. In this respect it enables them to continue to exist as moral beings in the face of the suffering and tragedy which characterise so much of the human experience of life. Nietzsche holds that in the absence of the truth of art human beings are overtaken by moral nihilism, since suffering, cruelty, and so on, become *unintelligible*.

This is the condition of modern human beings, who have neither the consolations of true Christian belief nor the profound truth of tragic art. Modern humanity is unable to answer the ancient, primordial question of human being: why do *I* suffer? (*OGM* III, 27). Only when modern humanity feels the *need* for art will it become a *spiritual* humanity. What Nietzsche was essentially saying to his fellow countryfolk was that unless they cultivated 'spirit' (*Geist*) within themselves, by thinking back to their real and true needs, their lives would be overtaken by the philistine power-politics of the German *Reich*.

PART II

Ancients and moderns

CHAPTER 3

Nietzsche and the Greeks: culture versus politics

INTRODUCTION

Nietzsche's early writings (1871–76), include *The Birth of Tragedy*, the *Untimely Meditations*, and two unpublished essays, *The Greek State* (1871) and *Homer's Contest* (1872).[1] The essay on the Greek state was written during the time that Nietzsche was aso engaged on his first major book, *The Birth of Tragedy*, which is generally assumed to have nothing to say on politics. However, a consideration of this posthumously published essay shows that the theory of art and culture that Nietzsche puts forward in the *Birth of Tragedy* rests on a particular conception of the political realm. In it we find a clear expression of Nietzsche's distinct political theory, with its emphasis on political life as a means to the production of great human beings and culture. For Nietzsche, modern politics is based on the delusion that it is possible to establish universal concord and justice on earth. He condemns as futile all attempts to ameliorate the human lot through modern political means.

GREEK TRAGEDY AND CULTURE

Nietzsche intended his first published work, *The Birth of Tragedy* (1872), to be a contribution to the young 'science of aesthetics'. The development of art is bound up with 'the *Apollonian* and *Dionysian* duality' (*BT* 1).[2] It is through two art deities, sculpture and music respectively, that the Greeks, according to Nietzsche, disclose the deep mysteries of artistic production. Apollo represents the dream experience; he is the 'shining one', the god of light, who provides the 'beautiful illusion' by which life is made worth living once we have looked deep into the abyss. The experience of 'beautiful illusion' provided by the Apollonian is one which provides the individual with trust and repose in the midst of a tormenting world. By contrast, the Dionysian experience is one of intoxication which shatters the '*principium individuationis*', and in which 'everything subjective vanishes into complete self-forgetfulness' (ibid.).

Nietzsche's fundamental argument is that the experience of emancipation from oppression (from nature, and from other human beings) is only possible through the medium of art. As he powerfully puts it:

Under the charm of the Dionysian not only is the union between man and man reaffirmed, but nature which has become alienated, hostile, or subjugated, celebrates once more her reconciliation with her lost son, man...Now the slave is a free man; now all the rigid barriers which necessity, caprice, or 'impudent convention' have fixed between man and man are broken. Now, with the gospel of universal harmony, each one feels himself not only united, reconciled, and fused with his neighbour, but as one with him, as if the veil of *maya* had been torn aside and were now merely fluttering in tatters before the mysterious primordial unity. (ibid.)

The Dionysian merely affords us a glimpse of universal harmony; it is not the task of art to incite us to revolution. Reflecting on the question of the origins of tragedy, for example, Nietzsche criticises the tradition which argues that the genre arose from the tragic chorus understood as an 'ideal spectator' such as 'the people'. His argument is that such a view injects into the origins of Greek drama an opposition between prince and people, 'indeed the whole politico-social sphere', which needs to be excluded from the purely religious origins of tragedy (*BT* 7). Nietzsche writes: 'Ancient constitutions knew of no constitutional representation of the people in *praxi*, and it is to be hoped that they did not even "have intimations" of it in tragedy' (ibid.). He insists that a 'chasm of oblivion' separates the two worlds of everyday reality and Dionysian reality in which an experience of primordial oneness with one's fellow-men is attainable. In this sense every human being who has been educated in the tragic experience of the Dionysian resembles the figure of Hamlet: he has been trained in the essence of things, gained knowledge, and experienced the nausea which inhibits action. He knows that it is ridiculous to suppose that anything he does today could have an effect on the future course of things, and that it is, therefore, futile and humiliating to suppose that he should be asked to put right a world that is out of joint. 'Knowledge kills action, action requires the veil of illusion', Nietzsche writes, 'that is the doctrine of Hamlet, not that cheap wisdom of Jack the Dreamer who reflects too much and, as it were, from an excess of possibilities does not get round to action. Not reflection, no – true knowledge, an insight into the horrible truth outweighs any motive for action' (*BT* 7).

For Nietzsche, a strong and vibrant culture is one which rests on a 'pessimism of strength'. The Greeks, Nietzsche says, knew and felt the terror and the absurdity of existence (*BT* 3). Out of the recognition of this terror and absurdity they invented art in order to experience life as an aesthetic phenomenon in which the human being transcends a merely individual nature and gains a glimpse of life as eternal becoming. Art provides the 'metaphysical comfort…that life is at the bottom of things, despite all the changes of appearances, indestructibly powerful and pleasurable' (*BT* 7). The Greek was a person susceptible to the tenderest and deepest suffering, who 'having looked boldly right into the terrible destructiveness of so-called world history as well as the cruelty of nature, and being' was 'in danger of longing for a Buddhistic negation of the will. Art saves him, and through art – life' (ibid.). The Greek experience of art is an affirmative one, for it offers the possibility of living beyond good and evil. Nietzsche writes:

Whoever approaches these Olympians with another religion in his heart, searching among them for moral elevation, even for sanctity, for disincarnate spirituality, for charity and benevolence, will be soon forced to turn his back on them, discouraged and disappointed. For there is nothing here which suggests asceticism, spirituality, or duty. We hear nothing but the accents of an exuberant, triumphant life in which all things, whether good or evil, are deified. (*BT* 3)

It is this attitude of a 'pessimism of strength', requiring the ability to affirm life in the face of its terrifying aspects, that Nietzsche argues is missing in modern culture. We have been 'emasculated' through Christianity – 'this womanish flight from seriousness and terror' (*BT* 11); our political theories are sentimental and fail to recognise that every culture must accept the necessity of slavery (Rousseau and socialism) (*BT* 18). Our contemporary view of the world is a scientific and theoretical one (as opposed to the artistic and mythic one of the Greeks Nietzsche depicts), the legacy of a 'Socratism' which believes that knowledge can penetrate the deepest abysses of being, and even correct and *improve* life (*BT* 13).

For Nietzsche, therefore, the Greek experience of art can instruct us in how it is possible to overcome nihilism, not through a utopian politics or an eschatological religion, but through the cultivation of an affirmation of the tragic character of existence. Like modern humanity, the Greeks felt themselves overwhelmed by the senselessness and meaninglessness of existence. But through tragic art they addressed the challenge of the wisdom of Silenus, which declared that the best thing of all is not to be born, not 'to be', and that the second best thing is to die soon. Art, for the Greeks, was not simply an imitation of nature, but 'a metaphysical supplement of the reality of nature, placed beside it for its overcoming and transfiguration' (*BT* 24). It is in this context that Nietzsche severely criticises an age reared on the bosom of Rousseau's sentimentalism, with its naive view of a benign and benevolent primordial nature:

Here we should note that this harmony which is contemplated with such longing by modern man, this oneness with nature...is by no means a simple condition which comes into being naturally and as if inevitably. It is not a condition which, like a terrestrial paradise, must *necessarily* be found at the gate of every culture. Only a romantic age could believe this, an age which conceived of the artist in terms of Rousseau's *Émile*...Where we encounter the 'naive' in art, we should recognize the highest effect of Apollonian culture, which must always first overcome an empire of Titans and slay monsters, and which must have triumphed over an abysmal and terrifying view of the world and keenest susceptibility to suffering through recourse to the most forceful and pleasurable illusions. (*BT* 3)

The two deities, Apollo and Dionysus, reveal for Nietzsche the deep tension in which the Greeks existed as creatures who could only overcome nihilism by cultivating an aesthetic appreciation of the spectacle of life – life as primordial pain, suffering, and self-contradiction. Through art the Greeks gained a Dionysian sense of the primordial unity of nature and of man, and, at the same time, were redeemed from its intoxicating effects through the pleasurable illusion afforded by the Apollonain. In the Dionysian experience excess reveals itself as 'truth', and contradiction speaks out from the heart of nature. Nietzsche's greatest fear, however, is that if it is interpreted politically, the Dionysian experience will incite people to change social and political institutions, and to reform them in accordance with the experience of oneness which the Dionysian reveals as the true ground of being.

In *The Birth of Tragedy* Nietzsche argues against any attempt to employ the Dionysian in the services of a rationalist (Socratic) politics. He considers Socrates to be 'the one turning point and vortex of so-called world history' (*BT* 15).[3] He is the 'prototype of the theoretical optimist' who believes that it is possible not only to know reality as it is in-itself, but to correct and improve it. For Nietzsche there is 'an eternal conflict between the theoretical and the tragic world-view' (*BT* 17). In contrast to the rationalism and optimism of the former, the tragic view esteems myth as the foundation of culture and society. The theoretical view deludes itself into believing that earthly happiness is possible for all, while the tragic view accepts the necessity of slavery (*BT* 18). Although there can be no final redemption from the suffering of life and history, an aristocratic culture can create the conditions for an heroic experience of the primordial pain, and pleasure, of existence. Nietzsche ultimately objects to Socrates' attempt to give a rational and conscious foundation to aristocratic rule. Not only was Socrates wrong in believing that it is possible to penetrate the deepest abysses of being, but his teaching has led to a theoretical optimism which believes that it is possible to transform society and establish a just social order founded on rational principles. Socrates did not set out to revolutionise the content of Athenian morality, or to create a new one, but to give common morality the *self-consciousness* it lacked.

Nietzsche holds that modern politics rests on a certain moral faith in truth and rationality which is derived from Socrates. For Nietzsche, however, it is necessary to revalue the value of science and knowledge if we are to properly appreciate the meaning of culture. This he does in the *Untimely Meditations*. He argues for a 'revolution in education' as the solution to the ills of modern society: 'Culture [*Bildung*] is liberation' (*SE* 1, p. 130). Culture is conceived as the domain of 'transfigured *physis*' (nature) (*SE* 3, p. 145), and defined as the 'unity of artistic style in all the expressions of the life of a people' (*HL* 4, p. 79). At the end of the meditation on history Nietzsche argues that the Greek experience of education and culture centres on the task of organising the chaos within ourselves by thinking back to our real needs. And 'thus the Greek conception of culture will be revealed... the conception of culture [*Cultur*] as a new and improved *physis*, without inner and outer, without dissimulation and convention, culture as unanimity of life, thought, appearance, and will' (*HL* 10, p. 123). In his meditation on history he argues that, 'the *goal of humanity* cannot lie in its end, but only *in its highest exemplars* (*HL* 9, p. 111). He makes it clear that his attempt to effect a major reform of education should be understood in terms of a striving for '*German unity*' in its highest sense. The untimely educators are to strive more ardently for 'the unity of German spirit and life after the abolition of the antithesis of form and content, of subjectivity and convention', than they are for 'political reunification' (*HL* 4, p. 82).

Nietzsche wants to show that 'instruction without invigoration', and 'knowledge unattended by action', are a 'costly superfluity and luxury'. He attacks the education system in Germany for burying the youthfulness and innocence of life under the weight of the past through the study of history. We certainly need history, Nietzsche says, but 'for reasons different from those for which the idler in the garden of knowledge needs it' (*HL* Foreword, p. 59). Thus, Nietzsche sets out to pose a decisive question to his age and its educators: 'Is life to dominate knowledge and science, or is knowledge to dominate

life? Which of these two forces is the higher and more decisive?'
(*HL* 10, p. 121).

Why is the present study of history in terms of an objective
science such a problem for Nietzsche? According to him there is
a deep conflict within the human being between the faculty of
memory and the power of forgetting, between knowledge and
innocence, between the past and the future. He posits as a
'universal law' that a living thing can only thrive, that is, be
healthy and strong, to the extent that it is bounded by a horizon
(*HL* 1, p. 63). Unlike an animal like the cow, which passes from
one moment to the next in blissful ignorance, the human being
possesses a consciousness of the past which it always carries with
it. The animal is able to live unhistorically, for its existence is
consumed solely by the present moment and with satisfying its
immediate needs and desires. An animal, Nietzsche says, cannot
dissimulate, 'it conceals nothing and at every instant it appears
as wholly as it is' (*HL* 1, p. 61). In contrast to the animal who
has no lasting memory and is unable to make promises man is
burdened by his knowledge of the past which 'pushes him down
and bends him sideways'. The grief of man consists in the fact
that life always reminds him of the 'it was', which Nietzsche
describes as 'that password which gives conflict, suffering, and
satiety access to man so as to remind him what his existence
fundamentally is – an imperfect tense that never becomes a
perfect one (ibid.).

The weight of the past prohibits a human being from living a
truly creative life. This is why Nietzsche says that the reader
must meditate on the proposition that '*the unhistorical and the
historical are required in equal measure for the health of an individual, of
a people and of a culture*' (ibid., p. 63). To be an authentic human
being is to live within this tension of the historical (knowledge)
and the unhistorical (ignorance). Nietzsche expands.

He who cannot sink down on the threshold of the moment and forget
all the past, who cannot stand balanced like a goddess of victory
without growing dizzy and afraid, will never know what happiness is
– worse, he will never do anything to make others happy. Imagine the
extremist example of a man who did not possess the power of
forgetting at all and who was thus condemned to see everywhere a

state of becoming: such a man would no longer believe in his own
being, would no longer believe in himself... and would lose himself in
this stream of becoming: like a true pupil of Heraclitus, he would in
the end hardly dare to raise a finger. (ibid., p. 62)

The capacity to live unhistorically is, Nietzsche contends, more
vital and more fundamental than its opposite, since 'it
constitutes the foundation upon which alone anything sound,
healthy and great, anything truly human, can grow' (ibid. p.
63).

It was in the atmosphere of a strong and unified Germany
(1866–74) that Nietzsche read Schopenhauer as the philosopher
of a regenerated Germany. It seemed self-evident to him that
the new political epoch in Germany would inevitably require a
cultural analogue. As one commentator has noted: 'Bismarck's
political solution had made possible, so Nietzsche thought, a
cultural blossoming under the aegis of Schopenhauer'.[4] It was
the aspiration of Nietzsche and his academic friends of this time
to turn Schopenhauer into the kind of inspirational figure for
the generation of 1866 that Hegel had been for the generation
of 1830. In 1877, for example, Wilhelm Wundt, a leading neo-
Kantian, could write that Schopenhauer had become 'the head
of non-academic philosophy in Germany'.[5] Although Nietzsche
later rejected Schopenhauer as his mentor, regarding his
philosophy as a continuation of the Christian-moral tradition,
at this stage he is the only German philosopher Nietzsche can
use against the orthodoxies – academic, educational, political –
of the age. Schopenhauer's philosophy teaches us to stop and
think, to stand apart from the masses and follow our conscience
which calls to us: 'Be your self! All you are now doing, thinking,
desiring, is not you yourself!' (*SE* 1, p. 127). Through an
engagement with Schopenhauer we are to become what we are,
and to discover 'the fundamental law of our own true self', for
our 'true nature', Nietzsche says, lies infinitely high above
(*über*) ourselves – or what we commonly take to be ourselves
(ibid., p. 129). For Nietzsche 'A happy life is impossible: the
highest that man can attain to is a *heroic one*' (ibid. p. 153).
Heroism consists in the ability of the individual to withstand the
flux of time and attain, however brief and fleetingly, a moment

of eternity; it lies in making oneself 'imperishable' (ibid., p. 155).

Nietzsche's emphasis on education and culture results in a denigration of political activity. He writes:

Every philosophy which believes that the problem of existence is touched on, not to say solved, by a political event is a joke – and pseudo-philosophy. Many states have been founded since the world began; that is an old story. How should a political innovation suffice to turn men once and for all into contented inhabitants of the earth? If anyone really does believe in this possibility he ought to come forward, for he truly deserves to become a professor of philosophy. (ibid., 4, p. 148)

There can be no ultimate redemption from the tragic character of existence. We should seek to transcend the narrow standpoint of a weak individuality, and affirm the eternal self-creation and self-destruction of life which is without final goal or purpose.

THE GREEK STATE

The early, unpublished essay on the Greek state is a significant piece of work in Nietzsche's corpus in several respects. His political thought is usually seen to rest on an uncompromising individualism, which allies him with liberalism.[6] But in this essay Nietzsche construes the ethical basis of the individual's relationship to the state in a way normally associated with Rousseau or Hegel. It reveals that, for someone who is supposed to be uninterested in politics, Nietzsche is familiar with the development of political theory, and is concerned to evaluate the new political ideologies, such as liberalism and socialism, in terms of what he regards as a degeneration in modern political thinking. He attempts to show the limits of a liberal politics and rejects a sentimental view of life. The 'cry of compassion' must not be allowed to tear down 'the walls of culture'.

Nietzsche's early political thinking is similar to that of Rousseau and Hegel in that it wishes to regenerate, in an epoch ruled by an atomised individualism, a sense of Greek political life with the emphasis on political discipline and conceiving the individual as part of an organic whole. Nietzsche's thinking on politics faces the same kind of dilemmas which confronted Rousseau and Hegel.[7] Modern political culture rests on a potentially anarchic individualism, in which those virtues which cultivate political discipline have been eroded. In the modern polity the basis of the individual's obligation to society rests almost entirely on prudential grounds. Thus, the political sentiments and virtues which Nietzsche requires for a rebirth of tragic, aristocratic culture are absent in the modern world: the 'ethical impulse' and the call to a 'higher destiny' are undermined and rendered redundant by the rise of liberal individualism.

The essay begins with a contrast between the views of the Greeks and 'we moderns' (*Wir Neuren*) on the nature of existence and work. The modern world is characterised as an age of work in which the most esteemed ideas are those of the 'dignity of man' and the 'dignity of labour'. The Greeks, however, Nietzsche argues, did not glorify labour through a work ethic because they knew that a life devoted to toiling makes it impossible for a person to become an artist. Nietzsche interprets the nature of modern politics in this context:

Cursed seducers, who have destroyed the slave's state of innocence by the fruit of the tree of knowledge! Now the slave must vainly escape through from one day to another with transparent lies recognisable to every one of deeper insight, such as the alleged 'equal rights of all' or the so-called 'fundamental rights of man', of man as such, or the 'dignity of labour'. Indeed he is not to understand at what stage and at what height dignity can first be mentioned – namely, at the point, where the individual goes wholly beyond himself and no longer has to work and to produce in order to preserve his individual existence. (*GSt* p. 5)

The main insight which Nietzsche draws from his interpretation of Greek life is that 'culture – defined as "a real need for art" – rests upon a terrible basis'; namely:

In order that there may be a broad, deep, and fruitful soil for the development of art, the enormous majority must, in the service of a minority, be slavishly subjected to life's struggle, to a *greater* degree than their own wants necessitate. At their cost, through the surplus of their labour, that privileged class is to be relieved from the struggle for existence, in order to create and to satisfy a new world of want. (ibid., pp. 6–7)

Nietzsche knows that he is saying something which runs counter to the cherished ideal of equality which characterises the modern polity. We moderns, he argues, refuse to accept the fact that *'slavery is of the essence of culture'*. Today politics is characterised by resentment against this fact. Nietzsche presents the reader with the choice between an aristocratic culture and a democratic polity in the following terms:

If culture really rested upon the will of the people, if here inexorable powers did not rule, powers which are law and barrier to the individual, then the contempt for culture, the glorification of 'poorness in spirit', the iconoclastic annihilation of artistic claims would be *more* than an insurrection of the suppressed masses against drone-like individuals; it would be the cry of compassion tearing down the walls of culture; the desire for justice, for the equalization of suffering, would swamp all other ideas. (ibid. p. 7)

It is 'out of the emasculation of modern man' (in the sense that we squeam at the thought of there being slaves) that the enormous social ills of the present age have been born. If it is the case, he suggests, that the Greeks perished through their slavedom, then it is a certain fact that we moderns shall perish through our lack of it. In the absence of a strong political discipline and a hierarchical social structure, the entire ethical and legal basis of society will collapse since it will be placed in the hands of egoistic individuals who view their relationship to the state solely in terms of the satisfaction of self-interest.

For Nietzsche, the state is the means by which the social process of imposing political discipline on the individual is performed. It may well be that man possesses a sociable instinct, but without the iron clamp of the state, Nietzsche says, following Hobbes, it would be impossible to educate the individual into a political animal: 'without the state, in the natural *bellum omnium contra omnes* society cannot strike root at all on a larger scale and beyond the reach of the family' (ibid., p. 12). The origins of the state are violent and bloody for it is in the nature of power that it 'gives the first *right*, and there is no right which is not at bottom presumption, usurpation, violence' (ibid. p. 10). This is a position Nietzsche maintains throughout his writings, and which he uses to combat a sentimental politics. The state should be regarded by those who have political insight as 'the goal and ultimate aim of the sacrifices and duties of the individual' (ibid. p. 11). It is only the state, in spite of its ignominious origins and violent birth, which is able to reveal to individuals their true worth, for at times, perhaps of battle, it calls upon them to make heroic sacrifices and to perform heroic deeds. Nietzsche describes the Greeks as the 'political men in themselves' (only Renaissance Italy comes anywhere palpably close, and even then that is remote) because they possessed political knowledge and freely subjected themselves to the discipline of the state.

It is because political instinct and virtues are absent in the modern period that Nietzsche discerns 'dangerous atrophies in the political sphere equally critical for art and society'. Instead of the state being a means to the production of culture, it is today in the process of being reduced to a means for the furtherance of the wishes of the egoistic individual:

If there should exist men who, as it were through birth are placed outside the national and state-instincts, who consequently have to esteem the state in so far as they conceive that it coincides with their own interest, then such men will necessarily imagine as the ultimate political aim the most undisturbed collateral existence of great political communities possible, in which *they* might be permitted to pursue their own purposes without restriction. With this idea in their heads they will promote *that* policy which will offer the greatest security to these purposes; whereas it is unthinkable, that they, against their intentions, guided perhaps by an unconscious instinct, should sacrifice themselves for the state: unthinkable because they lack that very instinct. (ibid. p. 13)

Nietzsche argues that the modern philosophy of the state stems from the 'liberal optimistic view of the world, which has its roots in the doctrines of French Rationalism and the French Revolution' (ibid. p. 14). The goal of modern politics is to free the state from the possibility of the incalculable convulsions of war and establish it on a purely rational basis for the pursuit of economic ends – what Nietzsche at one point in the essay calls the 'deviation of the state-tendency into a money-tendency' (ibid. p. 15). Nietzsche argues that war, in fact, is the only remedy to cure this decline of the state into liberal optimism, for it is war which shows the individual that the state is not simply a 'protective institution for egoistic individuals', but 'in love to fatherland and prince, it produces an ethical impulse, indicative of a much higher destiny' (ibid.). Nietzsche justifies his call for war in the following terms:

If I therefore designate as a dangerous and characteristic sign of the present political situation the application of revolutionary thought in the service of a selfish state-less money aristocracy, if at the same time I conceive of the enormous dissemination of liberal optimism as the result of modern financial affairs fallen into strange hands, and if I imagine all evils of social conditions together with the necessary decay of the arts to have either germinated from that root or grown together with it, one will have to pardon my occasionally chanting a Paean on war. Horribly clangs its silvery bow; and although it comes along like the night, war is nevertheless Apollo, the true divinity for consecrating and purifying the state. (ibid.)

It should come as no surprise that Nietzsche, like Rousseau, should sing the praises of the Spartans for their cultivation of military genius.

Nietzsche closes the essay by criticising modern political theories – he specifically mentions liberalism and socialism (as we shall see, Nietzsche interprets modern socialism in terms of an *exacerbation* of the atomistic and individualistic tendencies of liberalism, not as their overcoming) – for reducing the relationship between the individual and the state to a merely prudential one in which our obligation to society arises out of fear and insecurity, and in which its prime basis is that of rational self-interest. Although Nietzsche does not mention any particular thinkers here, it is clear that his reference to liberalism contains an implicit critique of Hobbes and Locke who construe political obligation precisely in the terms that Nietzsche depicts. As Richard Tuck has suggested in his study of Hobbes, if liberalism is the doctrine that the state primarily exists to protect natural, pre-political rights, then Hobbes and Locke can be fairly interpreted as the founders of an early liberal tradition.[8] Nietzsche defends a classical Platonic conception of the state in which the emphasis is placed on the ethical basis of political life, and in which the individual is valued to the extent that he or she fulfils their particular function in the social whole. Regarding the political theory of Plato's *Republic*, for example, Nietzsche writes that it is only here that the proper aim of the state – defined as 'the Olympian existence and ever-renewed procreation and preparation of genius' – is discovered 'with poetic intuition and painted with firmness'. The difference between Plato and Nietzsche is that, whereas for Plato the man of genius is represented by the man of knowledge (Socrates or the philosopher-king), for Nietzsche he is represented by the artist. Throughout his writings, in fact, Nietzsche never stopped praising Plato for his artistry. The problem of Plato for Nietzsche is that he failed to recognise the artistic basis of his own philosophy and presented it as eternal and objective truth.[9] For Nietzsche, any such truth is an illusion; what the artist or poet does is to *invent* a 'true' world. In politics, however, it may be necessary to disguise the artistic production of truth so as to give the appearance, the illusion, of a natural order of things (as in Plato's well-known noble myth, for example). In Plato's political thought one finds the 'great hieroglyph of a profound and eternally to be interpreted *esoteric doctrine of the connection between the state and genius*' (ibid. p. 18).

In *Homer's Contest* Nietzsche argues that the Greeks recognised that at the core of human nature were to be found violent and cruel impulses. He argues that just as the idea of Greek law emerged from murder and its expiation, so does nobler civilisation take its 'first wreath of victory from the altar of the expiation of murder' (*HC* p. 53). Nietzsche counters the view that humanity is different from nature. The so-called 'natural' qualities and the properly called human attributes have grown up inseparably. 'Man in his highest and noblest capacities is nature and bears in himself its awful twofold character'. The abilities and attributes widely considered terrible and inhuman are 'the fertile soil, out of which alone, can grow forth all humanity in feelings, deeds, and works' (ibid. p. 51).

For Nietzsche it is the contest (*agon*) (in politics, in the arts, in sport, and in festival) which serves to sublimate and channel the fearful and aggressive impulses of human nature, ensuring that the individual drives promote the 'welfare of the whole, of the civic society' (ibid. p. 58). Every Athenian, he argues, 'was to cultivate [his] ego in contest, so that it should be of the highest service to Athens and should do the least harm' (ibid.). Through the medium of the contest the Greeks were able to bridle and restrict selfishness. Individuals in Greek society lived within definite boundaries and clear horizons. Individuals in antiquity were freer than modern individuals because their aims were more tangible. Modern man, by contrast, has emancipated himself from the social bond and from traditional roles and hierarchies, but only to discover that his newly won infinite freedom is too great a burden (ibid. p. 59).

Nietzsche does not simply glorify the cruel basis of the state. Nor is his attitude that of a conservative apologist contemplating with false modesty the refinements of high culture. As one commentator has pointed out, our aim should be neither to excuse nor condemn Nietzsche for his views, but to show a greater appreciation of his sensitivity to the dilemmas of culture.[10] Nietzsche does not hide the fact that culture is built on the blood and misery of the oppressed. He expresses the contest between culture and politics in tragic terms. The 'cry of compassion' of the oppressed is a legitimate one, but if it is allowed to determine the fate of politics then the ethical basis of the state will be eroded and society will no longer exist for the sake of art and greatness, but for the satisfaction of a narrow egoism. He is astute in showing us the unpalatable truth that modern liberal democracy tends to undermine aesthetic greatness, heroic individuality, and aristocratic notions of freedom. For the liberal all values on life are relativised and rendered of equal worth. There is no recognition of the necessity of an order of rank in society and among values. Social life becomes characterised by a narrowly defined individuality in which the emphasis is placed on the cultivation of a *private* egoism. Nietzsche is showing us some of the dilemmas thrown up by modern democracy and the fateful consequences modern ways of thinking have for art and culture.

The arguments Nietzsche puts forward in defence of slavery and war perhaps seem alien and naive to us, not simply because they run counter to our ingrained liberal and democratic sentiments, but, more importantly, because of our knowledge of the horrors of war we have witnessed in the twentieth century. They are naive in their failure to relate Greek political virtues to the economic and military realities of work and war in the nineteenth century. In particular, Nietzsche makes no attempt to tailor his arguments to the changed conditions of work under the techniques of modern industrial production, grounding them instead in ideas which spring from an ancient slave culture. One of the most powerful aspects of Marx's critique of capitalism is his theory of alienation in which he exposes the crippling effects modern conditions of work have on the existential and psychological life of the worker.[11] The force of Marx's critique of capitalist society stems, to a large extent, from its appreciation of social ills generated by a class-divided society, in which politics becomes dominated by the economic clash of the rich and the poor. In contrast to the appositeness of Marx's critique, Nietzsche's grasp of the economic and social realities of modern society seems very superficial, no more trenchant or adequate than that of a typical 'romantic anti-capitalist'.[12]

CONCLUSION

Nietzsche's interpretation of the Greeks is political in the sense that it is motivated by ideological interests. In his attempt to discredit ancient and modern democracy and to elevate an aristocratic culture he presents us with a stark either/or logic. His political thought rests on a devaluation of politics as it was experienced in the golden age of democracy in Periclean Athens. In spite of his opposition to Socrates, Nietzsche shares his devaluation of the historically evolved *polis* as a democratic polity. What is missing in Nietzsche's portrait of the Greeks is any appreciation of the novel and original nature of their experience of politics. Greek democracy established new kinds of political relationships in that it replaced the rule of kinship and tribal custom, as well as the arbitrary rule of the master over his subject, with civic bonds and the rule of law. The Greeks establish a new form of communal relationship which is neither tribal nor a patriarchal and hierarchical household writ large. In the democratic *polis* 'Palace and king are replaced by a community of free men or *citizens*'.[13] It is not the king but the citizen-body which embodies the state.

Nietzsche's estimation of politics is an instrumentalist one. In its failure to appreciate the distinctive democratic features of the Greek *polis* it reduces politics to no more than an instrument of social control. He views action in purely amoral and aesthetic terms as perpetual virtuosity. While Nietzsche is often astute in showing us the reasons why we should opt for culture over politics, he does seem blind to the virtues of a democratic polity.[14]

Nietzsche's first published work on Greek tragedy and culture is full of youthful reflections which he himself later subjected to severe criticism. In 1886 he confessed that he found it 'a questionable book', which suffered from burdening ancient Greek culture with problems which were peculiarly modern. As he points out at the beginning of his 1886 'Attempt At A Self-Criticism', in the midst and wake of the Franco-Prussian War of 1870/1 a 'bemused and beriddled' young professor, suffering from romantic yearnings of a decidedly modern kind, wrote down his thoughts about the *Greeks*! He confesses that the book's aestheticism and romanticism reflected his own personal pessimism regarding the prospects for cultural regeneration in Germany. The question he wanted to pose, and which he still takes to be a valid and important one, is whether it is possible to identify a 'pessimism of strength'; that is, a pessimism which reveals an intellectual preference for the hard, gruesome, and evil aspects of existence prompted by well-being and over-flowing health. Nietzsche admits the paradox: a pessimism about existence which arises from health? What he now locates in both the music of Wagner and the philosophy of Schopen-hauer is a morbid 'romantic pessimism'. He avails himself of a 'dual interpretation' of the work of artists and philosophers, asking the crucial question: does the artist or thinker suffer and create from an overfullness or an impoverishment of life? If they

suffer from overflowing health then, he argues, their desire for
destruction and change can be an expression of a powerful
energy which is 'pregnant with future'; if, on the other hand,
they suffer from the latter condition, then such a desire is often
the expression of the hatred and resentment of the disinherited
and underprivileged (*GS* 370).

It is this type of questioning which becomes the prevailing
feature of Nietzsche's mature work. Nietzsche's inquiry in the
Genealogy of Morals, for example, is guided by the question: are
modern moral values signs of exuberant, creative life or signs
that humanity has become exhausted and weary of itself?
Reflection on the Greeks in *The Birth of Tragedy*, which
concentrates on aesthetic values, enabled Nietzsche to develop
his philosophical education and to begin the task of deciphering
the signs of modernity. In effect, Nietzsche was writing in his
early work a version of 'monumental history', that is, the type
of history which, as he states in his untimely meditation on the
subject, enables one to strive for greatness in the present by
recollecting past greatness. One is inspired by the example of
the past. Furthermore, in certain respects *The Birth of Tragedy*
already constitutes what Nietzsche later called a 'genealogy of
morals', that is, a 'history of the present' (how one becomes
what one is). Nietzsche was opening up the present, and its
possibilities for future development, by bringing to light a
different image of the past to the one which prevailed in
European culture at this time. The dominant picture of the
Greeks was developed by Johann Winckelmann (1717–68),
who portrayed the Greeks in terms of 'noble simplicity and
calm grandeur'.

In later life, therefore, Nietzsche's attitude toward his first
book was a deeply ambivalent one. On the one hand, he
considered it, 'badly written, ponderous, embarassing, image-
mad and image-confused, sentimental...a book for initiates'.
On the other hand, however, it revealed a knack for opening up
'new secret paths and dancing places' (*BT* 'Attempt At A Self-
Criticism', 3). Thus, beneath the rhapsodic tones of the sick
romantic, the 'dialectical ill-humour of the German', and the
'bad manners of a Wagnerian', it is possible to detect 'a *strange*

voice' and 'the disciple of a still "unknown God"' (Dionysus).
Nietzsche still upholds the fundamental claim of the book that
art is the truly life-affirming and life-enhancing activity of man.
Morality, by contrast, reveals a hostility to life, since it cannot
accept that life is based on semblance, on deception, on
perspectives, and on error. Morality has to be 'judged' (again
a paradox on Nietzsche's part) as a 'will to negate life, as a
secret principle of decay, diminution, and slander… the danger
of dangers' (ibid., 5). However, Nietzsche now wishes to
relinquish the romantic perspective governing his first book and
to call into question its emphasis on art as providing human
beings with 'metaphysical comfort' in the face of the terror and
absurdity of existence. He now holds the view that only
romantics and Christians need to be comforted *metaphysically*.
What is required of strong pessimists is that they learn what he
calls 'the art of *this-worldly* comfort', which is the art of *laughter*
(ibid. 7). What Nietzsche wishes to advocate fourteen years
after publishing his first book is not simply the importance of
recognising the *tragedy*, but, more importantly, the *comedy* of
existence. Thus, when viewed from the perspective of his mature
outlook, his first book might be more accurately titled 'The
Birth of Comedy'.

In contrast to the outlook of his first book, therefore,
Nietzsche's mature thinking is based on the recognition that one
must gain a distance from one's 'modernity' if one is successfully
to overcome it. The philosopher can do this by cultivating his or
her untimeliness (something Nietzsche begins to do shortly after
the appearance of *The Birth of Tragedy*). The problem of the first
book for the later Nietzsche is that it displays all that is
unhealthy and morbid about the present. In his later work he
sets himself a new task, the necessity of working through one's
decadence and sickness. He recognises that one cannot freely
choose whether one is born into an age that is healthy or one
that is decadent. Thus, neither Socrates nor Wagner *chose* to be
decadents; they were both artists who embodied the malaise
and degeneration of their time. What is necessary, however,
is to recognise the signs and symptoms of one's time, resist
modernity, and, in this way, achieve a degree of freedom. To

overcome one's own time requires, above all, that one is able to overcome one's prior aversion towards, and suffering from it (*GS* 380). Nietzsche can say he is a decadent (for he is a child of his time), but can also claim that he represents a possible new beginning since he *resists* his time. He thus describes himself as the teacher of the modern age *par excellence*, since his life-work embodies both morbid and healthy aspects. He represents *both* a danger and a promise. (*EH* 'Why I Am So Wise', 1).

In effect, what Nietzsche is doing in portraying himself in such terms is to encourage his readers to place their reception of his teaching beyond good and evil (beyond the simple 'yes' and 'no' of moral judgement), and so construe their confrontation with his work in terms of a fate (Nietzsche describes himself in *Ecce Homo* as a 'fatality'). Thus, when he says that in order to overcome Wagner one must first become a Wagnerian, the same could equally apply to the reader's own reception of Nietzsche (*CW* Preface).

CHAPTER 4

Nietzsche on modern politics

INTRODUCTION: ENLIGHTENMENT AND REVOLUTION

The writings of the period 1878–82 contain a set of coherent and instructive insights into the realities and dilemmas of modern social existence. In these writings we find a Nietzsche championing the aims of the Enlightenment, and promoting the cause of a rationalist, critical theory.

It is here that Nietzsche first begins his archaeological excavation of the historical evolution of moral concepts and judgements. Casting off the comforts of Schopenhauerian metaphysics he now supports modern philosophy in its attack on all unexamined authority, whether that authority be religious and metaphysical, moral or political. He supports the Enlightenment, but condemns any attempt to develop a philosophy of revolution out of its challenge to illegitimate authority. An opposition between 'enlightenment' and 'revolution' is presented in terms of a contrast between Rousseau and Voltaire. For Nietzsche a philosophy of revolution suffers from the delusion that once a social order has been overturned then 'the proudest temple of fair humanity will at once rise up of its own accord'. The modern theory of revolution is derived from Rousseau's belief that beneath the layers of civilisation there lies buried a natural human goodness; the source of corruption lies not within man, in human nature, but in the institutions of the state and society, and in education. Against this theory Nietzsche offers the following warning and advice:

The experiences of history have taught us, unfortunately, that every such revolution brings about the resurrection of the most savage

energies in the shape of the long-buried dreadfulness and excesses of
the most distant ages: that a revolution can thus be a source of energy
in mankind grown feeble but never a regulator, architect, artist,
perfector of human nature. It is not *Voltaire's* moderate nature,
inclined as it was to ordering, purifying, and reconstructing, but
Rousseau's passionate follies and half-lies that called forth the optimistic
spirit of the Revolution against which I cry: '*Ecrasez l'infame!*' It is this
spirit that has for a long time banished the *spirit of Enlightenment and of
progressive evolution*: let us see – each of us within himself – whether it is
possible to call it back! (*HAH* 463)

It is notable that the views enunciated in this passage are
continuous with Nietzsche's earliest political thinking; once
again he expresses the view that culture must override politics,
and warns against Dionysian excesses, especially if they lead to
the cultivation of revolutionary fervour in a directly political
sense. Nietzsche favours the Apollonian 'Voltaire', championing 'progressive evolution' over 'revolution'. Notwithstanding
the excesses of his last books, Nietzsche never abandoned his fear
and distrust of moral and political fanaticism.

In order to further the cause of moderation and progressive
evolution Nietzsche calls for a new mode of philosophising
which begins from the assumption that there are no eternal facts
and no absolute truths. Philosophers lack an historical sense.
The recognition that man has evolved should guide the
philosophy of the future. Nietzsche writes, on the way toward 'a
genealogy of morals':

Now, everything *essential* in the development of mankind took place in
primeval times, long before the four thousand years we more or less
know about; during these years mankind may well not have altered
very much. But the philosopher here sees 'instincts' in man as he is
now and assumes that these belong to the unalterable facts of mankind
and to that extent provide a key to the understanding of the world in
general: the whole of teleology is constructed by speaking of the man
of the last four millenia as of an *eternal* man towards whom all things
in the world have had a natural relationship from the time he began.
(*HAH* 2)

Nietzsche's attempt to carry out a critique of metaphysics and
philosophical authority reflects what he sees as significant

political changes taking place in modern European societies. For him the growing liberalisation and democratisation of society generates the need for a new 'historical' mode of philosophising which is to be both enlightened and critical. He becomes an advocate of both programmes of change and development, the philosophical *and* the political.

THE DECLINE OF AUTHORITY AND THE RISE OF THE MODERN STATE

According to Nietzsche it is necessary to recognise that in the modern age belief in unconditional authority and definitive truth is disappearing. What characterises the modern age is the secularisation of political authority. 'The period of the tyrant is past'. Nietzsche writes, 'In the sphere of higher culture there will always have to be sovereign authority, to be sure – but this sovereign authority will hereafter lie in the hands of the *oligarchs of the spirit*' (*HAH* 261). We find in this passage a continuation of Nietzsche's early concern that political reform and change in Europe should be accompanied by cultural reform and change, and a prefiguration of his later call for philosopher-legislators to be cultivated who would give direction to the future of Europe by legislating new values (*BGE* 211).

In the writings of this middle period Nietzsche is at his most compromising, prepared to concede a great deal to the tide of modern politics, and arguing that what is needed to cure social ills 'is not a forcible redistribution of property but a gradual transformation of mind: the sense of justice must grow greater in everyone and the instinct for violence weaker' (*HAH* 452). Absent from modern political life for Nietzsche is any real sense of customs and traditions. The capacity to build a new future depends on an ability to see a continuity with the strengths of the past (traditions). A certain way of thinking about politics and society (Nietzsche calls it a 'faith'), which would enable us to calculate and anticipate the future is dying out today. This is 'the faith that man has value and meaning only insofar as he is *a stone in a great edifice*' (*GS* 356).

With the decline in religious belief, modern societies lack the traditional means for legitimating authority. He argues, for example, that 'where law is no longer tradition, as is the case with us, it can only be *commanded*, imposed by constraint, so we have to put up with *arbitrary law*, which is the expression of the necessity of the fact that there *has to be* law' (ibid. 459). The decisive occurrence of the modern period for Nietzsche is the decline of a religious basis to the state. One of the major passages in *Human, All Too Human*, absolutely central for understanding Nietzsche's political thought during this period, is devoted to this topic. It reveals sentiments that make it possible to connect Nietzsche to a certain extent with the political thinking of the early liberal tradition of Hobbes and Locke.

The passage, entitled 'Religion and Government', begins by noting that the significance of religion in the life of a culture lies in the fact that it consoles the hearts of individuals in times of loss, deprivation, and fear; that is, in times when a government is powerless to alleviate the psychical sufferings of its people in the face of inevitable and unavoidable events such as famines and wars (or at least what appeared in earlier times as unavoidable). Religion is useful in that, through the cultivation of popular sentiment and a common identity, it secures internal civil peace and fosters the continuous development of a culture. Nietzsche claims that 'absolute tutelary government and the careful preservation of religion necessarily go together', because it is impossible – as Napoleon recognised – for political power to gain legitimacy without the assistance of the priestly class. However, this close association between religion and politics only holds good in a situation where the governing classes know the advantages they can accrue from religion and feel superior to it. Religion simply serves them as a useful instrument of popular control and political discipline. But in a democratic state the situation is quite different, for here it is more than likely that religion will be regarded as an instrument of the popular will, not as an 'above' in relation to a 'below', but merely as a function of the sole sovereign power, 'the people'. In this political framework, control of society through religious teaching will not be so easy, because teaching will be open to rational and enlightened debate and scrutiny. The only exception

Nietzsche envisages is where the party leaders in a democracy exercise an influence similar to that under an enlightened despotism. What is likely, however, is that in a society where the state is no longer free to profit from religion, and where society tolerates pluralism in religious beliefs and practices, religion will become merely a private affair, left to the conscience and customs of each individual.[1]

The result of this decline in the importance of religion in the cultural life of a community or a state is that the ethical basis of the individual's obligation to society is gradually eroded as egoistical sentiments come to dominate its sense of political obligation. Nietzsche regards the fundamental consequence of the rise of modern democracy to be the 'decline and death of the state'. One of the points he wishes to emphasise is that the modern secular state represents only the 'liberation of the private person', not of the 'individual'. This is a significant remark on Nietzsche's part because it shows that the widely held view of him as an extreme individualist, or an existentialist, solely preoccupied with the nature of an asocial, isolated individual, is profoundly misleading. As this remark shows, Nietzsche's commitment is to culture and to the citizen, not to the abstract private individual of modern liberal democracy. Like the political thinking of Rousseau and Hegel, Nietzsche's political thought is characterised from beginning to end by a desire to transcend the atomistic basis of modern societies and its narrow, 'bourgeois', individualism. The privatisation of society for Nietzsche means the *end* of society. Consider the following in which Nietzsche is exposing the effects of the decline of any ethical basis to political obligation, bearing in mind that he is addressing an audience of European readers in the late 1870s, not the 1980s or 1990s:

Henceforth the individual will see only the side of it [the state] that promises to be useful or threatens to be harmful to him ... None of the measures effected by a government will be guaranteed continuity; everybody will draw back from undertakings that require quiet tending for decades or centuries if their fruits are to mature. No one will feel towards a law any greater obligation than that bowing for the moment to the force which backs up the law: one will then at once set to work to subvert it with a new force, the creation of a new majority. Finally – one can say this with certainty – distrust of all government, insight into the uselessness and destructiveness of these short-winded struggles will impel men to a quite novel resolve: the resolve to do away with the concept of the state, to the abolition of the distinction between private and public. Private companies will step by step absorb the business of the state: even the most resistant remainder of what was formerly the work of government (for example its activities designed to protect the private person from the private person) will in the long run be taken care of by private contractors. (*HAH* 472)

In its 'historical form', Nietzsche contends, modern democracy represents the '*decay of the state*' (ibid.). Since the belief in a divine order in the realm of politics is of religious origin, with the decline in religion, a loss of reverence, which threatens to undermine civil peace and harmony, accompanies the emergence of modern states. Nietzsche is close to Hobbes on this point. With the decline in political absolutism sanctioned by divine law, there arises the possibility of society being split apart as it becomes 'governed' by a state of anarchy, or in Hobbes' famous words by a 'Warre of every man against every man'.[2] However, in conceiving what should be the appropriate response to the new realities of political life, Nietzsche is closer to a thinker like Locke than he is to someone like Hobbes. He hopes that the growth of the secular state will bring about a new period of toleration, pluralism, and wisdom. He invites the moderate and enlightened to take advantage of the opportunities which exist for social change, and place their efforts in the service of a tolerant and pluralistic society in order to 'repulse the destructive experiments of the precipitate and over-zealous' (ibid.). Nietzsche's optimism is reflected in his belief that when the modern state has performed its task, and 'when every relapse into the old sickness has been overcome, a new page in the storybook of humanity will be turned in which there will be many strange tales to read and perhaps some of them good ones' (ibid.). He believes that if the prudence and self-interest of modern human beings have become their strongest and most active instincts, and 'if the state is no longer equal to the demands of these forces', then what should follow is not chaos and anarchy, but the gradual and enlightened struggle for 'an invention more suited to their purpose than the state' (ibid.).

This is the liberal and enlightened task Nietzsche sets modern humanity in his middle period, confident in the belief that it has the power and capacity to overcome itself in this way. But Nietzsche's optimism was short-lived. The problem he faced in a few years time, the time of the *Gay Science* (1882), is one which Hegel recognised as the major problem of modern societies: how a new ethical life (what Hegel calls *Sittlichkeit*) is possible, given that modernity is characterised by an individualism that is deeply ambiguous. On the one hand, the attainment of individual liberty for all represents a progressive achievement. But, on the other hand, it is potentially destructive and despotic (the throne of bourgeois egoism which interprets values and beliefs solely from its own narrow perspective).[3] In section 356 of *The Gay Science* Nietzsche argues that we moderns are no longer political animals in the Greek sense that we know ourselves, and are able to organise ourselves, as 'material for society' (compare *BGE* 262). It is this insight which lies behind his caustic attack on socialism and what he sees as the *naïveté* of socialists who believe that it is possible simply to transform the individualism of modern societies and turn it in the direction of the creation of new communal individuals. In truth, what Nietzsche has identified here is a problem which afflicts all attempts to conceive a revitalisation of the political realm in which individuals transcend a narrowly conceived individualism. It is, for example, precisely this problem which bedevilled Rousseau in his strenuous attempts to formulate a notion of the general will on the basis of the enlightened self-interest of the 'possessive individual' of modern liberal democratic societies. Rousseau recognised that, in order to achieve the self-overcoming of bourgeois man into post-bourgeois man, 'we would have to be *before* the law what we should *become* by means of it'.[4]

There is no simple way round this paradox and, as we shall see, it is Nietzsche's problem too. It accounts for many of the contradictions of his political thinking.

DEMOCRACY, SOCIALISM, AND NATIONALISM

In *Human, All Too Human* Nietzsche significantly moderates his earlier Platonic conception of the state by conceding that if the goal of politics is to make life as endurable for as many people as possible (which he detects as the underlying utilitarian morality of modern life), then people should be allowed the freedom to determine what they understand by an endurable life, so long as 'everything does not become politics in this sense' (*HAH* 438). This means that society must provide space for the rare, the unique, and the noble; that is, a space for unpolitical sentiments and strivings so as to ensure that not everything in life becomes politicised and, as a result, vulgarised. This passage shows that Nietzsche regards modern democratic politics in a very different light from the concerns and fears he had expressed in the essay on the Greek state. He now seems to think that democracy does not inevitably mean the death of high culture and noble values, provided that the two – culture and politics – can come to an agreement about the aims of each and that space is provided for the practice of both. His view is that democracy is the political form of the modern world which is able to offer the best protection of culture. For example, in section 275 of *The Wanderer and his Shadow* (1880), after having remarked that 'the democratization of Europe is irresistible', Nietzsche goes on to argue that such a process can be seen to represent

a link in the chain of those tremendous *prophylactic measures* which are the conception of modern times and through which we separate ourselves from the Middle Ages. Only now is it the age of cyclopean building! We finally secure the foundations, so that the whole future can safely build upon them! We make it henceforth possible for the fruitful fields of culture again to be destroyed overnight by wild and senseless torrents! We erect stone dams and protective walls against barbarians, against pestilences, *against physical and spiritual enslavement*!

Nietzsche argues in favour of a future democracy which will overcome polarities of wealth and power and which, he hopes, will render obsolete what he regards as the two most dangerous ideologies of the modern period, nationalism and socialism.

Democracy, he suggests, aims 'to create and guarantee as much *independence* as possible: independence of opinion, of mode of life, of employment'. To achieve this, however, it must undermine the three main enemies of the independence it affords: political parties, the indigent propertyless, and the rich propertied class. He says he is 'speaking of democracy as something yet to come' (*WS* 293). He favours a social order which 'keeps open all the paths to the accumulation of *moderate* wealth through work', while preventing 'the sudden or unearned acquisition of riches' (ibid., 285). Nietzsche even endorses an enlightened labour policy which will guarantee to workers security and protection against injustice and exploitation. In this way, securing the contentment of the body and soul of the worker will ensure that his prosperity will be the prosperity of society too. Nietzsche writes in a passage that will surprise many of his readers:

The *exploitation* of the worker was, it has now been realized, a piece of stupidity, an exhausting of the soil at the expense of the future, an imperilling of society. Now we have already almost a state of war: and the cost of keeping the peace, of concluding treaties and acquiring trust, will henceforth in any event be very great, because the folly of the exploiters was very great and of long duration. (Ibid., 286)

Given these sentiments, what, we might ask, are the bases of Nietzsche's objections to socialism?

Nietzsche's objections are twofold: firstly, he regards social-ism as a doctrine of political violence that is dangerous because it is based on a naive 'Rousseauian' morality of natural goodness; and, secondly, he considers the socialist ambition of abolishing private property to represent a serious and un-necessary attack on the liberty of the private person. He draws a connection between Plato and socialism, and argues that both attempts to get rid of the individual right to own private property would result in the destruction of the sentiments of vanity and egoism which must be allowed to play their part in social life. He argues, that 'Plato's utopian basic tune, continued in our own day by the socialists, rests upon a defective knowledge of man' (*WS* 285). If all property is to become communal, then the individual will not bestow on it the same

care and self—sacrifice as he would if he owned it himself;
instead he will treat it 'like a robber or a dissolute squanderer'
(ibid.). Nietzsche does not seek a completely politicized existence in which a private realm of existence is abolished. On the
contrary, he wishes to preserve a private/public distinction. His
quarrel with modern liberal society is that, although its ideology
of the privatisation of politics allows individuals a tremendous
degree of private freedom, it does so at the cost of undermining
notions of culture and citizenship.

A second and more serious charge Nietzsche makes against
socialism is that in its deepest instincts and tendencies it is a
reactionary ideology. It is, he argues, 'the fanciful younger
brother of the almost expired despotism whose heir it wants to
be' (*HAH 473*). The reason for this, according to Nietzsche, is
that in order to bring about the transformation of society it
desires, which will require a massive extension of social control
over the private life of individuals (in order to guarantee that
they are 'good socialists'), socialism must desire the kind of
abundance of state power that one would normally associate
with the most fearful despotism. He writes, socialism

outbids all the despotisms of the past inasmuch as it expressly aspires
to the annihilation of the individual, who appears to it like an
unauthorized luxury of nature destined to be improved into a useful
organ of the community...it desires a more complete subservience of the
citizen to the absolute state than has ever existed before. (ibid.)

The real danger of socialism, Nietzsche argues, lies in its
extreme terrorism. Given that religion has declined and there is
no longer any ethical or divine basis to the state, socialism,
considered as an impious and irreligious creed bent on the
abolition of all existing states, can only exist through the
exercise of terrorism. Nietzsche attacks socialists for cultivating
an atmosphere of fear and for 'driving the word "justice" into
the heads of the half-educated masses like a nail so as to rob
them of their reason...and to create in them a good conscience
for the evil game they are to play' (ibid.).

One of the most striking claims Nietzsche makes about
socialism is that it does not prefigure a qualitatively new form of

society, but is rather to be seen as a reaction to the atomistic individualism of liberal society which seeks to extend freedom and happiness to every individual. It thus has no notion of the ends of the polity as a whole, and the only morality it can draw on to justify its policies is a utilitarian one. In Nietzsche's critique of socialism we find an opposition to the use of violence and revolution for political ends, such as bringing about radical social change. He fears revolutions because he believes that the result will not be a new world of social harmony, but the unleashing of destructive energies which will establish a politics of resentment not freedom. Nietzsche opposes socialism, therefore, because of its acceptance of terrorism as a legitimate political weapon, and its cultivation of moral fanaticism. These are trenchant criticisms.

The other major event which Nietzsche perceives as full of potential and promise in modern European politics is the decline of nationalism. Nietzsche would soon realise that this was mere wishful thinking on his part, but it is the case that he never ceased to oppose nationalism and support the cause of a united Europe as a way of overcoming the petty politics of nationalism, which he regarded as overtly racist. In the 1880s he completely abandoned his early support for Bismarck and became a declared enemy of the German *Reich*. In the writings of this period, Nietzsche, noting that all political powers of his day exploited the fear of socialism as a way of strengthening their own constituencies, argued that the winner of this attack on socialism would be democracy. The reason being that all parties, in order to combat socialism, must appeal to the people and place their aspirations high on their political agendas. The end result, Nietzsche argues, will be, paradoxically enough, the dissolution of the need for socialism by the people:

As socialism is a doctrine that the acquisition of property ought to be abolished, the people are as alienated from it as they could be: and once they have got the power of taxation into their hands through their great parliamentary majorities they will assail the capitalists, the merchants, and the princes of the stock exchange with a progressive tax and slowly create in fact a middle class which will be in a position to *forget* socialism like an illness it has recovered from. (*WS* 292)

The practical outcome of this victory of democracy will be, according to Nietzsche, 'a European league of nations, within which each individual nation, delimited according to geographical fitness, will possess the status and right of a canton'. He looks forward to future international relations in which diplomats will 'have to be at once cultural scholars, agriculturalists and communications experts, and who will have behind them, not armies, but argument' (ibid). Developments in industry, technology, and commerce, as well as the new nomadic life styles of everyone who does not own land, are bringing about the abolition of European nations. As a result of the continual mixing of race a new European humanity will emerge. Nietzsche writes about the attempt to counter this development with extraordinary perception:

This goal is at present being worked against, consciously or unconsciously, by the separation of nations through the production of *national* hostilities, yet this mixing will nonetheless go slowly forward in spite of that temporary counter-current: this artificial nationalism is in any case as perilous as artificial Catholicism used to be, for it is in its essence a forcibly imposed state of siege and self-defence inflicted on the many by the few and requires cunning, force and falsehood to maintain a front of respectability. It is not the interests of the many (the peoples), as is no doubt claimed, but above all the interests of certain princely dynasties and of certain classes of business and society, that impel to this nationalism; once one has recognized this fact, one should not be afraid to proclaim oneself simply a *good European* and actively to work for the amalgamation of nations. (*HAH* 475)

It is interesting to note that in the same passage Nietzsche argues that it is only in this context of nationalism that the 'Jewish question' can properly be understood. Again, with great perspicacity he writes:

the entire problem of the *Jews* exists only within national states, inasmuch as it is here that their energy and higher intelligence, their capital in will and spirit accumulated from generation to generation in a long school of suffering, must come to preponderate to a degree calculated to arouse envy and hatred, so that in almost every nation – and the more so the more nationalist a posture the nation is adopting – there is gaining ground the literary indecency of leading the Jews to the sacrificial slaughter as scapegoats for every possible public or private misfortune. As soon as it is no longer a question of the conserving of nations but of the production of the strongest possible European mixed race, the Jew will be just as usable and desirable as an ingredient of it as any other national residue. (ibid.)

Nietzsche's attitudes towards Jews are those of a typical gentile, not a rabid anti-Semite. He seeks the assimilation of their race and culture in the further development of the Occident, not their 'extermination'.

CONCLUSION

I do not believe that the sentiments Nietzsche expresses in the writings of this middle period either represent a dramatic break with his early political thought or signify a complete aberration from the political views usually associated with him and derived from his mature philosophy (often categorized under the title of 'aristocratic radicalism').[5] For a start, Nietzsche's commitment to culture over politics is unwavering. What has changed is the moderation he now brings to bear on his political judgements about modernity and his positive estimation of the growing 'liberalisation' of society. It is clear that in this period he is developing a mode of political thinking which can be seen to anticipate his later conception of 'great politics', which posits an elite class of philosopher-legislators who will create new values that will inspire we moderns to transform ourselves into good Europeans. The 'aristocratic radicalism' which characterises Nietzsche's later thinking is perhaps more of a means to an end – a means to bring about fundamental change and place politics on a new track beyond the narrow horizon of nationalism – than an end in itself. Nevertheless, his final position remains overly culturalist and aestheticist, and rests on a devaluation of the political realm as an arena which provides a space for the practice of democratic citizenship. Nietzsche's position at this time, however, does not rest on such a devaluation. Quite the contrary. He thinks that democratic politics can promote and further culture, not that it necessarily has to destroy it, or that it is synonymous with decadence and degeneration.

There are two key aspects to Nietzsche's political thinking at this time. The first is his opposition to political revolution in terms of an opposition to the political philosophy of Jean-Jacques Rousseau, which he mistakenly interprets as a philosophy of revolution.[6] This continues from his earlier effort to combat any political utilisation of the recognition of the dark and destructive Dionysian forces of nature. It is Rousseau, argues Nietzsche, who transformed the Enlightenment into a fanatical direction and whose 'semi-insanity, histrionicism, bestial cruelty...sentimentality and self-intoxication' constitutes the chief inspiration behind the modern theory of revolution. What is necessary now, Nietzsche argues, is that this process by which the Enlightenment degenerated into violence and terror must be reversed. He thus exhorts modern individuals 'to *continue* the work of the Enlightenment...and to strangle the Revolution at birth, to make it not happen' (*WS* 221).

The second is his recognition that, in the absence of any ethical universality in modern societies, it becomes foolish to impose the demands of morality upon individuals. He argues, in *Daybreak*, that only if humanity did possess 'a universally recognized *goal* would it be possible to propose "thus and thus is the *right* course of action"'. This fact does not, however, prevent a goal from being recommended as something which lies in the discretion of individuals. As he writes:

supposing the recommendation appealed to mankind, it could in pursuit of it also *impose* upon itself a moral law, likewise at its own discretion. But up to now the moral law has supposed to stand *above* our own likes and dislikes: one did not actually want to *impose* this law upon oneself, one wanted to *take* it from somewhere or *discover* it somewhere or *have it commanded to one* from somewhere. (*D* 108)

The principal difference between the Nietzsche of the middle period and the Nietzsche of the later years is that, whereas the former envisages social and moral change taking place through a process of liberal recommendation, the latter construes the same process in terms of an aristocratic legislation. In his mature political thinking Nietzsche accepts a machiavellism which in the thought of his middle period he associates with the despotism of socialism and clearly rejects because of its reliance on force and deception. We shall examine this major shift in Nietzsche's political thinking shortly.

Nietzsche's main insight into politics in the modern age is that, with the decline of religious authority, the decay of the traditional state, and the eroding of traditional law and custom, the relationship between the individual and society needs reconstructing and reevaluating. This insight is by no means unique or original to him, but as one of Nietzsche's overriding concerns it shows the extent to which the typical portrait of him as an unpolitical philosopher is deeply flawed and inadequate.

PART III

Man and overman

CHAPTER 5

Zarathustra's teaching of the overman

The present is always inadequate, the future is uncertain,
and the past irrecoverable.
Schopenhauer, *The World as Will and Representation* (volume II).

> Time present and time past
> Are both perhaps present in time future
> And time future contained in time past.
> If all time is eternally present
> All time is unredeemable.
> T. S. Eliot, 'Burnt Norton' (1935), *Four Quartets*.

On one occasion Zarathustra strictly defines his task – it is
also mine – the *meaning* of which cannot be misunderstood:
he is *affirmative* to the point of justifying, of redeeming even
the entire past.
Nietzsche, *Ecce Homo*, 'Thus Spoke Zarathustra', 8.

INTRODUCTION: WHO IS ZARATHUSTRA?

Written in a poetic, inspirational mode and in the form of
parables, Nietzsche's *Thus Spoke Zarathustra* is not widely
recognised as being a philosophical work, let alone as representing a contribution to political philosophy. However, a
reading of the book does yield important insights into the
preoccupations and problems of Nietzsche's political thought.
Despite some major studies by philosophers of the work in
recent years, there still exists no consensus as to the meaning and
significance of the principal teachings of the book. The two
main ideas are those of the 'overman' (*Übermensch* – often
translated as 'superman') and the 'eternal return of the same'.
There is much controversy as to the meaning of these notions,

and recent interpretations have cast doubt especially on the coherence of the ideal of the overman in Nietzsche's thought. The importance of *Zarathustra* is that, at least on one level, it is a book which dramatises and ironises the felt need for a politics of redemption in an age of nihilism. If this is the case, then it becomes impossible to construe the overman as an ideal which will bring mankind salvation. Nietzsche's yearning for a new humanity can itself be seen as an expression of the nihilistic condition he wishes us to overcome. It reveals a dissatisfaction with the present, with 'man', expressing the same kind of negative attitudes, such as revenge and resentment towards life as it is, which characterises the ascetic ideal.

Nihilism chiefly signals a crisis of authority.[1] In the wake of the death of God, humanity seeks new idols who will command and provide a new metaphysical foundation for morals. In *Zarathustra* Nietzsche dramatises the predicament in which modern human beings find themselves, and shows both the necessity *and* the impossibility of instigating a new legislation. How can new values be fashioned and legislated when the transcendental basis which would support them has been undermined? In the age of nihilism, not only is it imperative to rethink the value of truth, but equally the value of morality, of justice, and of law. Throughout the book Nietzsche has Zarathustra constantly call into question the legitimacy of his own authority, and in this way he keeps open the question of his identity, of who and what he is, and is to become. In the epoch of the 'twilight of the idols', in which God is dead and all idols are to be overthrown, the only honest guise the teacher can adopt is that of a self-parodist. In *Ecce Homo* Nietzsche describes Zarathustra as a 'type', he is 'the ideal of a spirit' who plays naively and impulsively with everything that has so far been called holy, good, untouchable, and divine. Such a type will appear 'inhuman', Nietzsche says, when it comes into contact with earthly seriousness so far. The figure of Zarathustra symbolises for Nietzsche what he calls 'the self-overcoming of morality'. It was the Persian prophet Zoroaster who first introduced the struggle between good and evil into the workings of the cosmos, and who translated morality into metaphysics.

Consequently, as Zarathustra created the most fateful of errors, morality, he must be the first to recognise and overcome it (*EH* 'Why I Am A Destiny', 3).

On many occasions in the notes from the period of the composition of *Zarathustra* Nietzsche portrays Zarathustra as a lawgiver (*Gesetzgeber*), ranking him alongside such figures as Buddha, Moses, Jesus, and Muhammad (*KSA* 9, p. 642). In Greek thought the lawgiver or legislator is the archetype of the political hero and the symbol of what uninhibited greatness might achieve. He is the figure who suddenly appears in order to save the life of the *polis* from disintegration and decay and to re-establish it on a fresh foundation. In Machiavelli the 'prince' is a ruler who possesses superhuman powers of courage and prowess, and who conducts political life in accordance with a purely pragmatic value system. In Rousseau the lawgiver is the figure who devises the particular set of laws for a people, a *nomothetes* like Solon in Athens or Numa in Rome. It is his task not to legislate as such, but to create the conditions under which civil association is to take place. In Nietzsche's hands, however, Zarathustra becomes a parody of the lawgiver. He hesitates when he should be firm in his pronunciations; he renounces authority when people are prepared to fall down on their knees before him and unconditionally obey him. With the death of God it is no longer possible for any political authority to claim divine sanction for its rule. The question which comes to the fore concerns the kind of justification of political rule which is possible in the modern age. Hitherto, the great legislators of humanity, such as philosophers and religious teachers, have presented their lawgiving in terms of ther 'good-in-itself', where the 'good' is conceived metaphysically and divinely. However, in an age in which it is no longer possible to appeal to a divine conscience, to 'god' or to 'eternal values', as a way of supporting one's legislation of values for 'man', then, 'the task of the legislator of values raises to a new fearfulness never yet attained' (*WP* 972; *KSA* 11, pp. 611–13).

For Nietzsche the chief problem facing politics in the current epoch of nihilism is that of creating the conditions under which the type 'man' can undergo further development and en-

hancement. The philosophers of the future, he argues, need to
address themselves to the 'great task and question' which is
approaching humanity inexorably as a terrible fate: 'How shall
the earth as a whole be governed? To what end shall "man" as
a whole – and no longer as a people or a race – be raised and
trained' (*WP* 957). This for Nietzsche is the problem of a 'great
politics'. *Thus Spoke Zarathustra* shows us a different Nietzsche
who recognizes that it is not easy, or desirable even, simply
to proclaim a new dispensation for man and to instigate violent
revolution on a grand scale. In the pages of *Zarathustra* it is
possible to locate a Nietzsche who advocates the necessity and
desirability of engaging in 'local rebellions'.[2] As Zarathustra
teaches in a discourse entitled 'Of Great Events': 'The world
revolves, not around the inventors of new noises, but around the
inventors of new values; it revolves *inaudibly*'.

Instead of proposing a world-historical solution to the
problem of man, Nietzsche attempts to teach a new ideal by way
of example. This is the ideal of a superabundant, healthy
human type who binds together all opposites into a new unity:
the 'highest and lowest forces of human nature, the sweetest,
most frivolous and most fearsome stream forth out of *one*
fountain with immortal certainty' (*EH* 'Thus Spoke Zarathustra' 6). In this ideal of 'greatness' we have nothing other
than 'the concept of Dionysus himself'. Zarathustra, Nietzsche
tells us, is the dancer who, in spite of having the most fearful
insight into reality, and who has thought 'the most abysmal
thought' (the eternal return of all things), finds in it no
objection to existence, but only one more reason '*to be himself* the
eternal Yes to all things... "Into every abyss I still bear the
blessing of my affirmation"' (ibid.).

THE TEACHING OF THE OVERMAN

In the prologue to the work, Zarathustra descends to humanity
after ten years of solitude and announces that man is something
to be overcome. In the market-square he teaches the *Übermensch*,
which is to be the meaning of the earth after the momentous and
world-historical event of the death of God (see *GS* 125):

The overman *shall be* the meaning of the earth!
I entreat you, my brethren, *remain true to the earth*, and do not believe those who speak to you of supra-terrestrial hopes! (*Z* Prologue, section 3)

Uncanny is human existence and still without a meaning ... I want to teach human beings the meaning of their being: which is the overman, the lightning from the dark cloud of man. (*Z* Prologue, section 7)

In order to go over or across (*übergehen*) to the future of man (*Mensch*), which can only be a different kind of humanity, we must first learn how to go under or perish (*untergehen*). There has never been an *Übermensch*, Zarathustra says, for man has yet to learn *how* to go under. When we do go under we experience 'the hour of the great contempt', the hour in which our present happiness, reason, pity, justice, and virtue grow loathsome to us. In the discourse entitled 'Of the Way of the Creator' in book one, Zarathustra declares that he loves the person who 'wants to create beyond (*über*) himself, and thus perishes'. It is through the teaching of eternal return that Zarathustra shows how one can learn to go under. It is the doctrine of return, therefore, that provides the bridge (the way) across (*über*) to the overman. At the same time, however, it is the vision of the *Übermensch* which is designed to inspire in human beings a desire for the experience of going-down and beyond (*über*) man.

In the prologue we find Zarathustra attempting to teach self-overcoming as the law of life in order to show humanity how it can go beyond the event of the death of God and the reign of nihilism. We have to learn that man is only a bridge and not a goal; he is a rope tied between animal and *Übermensch* as over an abyss, a dangerous going-across and wayfaring. The opposite of this desire for self-overcoming is the desire for self-preservation which characterises the attitude towards life of 'the last man'. The last (or ultimate) man denotes a humanity which has discovered happiness and is content with preserving itself; it no longer believes in taking risks or in experiments, it no longer really believes in anything. It is without passion or commitment. The attitude of this type of humanity is that of an empty relativism in which there are no longer any distinctions or judgements of taste since every viewpoint is recognised as having equal validity; there are no good and bad, no rich and poor, no commanding and obeying, no rulers and ruled: 'Everyone wants the same thing, everyone is the same: whoever thinks otherwise goes voluntarily into the madhouse' (ibid. 5). The prologue ends with Zarathustra declaring that he seeks not disciples but companions who he calls 'fellow-creators and rejoicers'. He shall not be herdsman to the herd, but instead shall teach by way of example, 'I will show them the rainbow and the stairway to the *Übermensch*' (ibid. 9).

With the notion of the overman Nietzsche is seeking to re-establish a notion of noble human agency. Whereas the last man pursues only material comfort, the overman is prepared to squander his life in the pursuit of great deeds. To be 'great' is to stand willingly beyond good and evil. It is to be 'beyond' morality as it is understood by the herd. Creative action is action which necessarily exceeds the judgement of morality since it establishes new rules and new norms (this is what we understand by the 'genius'). To be creative is to expend one's energies in the moment and not to be deterred by any anticipation of the consequences of one's actions.

For several decades now, generations of English-speaking commentators of Nietzsche have wrestled with the problem of how best to translate the word *Übermensch*. The question which any new reader of Nietzsche wants to ask is: what is meant by the term *Übermensch*? Is it, for example, the type of being in possession of superhuman powers, the superman of Nietzsche legend? Or is it the symbol of the humanity of the future which has overcome the nihilism of the modern epoch and the world-weariness of modern humanity? Nietzsche provides a hint in *Ecce Homo*, when he declares that the notion of *Übermensch* is not in any way to be conceived along Darwinian lines or as representing a transcendental ideal (*EH* 'Why I Write Such Good Books', 1). The *Übermensch* is not an ideal that is posited in terms of an infinite future beyond the reach of mere mortals; it is not 'super' or 'above' (*über*) in this sense. 'I love him', Zarathustra says, 'who justifies the humanity of the future and redeems the humanity of the past, for he wants to perish by the humanity of the present' (*Z* Prologue 4). To the last men who are gathered in the market-place, bemused by the madman who announces the death of God, the person who strives for something higher and nobler will always appear as super-human. This shows that Nietzsche, as Walter Kaufmann pointed out in his classic study of 1950, is playing with the connotations of the word '*über*' (across, over, beyond).[3] He is trying to show that the desire for change within the self involves both a process of the old perishing and of the new striving to be brought into existence. How can this moment of self-trans-formation be constituted, and how can one sacrifice the present for the future in a way that is free of resentment?

With the notion of the *Übermensch* Nietzsche does not intend Zarathustra to teach something utterly fantastical. In the discourse in *Zarathustra* entitled 'Of the Afterworldsmen', for example, Zarathustra says that he teaches a 'new will' which is designed to teach human beings to desire not a new path but the one that they have hitherto blindly followed and to 'call it good'. It is a question of learning how to *become* what we *are*. In the discourse entitled 'On the Blissful Islands' which appears at the beginning of part two of the work, Zarathustra says that we should reach no further than our 'creating will': 'Could you *create* a god? – So be silent about all gods! But you could surely create the overman'. Zarathustra teaches the following (supra-moral) imperative: we must create within the realm of terrestrial possibilities and, in creating, 'remain true to the earth'.

On one level the teaching of the overman represents Nietzsche's preoccupation with the problem of the further discipline and cultivation of the human animal once the Christian-moral view of the world has lost its authority and ascendancy. This is the specific historical context – the death of God and the devaluation of humanity's highest values – in which the ideal is introduced by Nietzsche. Nietzsche is trapped within the logic of the 'ideal', in spite of his vicious attack on all idols (his word for 'ideals'), because the 'overman' gives him hope for the future and enables him to overcome his feeling of contempt towards the present. On this level, the overman represents Nietzsche's consolation for the future in the face of his intense dissatisfaction with existing humanity and the present.

THE THOUGHT OF ETERNAL RETURN

After the prologue the book develops in four parts or acts. In part one Zarathustra sets out to show human beings 'the way of the Creator'. All willing is creating. Behind the positing of the values of good and evil there stands the creator and destroyer of values (the 'will' is 'will to power'). The first part closes with the expectation of a great noontide – the moment of *Untergang* – when man will stand in the middle of his journey between animal and overman and celebrate it as his highest hope, for it is the bridge to a new beginning. Going under man will bless himself for he is going over to something greater and nobler. He will be able to declare proudly and defiantly: 'All gods are dead now: we want (*wollen*) the overman to live' (*Z* 'Of the Bestowing Virtue', 3).

Part two of the book centres on the meaning of the doctrine of life as will to power and contains two key discourses on 'self-overcoming' and 'redemption' (*Erlösung*). It is in the latter discourse, which appears towards the end of the second part or act, that Zarathustra hints at the doctrine of eternal return. In this discourse we witness Zarathustra searching for a doctrine which will teach the human will that it is a will to power, denoting a creative and legislative will. The great problem of the will is that it is overwhelmed by the burden and weight of the past which casts a dark shadow over the future. The human will feels impotent in the face of what has been, since it recognises that one cannot change what is past. It sees itself as a victim of the past and in a fit of rage it takes revenge on life. The will is afflicted since it cannot will backwards and break time's law of change, becoming, and constant movement. 'The spirit of revenge', Zarathustra announces, has up to now been mankind's chief concern; 'where there was suffering, there was always supposed to be punishment'. Zarathustra seeks a doctrine which will liberate the will from its fixation on the past.

He requires a doctrine which will restore for man the 'innocence of becoming', that is, the view of existence which is able to recognise that ultimately life is without meaning and beyond justification; or rather, that human life contains within its eternal movement of creation and destruction, of change and development, of pleasure and pain, of joy and suffering, its own justification.[4] The meaning of life is to be found nowhere but within life itself as we live it and shall live it. But instead of such an insight crippling us, we should be inspired by it – to the extent that we are able to affirm unconditionally the eternal return of all the moments of our existence because we recognise that every one of those moments is necessary to who we are. The discourse on redemption ends by prefiguring the major doctrine of eternal return:

Has the will become its own redeemer and bringer of joy? Has it unlearned the spirit of revenge and all teeth-gnashing?
And who has taught it to be reconciled with time, and higher things than reconciliation?
The will that is the will to power must will something higher than any reconciliation – but how shall this happen? Who has taught it to will backwards, too? (*Z* 'Of Redemption').

The central teaching of part three, and arguably of Nietzsche's whole philosophy, is that of eternal return. In *Twilight of the Idols*, Nietzsche states that he is the last disciple of the philosopher Dionysus and 'the teacher of eternal recurrence' (*TI* 'What I Owe to the Ancients' 5).[5] Nietzsche himself located the roots of the thought in Heraclitus. My treatment of it here will inevitably be superficial. I am able to give only the barest sense of what it might mean, and touch on some of the problems attached to the teaching.

In *Ecce Homo* the thought (*Gedanke*) of eternal return is said to be the most fundamental conception of *Zarathustra*, representing the highest formula of affirmation attainable (*EH* 'Thus Spoke Zarathustra', 1). The significance of the doctrine is twofold: it is intended as a teaching on the nature of time and as an experience which affirms the creative unity of all things, including that of good and evil. It is out of the experience of return that the overman will emerge as the one who embodies the creative and innocent will to power. The overman is to be understood as the *vision* which emerges out of the *riddle* of eternal return.[6] Nietzsche understands the thought of return as leading to the constitution of an over-humanity. However, the thought can only have meaning and significance for beings who are moral (sovereign). In undergoing the thought-experiment of eternal return it is *not* a case of simply transcending the level of the human, all too human, but of *deepening* it. The 'human' and the 'overhuman' do not stand radically opposed to one another. Just as the experience of the 'extra-ordinary' is at the heart of our everyday, ordinary existence, so too must be the experience of the overhuman be seen as fundamental to the human being's existence (*Dasein*). It is perhaps the great paradox of Zarathustra's vision of the overman that we seek within it something fantastic and monumental. As Nietzsche says in a note of 1882/3, all signs of the 'overhuman', will appear as signs of illness or madness to the human herd (*KSA* x, p. 217).

The thought descends upon Zarathustra in the form of a riddle and as the vision of the most solitary man. As he tries to climb ever higher upward, his arch-enemy, the spirit of gravity, draws him back down towards the abyss. The spirit oppresses Zarathustra and it is to him that he presents the riddle of eternal return as his most abysmal thought. The two stand before a gateway which has two aspects and where two paths come together: no one, Zarathustra informs the dwarf, has ever reached their end for the two lines go on for ever unto eternity. They merge together, however, at the gateway at which they are standing and above which they can read the word 'moment' (*Augenblick* – literally 'glance of the eye'). Zarathustra scolds the dwarf for treating the riddle lightly when it naively declares: 'Everything straight lies... All truth is crooked, time itself is a circle.' For Nietzsche, however, the thought of return does not simply posit a circular conception of time. Such a concept can lead only to a crushing fatalism which declares that 'everything is in vain'. Zarathustra responds by suggesting that, if we behold the moment, we see that from its gateway a long, eternal lane runs back, which is eternity itself. He is led to raise the question: must not everything that can happen have already happened? Must not this gateway and this moment have already happened? Moreover, is not everything bound fast together in such a way that this 'moment' draws after it all future things? But this awakening of the 'moment' cannot be the awakening of ourselves to the experience of life literally returning in terms of repeatable cycles. Rather, the doctrine has to be read in terms of the existential constitution of time. In undergoing the experience of eternal return we experience for the first time the passing away and infinite movement of time in an existential manner. We no longer simply experience time in terms of a straightforward seriality of past, present, and future, but experience the dimensions of time as fundamentally interconnected, and in terms of the dramatic happening of the 'moment'. In willing the eternal return of the moment we are willing the law of life itself and recognising that life is the unity of opposites, of pleasure and pain, of joy and suffering, of good and evil. 'Good and evil ... and all the names of the virtues: they should be weapons and ringing symbols that life must overcome itself again and again!' (*Z* 'Of the Tarantulas'). It is this existential experience of the 'moment' which the dwarf fails to undergo.

Taken literally, as a cosmological hypothesis, the thought of eternal return is absurd.[7] However, if viewed in terms of an imaginative response to the problem of time and time's 'it was' (the problem of the present being overwhelmed by the past), we see that it proposes an affirmation of the nature of time, of time's passing away, of its becoming and its perishing. The peculiar challenge that the thought presents lies in the question that confronts the person who undergoes its experience. Can I accept the destiny of my being in such a way that I can also accept the necessity of my past because, as a creator of the future, I 'willed' it? The test of return teaches a new will by teaching the individual to will creatively the existence which hitherto it has led only blindly and unknowingly. How well-disposed towards life would we have to be to desire nothing more fervently than its eternal self-overcoming? Do we have the strength and courage to affirm the eternal return of the 'moment', or are we full of pity for life and desire only its self-preservation? It is these

kinds of questions we find in section 341 of the *Gay Science* where
the doctrine of return is first presented in Nietzsche's published
work.

The doctrine of return is presented here as the 'greatest
weight' because it endows our personal existence with meaning
and significance. It teaches us to affirm life and not to seek
redemption from its tragic character. The doctrine teaches that
in undergoing the experience of the moment – what I would
like to call 'the time of return' – what the will must will is the
return of one's life with every pain and every joy, every thought
and every sigh, and everything unutterably small and great all
in the same succession and sequence. Why? Because everything
we have done, and the manner in which we have done it, is
necessary to who we are. The question is: do we wish to *become*
those who we are? The individual has a choice in that he or she
can decide whether or not to assume responsibility for what they
have become and for who they wish to become. The past itself
is not transformed in the experience of return, but only our
attitude towards it.

In the *Nachlass* (posthumously published notes) of the period,
Nietzsche considered a political application of the eternal
return. He construes it as a cultivating thought which will
strengthen the strong and paralyse the world-weary. A note
from the winter of 1883/4, for example, refers to a 'book of
prophecy' in which the teaching of eternal return is to be
presented, and its theoretical presuppositions and consequences
stated. In addition there is to be a proof (*Beweis*) of the doctrine,
a guide to the means of how to endure it, and an examination of
its role in history as a 'mid-point' (*Mitte*). The thought is to lead
to the 'foundation of an oligarchy over peoples and their
interests: education to a universally human politics (*allmensch-
lichen Politik*]'. The thought of return will introduce a 'new
Enlightenment' and a new order of rank (*KSA* 10, p. 645; 11,
pp. 212–13). In *Zarathustra*, however, Nietzsche does not place
the idea of eternal return in the service of a new politics, but
simply employs it as a doctrine which reveals the affirmative
attitude towards life which is able to liberate human beings
from the tyranny of the past and the 'spirit of revenge'.

The thought of eternal return seeks to establish the conditions of possibility for an existential experience of time. It affirms the irreversibility of time, but does not accept the brute facticity of the past. Failure to appreciate this point results in a number of commentators claiming that the thought does not succeed in its declared objective of overcoming the spirit of revenge. Arthur Danto, for example, claims that the thought does not lead to an affirmation of the eternal flux of life, of being as 'becoming', but to 'an eternally frozen mobility'. In the end, he argues, there is no passing away and no true becoming in the world.[8] Joan Stambaugh is astute in pointing out that what Nietzsche is seeking to affirm with the thought of return is the very timeliness of time (the momentariness of the 'moment').[9] In conceiving the 'moment' in terms of an eternity, Nietzsche is trying to overcome the negative concept of time found in the tradition of Western metaphysics, where eternity is seen as the *negation* of time and spiritual freedom is identified with a changeless condition. In affirming the eternal return of the same, one is affirming the ceaseless and restless motion of time itself, in which eternity does not negate the moment, but fulfils it. This amounts to the experience of perpetual novelty, not frozen mobility.

One of the most impressive interpretations of the teaching of eternal return is that put forward by the French philosopher of difference, Gilles Deleuze. His reading reveals some of the major problems arising from Nietzsche's formulation of the doctrine. Deleuze interprets the thought of return in terms of a kind of Kantian categorical imperative which invites an individual to ask itself of any given action: can I will what I am about to will in such a way that I can will its eternal return? The main significance of the thought, Deleuze argues, however, is that it affirms only the return of active forces. He thus reads it as a discriminating thought in which only active forces come back and reactive ones perish: 'reactive force will not return', he states.[10] The eternal return is an affirmative thought which conceives the innocence of becoming – of time – beyond the spirit of revenge and the negative force of resentment. If the reactive forces did return this would result in a depressing doctrine foretelling the eternal return, not of the 'overman', but of 'man'.[11] Deleuze interprets Nietzsche's teaching as putting forward an affirmative, spontaneous, and joyful experience of life; it is the kind of experience of life enjoyed by the 'master', not the 'slave'.

There are a number of problems with Deleuze's inventive interpretation of the doctrine. I shall concentrate on two. It might seem that contemplation of eternal return imposes upon us a tremendous weight of responsibility which would not facilitate action, but prohibit and depress it. In considering whether or not one wishes to will an action's eternal return, is one not robbing life of its innocence and spontaneity, precisely the opposite of what the teaching is designed to achieve? Of course, Nietzsche, or Deleuze, might reply by saying that this is how the thought would be experienced by the weak person who worries about life, not the strong type who acts freely and innocently and who affirms life as a totality. But, one might argue, surely the strong human being would have *no need* of a thought such as eternal return. Must one not already be suffering from life in order to feel the need to undergo its experience? Does it not, when expressed in the form of an ethical imperative, impose a consequentialist aspect on action which an affirmation of the innocence of becoming needs to disregard? Deleuze insists that the thought of return will eliminate the world-weary and the sick, and result in the performance of bold action (one does not contemplate the consequences of one's action in undergoing the thought, but transports oneself beyond moral judgement by affirming action as being beyond good and evil). But it is just as likely that it will 'corrupt' the strong human being (by making him *think* about his existence), and, in this respect, can be construed as quite a 'slavish' thought. How can the thought of eternal return not make us reflect deeply on life in a way which would prevent us from acting purely spontaneously?

The problem I have identified here touches upon a central difficulty in Nietzsche's thinking. As we shall see in the next chapter, Nietzsche depicts history in terms of the triumph of a negative and reactive slave morality. As Deleuze interprets it, with some legitimacy, the thought of eternal return is designed as an imperative which will lead to a new affirmative master 'morality'. But if it is the case that we have become slaves (by which Nietzsche means self-reflective, moral beings), how can we will the eternal return in any other way than as a moral doctrine? I will 'come back' to this point.

The second problem with Deleuze's reading centres around his contention that reactive forces do not return when one wills eternal return. Here, I would argue, Deleuze misses the true import of the doctrine as Nietzsche conceives it. For Nietzsche, the active forces require the opposition of reactive forces in order to define and assert themselves as 'active'. Moreover, a point Deleuze never considers is that the assertion of active force, far from leading to the elimination of reactive forces, is likely to generate them by creating the passions or sentiments of envy and resentment in those 'below' them. Nietzsche, in contrast to Deleuze, recognises this fact, which explains why he presents the ultimate test for Zarathustra in terms of his ability to affirm the *realisation* which descends upon him that the small man whom he views with contempt will also eternally recur. Unlike Deleuze's thought, Nietzsche's rests on principles of domination and hierarchy. It is only through a comparison of values that the master's affirmation of noble values can take place.[12] For Nietzsche, this comparison takes place, not through concordant relationships, but via ones of opposition and dominion (what he calls the 'pathos of distance').

Deleuze's reading of eternal return is instructive because it exposes two dimensions of the teaching which do not cohere, and which might explain why it continues to baffle and to generate different interpretations. On one level, it provides an experience of the affirmation of life in its totality and unity (providing a feeling of cosmic oneness with the universe); on another level, which is brought out by Deleuze's reading, it exists as a kind of ethical imperative. My argument is that if eternal return is to be viewed in the latter terms, then it cancels out the attitude of total affirmation implied in the cosmic view, and imposes on human beings the necessity, *as moral beings*, of making judgements on life: not only saying yes, I will that again and again, but also saying, no, never again. The thought can, I believe, only make sense for moral (self-reflective) beings, and an essential part of being a moral person is the exercise of judgement.[13] To be human is also to be over- or super-human: one says 'yes, yes', and one says 'no, no'.

THE PROBLEM OF THE OVERMAN IDEAL

How coherent is the notion of the *Übermensch*? Can Nietzsche's promotion of the idea of a humanity 'beyond' (*über*) man be taken seriously when his whole thinking is premised on the conviction that all modern ideals which encourage human beings to sacrifice the present for the future are no more than relics of our Christian–moral past, which need to be discredited by subjecting them to the philosopher's hammer? As Nietzsche himself had declared in his autobiography, *Ecce Homo*:

The last thing *I* should promise would be to 'improve' mankind. No new idols are erected by me; let the old ones learn what feet of clay mean. *Overthrowing idols* (my word for 'ideals') – that comes closer to being part of my craft. One has deprived reality of its value, its meaning, its truthfulness, to precisely the extent to which one has mendaciously invented an ideal world. (*EH* Preface, 2)

Another problem affecting the coherence of the notion arises from determining its precise relationship to the doctrine of eternal return. As far back as Georg Simmel, commentators have pointed out that the ideas of the overman and the eternal return seem to be fundamentally at odds with each other. In his study *Schopenhauer and Nietzsche*, first published in 1907, Simmel argues that it would appear that 'the infinity of the overman's task cannot be reconciled with the finitude of cosmic periods' which is presupposed in the thought of eternal return. As he put it:

within each period, humanity could be vested with only a limited number of forms of evolution, which could be constantly repeated, whereas the ideal of the overman demands a straight line of evolution heading toward the future.[14]

In other words, the overman ideal seems to require a linear conception of time, while the doctrine of the eternal return presupposes a circular, or cyclical, notion of time.

The view that the two major doctrines of *Thus Spoke Zarathustra* are incompatible has recently been forcefully expressed by Erich Heller, who argues that the overman and the eternal return are 'the paradigm of logical incompatibility'. Whereas the teaching of the overman is designed to inspire us to create something new and original, the doctrine of eternal return contains the crushing thought that the same will return eternally, and, therefore, all creation is in vain. The doctrine of eternal return teaches that nothing could come into existence that had not existed before, while in *Zarathustra* Nietzsche has his eponymous hero declare that 'there has never yet been an overman' (*Z* 'Of the Spirit of Gravity'). For Heller, Zarathustra should, in all honesty, declare that 'there *never* will be an overman'. He writes:

the expectation of this majestic new departure of life, indeed the possibility of any new development, seems frustrated at the outset, and the world, caught forever in a cycle of gloomily repeated constellations of energy, stands condemned to a most dismal eternity.[15]

We have already seen to what extent, however, the thought of return does not posit a circular notion of time. This is to think the doctrine literally. If we think of it in terms of an imaginative thought-experiment it is possible to see that there is no necessary 'logical incompatibility' between the two doctrines. The overman is simply the human type which is able to positively experience the eternal return (it does not crush him but changes him) in terms of a constitution of time in which 'time' becomes 'temporal'.

Perhaps the most powerful critique of the coherence of the overman ideal, in terms of it representing Nietzsche's vision of a new humanity, is to be found in a recent study by Maudemarie Clark. She argues, that the overman ideal expresses Nietzsche/ Zarathustra's own need for revenge.[16] The doctrine of eternal return, however, undermines the import of the overman ideal. In its final form the thought of return teaches Zarathustra that even that which he most despises and feels contempt for, the small man, will return again and again. It is obvious, therefore, Clark argues, that the eternal recurrence is incompatible with the possibility of establishing the overman and overcoming the small man.[17] Moreover, the overman is to be understood as yet another expression of the ascetic ideal (to be examined in the next chapter), that is the ideal of self-denial espoused by philosophers and priests. In construing humanity as a bridge, not an end, Nietzsche/Zarathustra devalues human life in the same manner as the Christian priest. Human life is valued as a means to something which is its own negation. The past is to be overcome, and the present negated, for the sake of the future and the creation of the overman. What this shows, Clark argues, is that, in positing the overman ideal, Nietzsche/Zarathustra is evidently dissatisfied with the process of life, to the extent that he cannot view it as an end sufficient in itself.

Certainly, it is true, I would agree, that the overman represents, on one level, Nietzsche's consolation in the face of what he sees as the feeble nature of modern man. With this notion it is possible for him to conceive of a human type which is able to endure and affirm the thought of eternal return. However, this does not necessarily mean that the ideal represents Nietzsche's revenge against human life. It could be argued that what we are provided with at the end of the book is a reformulated notion of the overman. While in the prologue the notion of the overman is declared in terms of an ascetic ideal, at the end of the book it is not possible to think of the overman apart from the thought of return. The overman is now to be understood as a human type which is able to affirm the deepest and darkest implications of eternal return, including the infinite return of the small man of whom Zarathustra is weary. What Zarathustra learns is that the return of the small man is, in the end, not a barrier to the attainment of the overman, but its condition. Without the 'pathos of distance' created by viewing itself in relation to the small man, it is impossible for the overman to engage in self-overcoming. As Zarathustra declares at one point: 'Good and evil, and rich and poor, and noble and base…they should be weapons and ringing symbols that life must overcome itself again and again!' (Z 'of The Tarantulas'). The notion does not posit the transcendence of the human animal; rather it denotes its future creative possibilities. The overman, one could say, is an ever present possibility of the human. The overman fulfils the fundamental law of life (self-overcoming); it does not signify its negation.

The problems associated with the ideal of the overman, including the fact of its problematic relationship to the idea of eternal return, have led other commentators to argue that the teaching of the overman cannot be sustained and is, in fact, an ideal never seriously espoused or promoted by Nietzsche. Laurence Lampert, for example, believes that any interpretation which places the doctrine of the overman at the centre of Nietzsche's thought is wrong, since it imposes on it a notion of the eschatological fulfilment of time which Zarathustra wishes to overcome. Nietzsche's Zarathustra, he argues, overthrows what the Persian prophet Zoroaster bequeathed to humanity, namely a prophetic religion that forces earthly, mortal existence to be lived and endured 'under the terrible gravity of a future Day of Judgement in which eternal doom or eternal bliss will be decreed'.[18]

A similar argument to Lampert's has been put forward by Daniel Conway. He argues that we do Nietzsche a disservice if we succumb to the temptation of giving the notion of the overman a world-historical meaning and significance. When Nietzsche himself speaks, at the end of the second essay of the *Genealogy of Morals*, of the imminent arrival of a man 'who must come one day', a redeemer of sorts, he is 'betraying a nihilistic commitment to the deficiency of the human condition'.[19] In fact, argues Conway, Nietzsche does not seriously promote such a world-historical ideal. When speaking of the 'man of the future' and the 'great redeemer from nothingness and God' (*OGM* ii, 24), he is being merely ironic. The overman ideal is only posited in the first two parts of *Zarathustra*, he argues, and in the second half of the book Zarathustra renounces the ideal of a future redemption through a notion of the *Übermensch*. Instead of promoting an *ideal* of perfection and greatness, Zarathustra now sets out in the second half of his voyage of discovery to influence through the example of his pedagogy and to promote self-creation through exemplification. He has abandoned, Conway argues, the notion of a world-historical *Übermensch* in favour of the idea of a 'local rebellion' against nihilism, which is to be achieved by pursuing the path of a 'quiet *Übermensch*'.

The criticisms made by these commentators are not, I believe, fatal to the coherence of Nietzsche's teaching of the overman. I would argue that they share the same weaknesses I have identified with Clark's critical reading of the idea(1). But commentators like Conway do draw attention to the ironic use to which a teaching of redemption is put in *Thus Spoke Zarathustra*. A serious point is being made about the problem of redemption. The desire to transfigure the world often betrays resentment against it and represents the distressed cry of an impotent or suffering will which needs to posit an ascetic ideal for its own salvation. What Zarathustra himself learns in the course of his travels is that his own desire for a transfiguration of humanity into an over-humanity reflects his own sickness and morbid, dissatisfied condition. On an important level the story of Zarathustra's wanderings can be read as a critique of our yearning for a redemption from the human condition.

Thus Spoke Zarathustra is significant in showing a dimension to Nietzsche's thought which is often overlooked and neglected: the self-referential nature of his teaching and its penchant for self-parody. The book dramatises the problem of the legislator, showing that the present suffers from a crisis of *authority*. How is it possible to legislate new values in the epoch of nihilism? In Nietzsche's next work, *Beyond Good and Evil*, to be examined in chapter seven, he shows few self-parodic tendencies and identifies a new machiavellism as the most appropriate response to the crisis of values, of authority, which afflicts the modern age. For Nietzsche, politics should now abandon the illusions and deceptions of morality and place itself in the service of the aesthetic task of overcoming 'man' and creating an over-humanity.

CHAPTER 6

A genealogy of morals

All things that live long are gradually so saturated with reason that their origin in unreason becomes improbable. Does not almost every precise history of an origination impress our feelings as paradoxical and wantonly offensive? Does the good historian not, at bottom, constantly *contradict*?

Nietzsche, *Daybreak*, I

Morality as it has hitherto been understood – as it was ultimately formulated by Schopenhauer as 'denial of the will of life' – is the *instinct of decadence* itself...it is the judgement of the judged.

Nietzsche, *Twilight of the Idols*, 'Morality as Anti-Nature', 5

INTRODUCTION TO A 'GENEALOGY' OF MORALS

The *Genealogy of Morals* is a work of key importance for understanding Nietzsche's political thought. In this work Nietzsche rejects the approach of the natural law tradition of modern political thought (Hobbes, Locke, Rousseau, etc.), which seeks to establish the legitimacy of political rule by means of the notion of social contract. Nietzsche suspends questions of political obligation and legitimacy (why should the individual obey the state? What are the grounds of legitimate power?), in favour of a historical and psychological analysis of man's evolution as a moral animal. For Nietzsche, man is not naturally a political animal, but has undergone a process of training and

cultivation through the evolution of morality and centuries of
social development. The product of this process is the sovereign
individual, the proud owner of conscience and a free will, who
can be bound to social contracts and held responsible for his
actions. The historical development of the animal 'man' has
taken place in terms of a process of 'moralisation'. This is the
process by which legal concepts of obligation, duty, guilt, law,
and justice, which first emerged in specific material contexts,
such as the civil law relationship of creditor and debtor, assume
(with the rise of the *bad* conscience and the spread of
Christianity) a uniquely *moral* meaning and significance: guilt
for example, no longer means (legal) debt, but (moral) sin.

The evolution of the bad conscience is both a dangerous and
a promising one since it contains ambiguous possibilities. With
the knowledge of 'good', man now also has a corresponding
knowledge of 'evil'. It is the latter that Nietzsche wishes a new
(aristocratic) social order to cultivate in order to invert and
challenge the Christian-moral tradition and its secular succes-
sors. It is Nietzsche's insights into history and culture which
determine his conception of great politics – a conception of
politics which seeks to overcome morality and the moral view of
the world and posit a vision of the animal 'man' as 'beyond
good and evil'. History shows that, at least on the level of
culture, man's so-called evil affects and passions have been as
necessary to his evolution, and have contributed to his self-
preservation, as much as the 'good' affects and passions (see *GS*
1). When viewed from the perspective of the 'general economy
of the whole', may the 'evil man' not be of higher value than
the 'good man' praised by moralists?

In calling for the 'self-overcoming of morality' (of the
Christian-moral world-view) Nietzsche argues that we should
regard our present form of morality as one which is governed by
the necessity of carrying out a critique of morality. The aim
should not be to carry out a simple outright condemnation of
morality: 'Profoundest gratitude for that which morality has
achieved hitherto: but now it is only a burden which may
become a fatality! Morality itself, in the form of honesty,
compels us to deny morality' (*WP* 404). For Nietzsche, the

project of a genealogy of morals is inseparable from the task of 'becoming those that we are' (*GS* 335). The past has determined us in myriads of ways of which we are unaware. Nietzsche carries out not simply a 'history' of morals, but a *genealogy* of morals in order to emphasise that creating the future means to coming to terms with, confronting, and appropriating, the past. The past is never simply that ('past'); on the contrary, the past only gains its significance from the concerns of the present, concerns which themselves are largely determined by a desire to create a new future out of the present. If we are to go 'beyond' nihilism and create new values, it is first necessary that we examine how we have become what we are. The only way to do this is by revaluing the values, morals, and ideals that have defined and determined us, in order to discover their *value*.

For Nietzsche, the values in need of revaluation are largely altruistic and egalitarian ones, such as pity, self-abnegation, and equal rights. The political significance of this critique, for Nietzsche, lies in the fact that modern politics rests largely on a secular inheritance of these Christian values (he interprets the socialist doctrine of equality, for example, in terms of a secularisation of the Christian belief in the 'equality of all souls before God'). To pose the question of the value of our values is partly to ask the question whether these values reflect either an ascending or a descending mode of life, that is, either one which is superabundant and rich in its own self-affirmation, or one which is weak and exhausted. Nietzsche makes it clear in the preface that he is not concerned simply with 'hypothesis-mongering on the origin of morality', but with something quite different and much more vital; the awesome question of the very *value* of morality (preface 5). He invites his readers to experiment and to invert and overturn all that they have been led to believe so far about good and evil. 'The task', he writes in section 7 of the preface, 'is to traverse with quite novel questions, and as though with new eyes, the enormous, distant, and so well hidden land of morality... and does that not mean virtually to *discover* this land for the first time?'

This revaluation of values requires a new kind of knowledge: 'a knowledge of the conditions and circumstances in which they grew, under which they evolved and changed'. It is necessary to consider morality in all its various guises – morality as 'tartuf-ferie', as 'illness', as 'misunderstanding', as 'cause', as 'rem-edy', as 'restraint', etc. It is this kind of knowledge of 'conditions and circumstances' that Nietzsche seeks to develop. His title is intentionally ambiguous because the German prefix '*Zur*' can mean either 'On' or 'Toward'. It is necessary to preserve the ambiguity of Nietzsche's polemic, recognising that it is both a contribution to something that is already in existence (a certain historical appreciation of morality) *and* a redefinition of the parameters and objectives of the subject. Several times in the book Nietzsche refers to the way in which certain philo-sophers (those who undertake a 'history of morality') have 'bungled their moral genealogy' (I, 2 and II, 4) – a process which comes to light when one looks at the manner in which they carry out their inquiry into the origin (*Ursprung*) and descent (*Herkunft*) of certain concepts (the examples Nietzsche gives are 'good' in the first essay and 'guilt/debt' in the second essay). If we take the concept and judgement 'good', Nietzsche argues, we find that moral genealogists impose the altruistic prejudices of the modern age by interpreting the descent and lineage of the concept 'good' in altruistic terms. That is, they argue that, as a value judgement, 'good' originates in terms of those to whom goodness is shown. Nietzsche counters this argument with an aristocratic one of his own by arguing that the judgement 'good' first arose out of a 'pathos of distance' in which the noble and powerful established themselves and their actions as good independently of any altruistic concerns. He attempts to establish this point by showing the etymological significance of the designations for 'good' coined in various languages, showing that 'everywhere "noble", "aristocratic" in the social sense, is the basic concept from which "good" in the sense of "with aristocratic soul", "noble"...necessarily developed' (I, 4). In the *Genealogy* Nietzsche employs this study of the etymology of words in order to trace the metaphoric process by which material terms, such as guilt, gradually take on moral meanings. Nietzsche views meaning as radically historical.[1]

One of Nietzsche's key points about the performance of a genealogy of morals is that one must not confuse 'origin' and 'purpose'; for example, the current 'purpose' of law may reveal nothing about its – unlawful – 'origins'. In section 12 of the second essay Nietzsche sets out some of the methodological rules of a genealogy of morals. Here he argues that existing moral genealogists err when they confuse the evolution of something into a purpose with its origin. These moral genealogists lack a genuine historical sense and end up writing not genealogy, but what he calls '*Entstehungsgeschichte*' (the history of the emergence of a thing). Nietzsche writes:

'The purpose of law', however, is absolutely the last thing to be employed in the history of the origin of law: on the contrary, there is for historiography of any kind no more important proposition than the one it took such effort to establish but which really *ought to be* established now: the cause of the emergence (*Entstehung*) of a thing and its eventual utility, its actual employment and place in a system of purposes, lie worlds apart; whatever exists, having somehow come into being, is again and again reinterpreted to new ends, taken over, transformed, and redirected by some power superior to it; all events in the organic world are a subduing, a *becoming master*, and all subduing and becoming master involves a fresh interpretation, an adaptation through which any previous 'meaning' and 'purpose' are necessarily obscured or obliterated. (II, 12)

It is at this juncture that Nietzsche introduces the notion of the will to power as a methodological principle of the task of revaluation he is performing in the *Genealogy*. His major point is that the 'purpose' and 'utility' of a social custom or a legal institution reveal nothing about their origin, because 'purposes and utilities are only *signs* that a will to power has become master of something less powerful, and imposed upon it the character of a function'. We must recognise that the history of a thing can 'in this way be a continuous sign-chain of ever new interpretations and adaptations'. By uncovering a will to power behind the positing of moral values, and by tracing the origin and descent of values, it is the aim of a genealogy of morals to undermine the universalist and humanist pretensions of moral values. Genealogy is an important critical exercise since it shows that all values and ideals are products of historical change and development. Every concept, every sentiment, and every passion has a history.[2] As such, nothing is fixed and immutable; everything which exists, including legal institutions, social customs, and moral concepts, has evolved and is the product of a specific form of will to power. In analysing 'origins' Nietzsche wants to show that at the beginning of things are found conflict, struggle, and contestation. In reconstructing the past Nietzsche's goals are practical ones. He wishes to counter the prejudices of the present age which impose on the past an interpretation in order to support its democratic and altruistic values.

In the first essay Nietzsche concentrates his attention on the notion of the 'self', contrasting aristocratic and Christian conceptions of human agency, and identifying the moment when the notion of a self viewed as separate from nature and history is conceived (this amounts to the invention of the private self which inhabits a realm of inner freedom). In the second essay, his aim is to reveal an aristocratic ancestry to notions of law and justice in order to challenge the 'reactive' view which locates their origins in the collective needs of weak and insecure individuals.[3] In showing that morality has a history (it is something that has evolved and changed), and that there are different *types* of morality, Nietzsche wants to persuade us that there exists no single, universal morality which is valid for all human types. Today we are governed by a herd-animal morality which refuses to acknowledge that it is only one particular, partial perspective on the world. It is the hegemony of this morality type which he sets out to challenge.

Nietzsche employs history, therefore, in the service of practical interests: interpretation as transfiguration. However, the significance of the book is not restricted to its declared aristocratic aims and objectives. It is an original and provocative attempt to show us that moral and legal notions have a history and that 'man', considered as a political and moral animal, has 'become'. Almost everything that exists, Nietzsche is telling us, is open to interpretation; life itself is nothing but a contest and conflict of values and a struggle over the interpretation of ideas and ideals. 'Genealogy' reveals the *agon* at the heart of 'the art of interpretation' (*Kunst der Auslegung*).

In his autobiography, *Ecce Homo*, written in the autumn of 1888, Nietzsche reflects on his life's work and reviews his progress towards himself, that is, he reflects on how he became what *he* is: Nietzsche as educator. He divides his work into two distinct phases, a yes-saying part (the works written between 1878 and 1885) and a nay-saying part (the works written after 1885). The nay-saying part of his task refers to the revaluation of all values, 'the great war – the conjuring up of a day of decision'. What Nietzsche learns, as he himself recognises in *Ecce Homo*, is that in order to affirm (to say yes) one must also negate (say no): 'negating *and destroying* are conditions of saying Yes' (*Ecce Homo*, 'Why I Am A Destiny', section 4).

The dividing line between the two parts of his task is the work *Beyond Good and Evil* published in 1885, which Nietzsche later described as 'in all essentials a *critique of modernity*'. On the title page to the *Genealogy of Morals*, Nietzsche informs his readers that it is a work that is designed 'to supplement and clarify' *Beyond Good and Evil*. In the final section of the preface to the *Genealogy* he states that, if the book 'is incomprehensible to anyone and jars on their ears', the fault is not necessarily his, as he must presuppose that the reader is acquainted with his earlier writings. Moreover, a clue as to how we should perceive his writings, taken as a whole, is given in section 3 of the preface. Here Nietzsche reveals that the division he gives to his work in *Ecce Homo*, in terms of yes-saying and nay-saying writings, is misleading and, to a large extent, arbitrary. It is fitting for a philosopher, he tells us, that all his work grows from the *one* soil: 'our ideas, our values, our yeas and nays, our ifs and buts, grow out of us with the necessity with which a tree bears fruit – related and each with an affinity to each, and evidence of *one* will, *one* health, *one* soil, *one* sun'.

The *Genealogy* is made up of three essays which represent,

Nietzsche tells us in *Ecce Homo*, 'three decisive preliminary studies by a psychologist for a revaluation of all values'. The first inquiry concerns itself with tracing the birth of Christianity out of 'the spirit of *ressentiment*'; the second inquiry develops a 'psychology of the conscience', where 'conscience' refers not to the voice of God in man, but to the instinct of cruelty which has been internalised after it was supressed; the third and final inquiry looks into the meaning of ascetic ideals, and, in particular, inquires into how the ideal of the 'priest' derives its great power over humanity.

Master morality and slave morality

Perhaps the principal aim of the first and second essays is to show that one of the central ideas of moral and political theory, that of the human subject in possession of conscience and a free will, is not a natural given, but has to be seen as the result of an historical and psychological evolution. As Nietzsche dramatically poses the question at the start of his second inquiry, is not the real and paradoxical problem of man that of how he has been bred as a political animal, that is, as an *animal* which is able to make *promises*? The production of individual conscience has to be seen as a late fruit, not as something which stands at the beginning of human evolution.

Moral philosophy tends to presuppose the existence of a human subject which has the freedom to act. Modern thinking separates the doer from the deed and ascribes a value judgement to someone's actions in accordance with what it takes to be good or bad intentions behind their actions.[4] But this, Nietzsche argues, was not always the case. In what he calls the decisive 'pre-moral period of man', the period of the 'morality of custom' (see *BGE* 32), action was not judged on the basis of individual intentions. Instead, the rightness and wrongness of actions was judged solely in terms of the authority of tradition and the power of established custom. In societies or communities based on this morality of custom, to be an individual was to stand outside and apart from the social group, so that 'one was sentenced to individuality' as a form of punishment (see *GS* 117). In the first essay he accounts for the evolution of the idea of the human subject, conceived as a self-reflective ego separate from nature, society, and history, by analysing what he calls the 'slave revolt in morality'. This revolt consists of two things: the first is replacing a non-moralistic distinction of good/bad held by the masters and nobles, with a moralistic distinction of good/evil; the second is originating notions of free will, soul, and guilt.

Nietzsche had first introduced a typology of master and slave moralities in his work in section 45 of *Human, All Too Human*. He takes it up again in section 260 of *Beyond Good and Evil*, and the distinction governs the analysis in the first inquiry of the *Genealogy*. The typology denotes distinct psychological types of human agency which first arise out of political distinctions made between social classes. In the *Genealogy* Nietzsche makes it clear that what interests him about an aristocratic code of morality is not so much the political power a ruling class wields, but rather the 'typical character traits' by which it defines and affirms itself. He does, however, recognise the historical inseparability of oligarchy and aristocracy. He argues that modern Europeans are the product of both types of morality, and that in all higher and mixed cultures there are attempts at a mediation between the two types of morality (*BGE* 260). The discrimination of values has originated either among the rulers or the ruled. In the first case, the possession of a consciousness of difference, which separates the rulers from the ruled, results in feelings of pride and delight among the rulers. On account of their dominion over the ruled, the nobles esteem life in terms of a feeling of overflowing power. They possess a consciousness of wealth which wants to give and bestow. The noble human being is able to honour itself as a being which has achieved power over itself. But it is only able to do this through the 'pathos of distance' which divides it from the lower ranks. In contrast, the slave type of morality, the morality of the weak and the oppressed, results in a pessimistic suspicion about the whole human condition. The eye of the slave turns unfavourably towards the virtues of the powerful; it esteems those qualities, such as pity, humility, and patience, which will serve to ease its existence.

The first essay sets out to show that it is only through the act of a slave rebellion in morality that there is introduced into history the idea of a human subject which is free to act and whose existence is interpreted in distinctly moral terms. The slave revolt in morality refers largely, although not exclusively, to what Nietzsche understands and interprets as the Jewish revolt against the dominion of noble values (the other example of such a revolt for Nietzsche is to be found in the case of Socrates). It is 'Israel with its vengefulness and revaluation of all values' which has 'triumphed' over all noble ideals. Jesus, the 'Redeemer' of the weak and the poor, represents the great seduction to this Jewish revaluation of noble values: for Nietzsche such a revolt represents the 'grand politics of revenge' (*OGM* I, 9). Master or noble morality spontaneously affirms itself as 'good', and only after this self-ascription feels the need to extend the word 'bad' to what it considers lowly and inferior to itself. The slave morality, typified by Christianity, can only define itself as 'good' by first negating others – masters, nobles, other religions and races – as 'evil'. In other words, the slave morality is not a morality of self-affirmation, but is parasitic on what it must negate. To this end it invents the idea of the human subject who is free to act, and a whole new moral vocabulary (of sin, guilt, redemption, etc.), in order to attribute 'blame' to the nobles for being what they are (strong and powerful), and to glorify the weak for 'freely' choosing to be humble, meek, and so on. As Nietzsche says in section 13:

The subject (or, to employ a more popular expression, the *soul*) has perhaps been believed in hitherto more firmly than anything else on earth because it makes possible to the majority of mortals, the weak and oppressed of every kind, the sublime self-deception that interprets weakness as freedom, and their being thus-and-thus as a *merit*.

The defining attitude of this slave type of morality is one of resentment. In contrast to the master morality which affirms itself in its own uniqueness, the slave morality says 'no' to what is outside and different to itself: 'This inversion of the value-

positing eye', Nietzsche writes', 'this need to direct one's view
outward instead of back to oneself – is of the essence of
ressentiment: in order to exist, slave morality always first needs a
hostile external world; it needs, physiologically speaking,
external stimuli in order to act at all – its action is fundamentally reaction' (*OGM* I, 10).

Nietzsche's analysis of types of morality makes two important
claims: One is that moral designations were first applied to
human beings and only later, and derivatively, were they
applied to actions considered apart from the human type
performing them. The second is that, as far as modern human
beings are concerned, a master morality is something quite
alien. We find it hard to empathise with today, and it is even
harder to 'dig up and uncover' (*BGE* 260).

It would be a mistake, I believe, to think that Nietzsche is
simply condemning the triumph of the slave type of morality
over master morality. It is only with the development of the
priestly form of existence, which intensifies through the spread
of Christianity, that man becomes 'an interesting animal' on
account of his development of a soul and hence a knowledge not
only of good, but also of *evil* (*OGM* I, 7). However, *contra* a
political theoriest such as Rousseau, Nietzsche does not argue
that civilisation has corrupted man, but laments the fact that it
has not corrupted his sufficiently. Such a strange judgement of
the figure of Rousseau has to be seen as part of Nietzsche's wider
attempt to subvert our assumptions about good and evil and our
estimation of the role they play in the general economy of life
(see especially *GS* I). As Nietzsche says in one of his ultimate
challenges as an immoral philosopher: 'In the great economy of
the whole, the terrible aspects of reality (in affects, in desires, in
the will to power) are to an incalculable degree more necessary
than that form of petty happiness which people call "goodness"'
(*EH* 'Why I Am A Destiny', section 4).

With a genealogy of morals Nietzsche wants to show that
there existed a pre-moral time when the human animal did not
view its actions self-reflectively in terms of categories of good
and evil. The 'blond beasts' he speaks of, for example, did not
act intentionally with a view to inflict pain and injury on other

weaker types. They simply gave immediate and spontaneous expression to their instinctual, unconscious will to power, which, prior to the formation of society, assumed an aggressive form. They could not consider themselves accountable for their actions since they lacked a notion of free will which would have enabled them to do so. Today, we would view the actions of these beasts as lacking in compassion and as harsh and cruel. What is not clear from Nietzsche's argument, however, is whether, in his attempt to persuade modern human beings to struggle for the revitalisation of the 'evil' affects and passions, he is advocating the *conscious* cultivation of evil as a means of overcoming nihilism. Although this is not an issue which Nietzsche adequately deals with in his work, I would argue that it is an important one. If he is advocating the conscious practice of evil, then his thinking faces some grave difficulties and becomes highly disturbing. What these difficulties might amount to will be examined in the next chapter when I look at how Nietzsche attempts to apply his philosophy beyond good and evil to the political realm with a notion of 'great politics'. All that needs to be noted at this stage is the immense problem confronting Nietzsche's recommendation of 'evil' and his devaluation of 'goodness': if we, as modern human beings, are no longer capable of a master morality in its original form, and if we are now constituted as moral agents, then how is it possible for us to transform ourselves into the kind of creatures we would have to be in order to be 'beyond good and evil' and to engage in the 'self-overcoming of morality'? (We have already seen that the cultivating thought of eternal return stumbles at this fence.)

In the first essay Nietzsche wants to show that the 'soul' has evolved, and that before Christianity there prevailed a different understanding of human action. As modern human beings we are those individuals who consider themselves agents capable of free action, exercising judgement, and being held accountable for their actions. The ancient Greeks, however, saw character in terms of destiny, and did not separate the 'soul' from the body in the way Christianity does. What drives the self are often dark, unconscious forces over which the individual has no control. It is not a question of free will in the sense in which a Christian would conceive it, but rather a question of becoming what one *is*. The classic story in which this view of character is presented in Greek tragedy is that of *Oedipus Rex*. This is a play about the insecurity of the human condition and the blindness of man. Oedipus is a character who is granted a terrible fate, that of killing his father and marrying his mother.[5] Oedipus gropes in the dark, as we all do, not knowing who he is, or understanding why he suffers. The path to self-knowledge is a painful one. The play is also about human greatness and how Oedipus can achieve greatness through accepting his terrible fate. At one point in the play, he says, in instantly recognisable 'Nietz-schean' terms, 'This horror is mine, and none but I is *strong* enough to bear it'. As E. R. Dodds points out, Oedipus is great because he accepts responsibility for all his acts, 'including those which are objectively most horrible, though subjectively in-nocent'.[6] What ancient thought did not forget, and which is ever present in Greek tragedy, is the realisation that even a person's deliberate acts are in large measure the result of innumerable causes in their past over which they had little control. This did not mean, however, that one could not assume 'responsibility' for them. This conception of responsibility neither rests on a notion of free will (character as fate not as free choice) nor espouses a notion of sin.

By contrast, Nietzsche regards the Christian conception of personality as ignoble and cowardly. It is preoccupied with questions of sin and guilt which rob human character of its innocence. It removes the conditions of human agency from the actual, historical world and places them in a transcendental realm, a 'beyond' (see *AC* 25). As one commentator notes, the creation of the individual human personality has been vital to the development of morals and of civilisation.[7] The civilising role played by Platonism and Christianity has been to tend the needs of the soul, which requires first a notion of conscience and then a notion of the freedom of the will. But one of the results of this process of the cultivation of the soul is that the autonomous will becomes abstract, the soul severed from its connections with the body and from its connections with other bodies in the universe. With the notion of the *Übermensch* Nietzsche is seeking to revive a noble model of human agency in which character is viewed as fate and life as an experiment. One is what one does and one has to accept total responsibility for what one is. This is the – difficult – task of the proud, sovereign individual.[8]

Nietzsche is often accused of an empty formalism in positing his ideal of a noble selfhood, but this is to miss an important point. What Nietzsche is concerned with is a *style* of character, not with prescribing a specific set of rules of conduct, legislating what is good and what is evil for all. For Nietzsche, in becoming what one is the task is to fit together one's strengths and one's weaknesses into an artistic plan, 'until every one of them appears as art and reason and even weaknesses delight the eye' (*GS* 290).

Bad conscience

In the second essay Nietzsche focuses his attention on the psychological factors involved in the process by which the human animal becomes trained and disciplined as a social animal (a creature which can make promises and be held accountable for its actions). What concerns Nietzsche most in this essay is how the rise of Christianity represents a deformation of this process – how the development of conscience is transformed by Christian-moral culture into a kind of bad conscience which is unable ever to relieve itself of its feeling of guilt.

The task of cultivating an animal which is able to make promises, requires a 'preparatory task' by which man is made 'regular, calculable, and uniform'. This 'preparatory task' refers to the discipline of the human animal afforded by the 'morality of custom'. It is the morality of custom which cultivates in man a memory and a sense of responsibility. The disciplining of the human animal into a moral agent, or political animal, takes place not through any gentle methods of social control, but through the harsh and cruel measures of discipline and punishment associated with traditional morality. 'Perhaps', Nietzsche writes in section 3 of the second essay, 'there was nothing more fearful and uncanny in the whole prehistory of man than his *mnemotechnics*'. It is the 'oldest psychology on earth' that if you want something to stay in the memory (such as that stealing is wrong) the best way to ensure success is to *burn* it in (the burning off of the hand of the thief). What are all religions at bottom, Nietzsche asks, if not highly refined systems of cruelties? The potential 'fruit' of this labour of culture (*Kultur*) performed on man by the morality of custom is the 'sovereign individual', an autonomous and supra-ethical (*über-sittlich*) individual who is master of a free will, able to make promises, and is like only to him or herself. The autonomous individual has transcended the level of the morality (*Sittlichkeit*) of custom (*Sitte*) and is able to hold itself responsible for its actions.

In this picture of human evolution, conscience is not viewed as some kind of metaphysical entity unique to each individual, but as a moral faculty which is the product of a historical labour of culture or civilisation. The paradox of man's moral training can be stated as follows: the process by which man's existence becomes moralised is one which, in its beginnings, operates by coercion and violence; but once the human animal has become disciplined it is, at least potentially, capable of living beyond morality (*Sittlichkeit*) and autonomously.

It may be worthwhile at this point to state precisely where Nietzsche departs from Kant in his understanding of autonomy. Like Kant, Nietzsche does hold that autonomy is a precondition of being 'moral'. However, Nietzsche views the achievement of autonomy in terms of a moment of individuation and difference which distinguishes the self from other human beings, especially those who have not attained autonomy and have thus failed to earn the right to make promises. As Nietzsche puts it in his inimitable style, the 'free man' possesses 'his *measure of value*: looking out upon others from himself, he honours or he despises; and just as he is bound to honour his peers, the strong and reliable ... whose trust is a mark of distinction ... he is bound to reserve a kick for the feeble windbags who promise without the right to do so' (II, 2). To be 'moral' in this sense is to be a reflective, independent agent who has a 'will to self-responsibility'. But it does not entail for Nietzsche, as it does for Kant, that one believes that all human beings must conform to the

same universal maxims of action. Kant insists that in considering the maxim informing any given action we must ask
ourselves – in order to assess its rightfulness – whether it can be
universalised so as to apply to all rational human beings. But an
essential part of Nietzsche's thinking beyond good and evil is
that a virtue has to be the personal invention of each individual:
'The profoundest laws of preservation and growth demand the
reverse of Kant: that each one of us should devise *his own* virtue,
his own categorical imperative' (*AC* 11).

After the opening sections of the second essay Nietzsche
focuses his attention on the deformation that the creation of
conscience undergoes within Christian-moral culture. In anticipation of Freud, whose essay *Civilisation and Its Discontents* is
in many ways a psychoanalytical reworking of the *Genealogy of
Morals*, Nietzsche develops an understanding of the evolution of
civilisation in terms of the repression of instincts.[9] Thus, for
example, in section 7 of the second essay, he argues that 'The
darkening of the sky above mankind has deepened in step with
the increase in man's feeling of shame *at man*... the morbid
softening and moralisation through which the animal "man"
finally learns to be ashamed of all his instincts.' Nietzsche
explains how this moralisation of the animal 'man' takes place
by showing how the notion of guilt (*Schuld*) has changed
fundamentally from the ancient civil law relationship between
a creditor and a debtor, in which it primarily denotes a debt
that one has to honour in order to prove oneself as an animal
who has earned the 'right' to make promises, to the moral one
of a Christian culture in which one feels guilt in the sense of
original sin: one is not in debt to a creditor in terms of social or
legal relationship of equals, but simply on account of *being born*.
This process reaches its climax in the Christian teaching,
because here there is conceived the incredible spectacle where
the guilt felt in a relationship between a creditor (God) and a
debtor (man) is so great that an atonement equal to the sin
cannot be conceived. (In section 20 Nietzsche poses the question
whether the rise of atheism – which has the *potential* to be a
second kind of innocence – represents a new period of history in
which man will emancipate himself from this moralised exist-

ence. It is not until the third essay that he gives his answer to this question: 'Unconditional honest atheism ... is the awe-inspiring *catastrophe* of two thousand years of training in truthfulness that finally forbids itself the *lie involved in belief in God*') (*OGM* III, 27).

The most important thing to note about the bad conscience is that its rise preceded resentment and precluded all struggle. Its development has to be seen, therefore, in terms of 'an ineluctable disaster', a profound leap and break with what went before. The bad conscience is the inevitable development which happens when the human animal becomes 'enclosed within the walls of society and of peace'. Nietzsche compares this evolutionary leap to the situation which must have faced sea animals when they were forced to become land animals or perish. The bad conscience evolves through a process he calls 'the internalisation of man', the process whereby the instincts are not discharged externally but are turned inwards. These instincts are those of 'wild, free, prowling man' – 'hostility, joy in persecuting, in attacking, in change, in destruction' (*OGM* II, 16). In section 17 Nietzsche refers to the 'will to power' as the most basic and fundamental instinct, and it is this which becomes repressed in the development of the bad conscience. The will to power is the instinct for growth and development, what Nietzsche calls the 'instinct for freedom'. The key point is that the rise of the bad conscience originates prior to the slave revolt in morality. What it refers to, in effect, is a pre-moralised sense of accountability which is the result of aggression being redirected against the individual 'self'. On entering society it is no longer possible for the human animal to engage in the immediate discharge of its aggressive energy and expansive forces. The psychical structure of pre-moral guilt created by the bad conscience, however, is certainly what makes the slave revolt in morality possible.

For Nietzsche this strange leap in man's evolution as a creature of the earth transforms him from a limited, stupid animal of instinct into an animal with tremendous possibilities for development. The bad conscience, he tells us, is an illness, but only in the sense that pregnancy can be regarded as an illness:

From now on, man is *included* among the most unexpected and exciting lucky throws in the dice game of Heraclitus' 'great child', be he called Zeus or chance; he gives rise to an interest, a tension, a hope, almost a certainty, as if with him something were announcing and preparing itself, as if man were not a goal but only a way, an episode, a bridge, a great promise. (*OGM* ii, 16).

The metaphors of this passage refer us to an earlier work of Nietzsche's, namely *Thus Spoke Zarathustra*, in the prologue of which, man is defined as a rope tied between animal and *Übermensch*, and it is declared that what can be loved in man is the fact that he is a bridge and not a goal. Thus, it is significant that the second essay closes with a prefiguration of Zarathustra and his teaching (sections 24 and 25).

We modern human beings are the heirs of the conscience-vivisection and self-torture of millennia ... Man has all too long had an 'evil eye' for his natural inclinations, so that they have finally become inseparable from his 'bad conscience'. An attempt at the reverse *in itself* would be possible – but who is strong enough for it?... To whom should one turn today with *such* hopes and demands? (ii, 24)

Nietzsche's answer is 'Zarathustra', the 'Antichrist and anti-nihilist', the 'victor over God and nothingness' – '*he must come one day*'. It is at this stage in the evolution of the animal 'man' that the figure of Zarathustra is to appear in order to teach man that God is dead and now the overman shall be the meaning of the earth. At this point in social evolution another saga in the history of the human soul begins. In section 7 of the preface to the *Genealogy*, for example, Nietzsche describes the critique of morality in terms of unfolding another chapter in the great 'Dionysian drama on the destiny of the soul' – Dionysus being, for Nietzsche, the god of life (life conceived as will to power which is beyond good and evil).

It is in the second essay that Nietzsche speculates on the origins of society and rejects the social contract view found in the natural law tradition. He is very much concerned with combating what he takes to be a 'reactive' view on this question: the view that the origins of social order lie in the passions and needs of weak and insecure individuals. In contrast to this view, which he associates with the German thinker Eugen Dühring, but which can be found in thinkers as different as Hobbes and Rousseau, Nietzsche wishes to put forward the argument that the institutions of law and justice are creations of strong and powerful individuals who aim to impose measure on the reactive feelings and put an end to the 'senseless raging of *ressentiment* among the weaker powers' (II, 11). The initial purpose of law, Nietzsche argues, is to establish a supreme power which takes disputes out of the hands of rancorous and revengeful individuals. Nietzsche follows Hobbes in arguing that what is 'just' and 'unjust' can only be decided after the institution of law has been set up: outside of this context there can be no notions of justice and injustice (compare *HAH* 99).[10] However, Nietzsche does not follow Hobbes in deducing from a state of anarchy or moral licence absolutism as the only valid form of political rule. In fact, nowhere in the *Genealogy* does Nietzsche provide his readers with a picture of what he considers to be the most desirable political order (for this we have to turn to sections 257–9 of the previous work, *Beyond Good and Evil*); the only statement Nietzsche makes on this is the following in section 11 of the second essay:

A legal order thought of as sovereign and universal, not as a means in the struggle between power-complexes but as means of *preventing* all struggle in general... would be a principle *hostile to life*.

It is significant that in his discussion of the origins of law and justice in the second essay of the *Genealogy of Morals* Nietzsche does not address himself to the modern question of what constitutes legitimate political power (authority), or discuss the relationship between the individual and society in terms of a social contract. He suspends these kinds of questions and ends the essay with a prefiguration of the teaching of Zarathustra: that God is dead and that we should now will the overman as the meaning of the earth. This omission of the question of legitimacy on Nietzsche's part is not accidental; on the contrary, it accords with his view that the goal of humanity cannot lie in a moral end or goal, but only in the creations of its 'highest exemplars' (great human beings). The notion of the 'overman' cannot be presented in terms of legitimacy since it is '*the lightning*' which strikes out of 'the dark cloud man'.

Nietzsche dismisses as a piece of sentimentalism the view which considers the origins of the state in terms of a social contract, and revives the old idea which views its origins in terms of conquest. He imagines a pack of

blond beasts, a conqueror and master race which, organized for war and with the ability to organize, unhesitatingly lays its terrible claws upon a populace perhaps tremendously superior in numbers but still formless and nomad... He who can command, he is who is by nature 'master', he who is violent in act and bearing – what has he to do with contracts! (II, 17)

What Nietzsche neglects is the fact that social contract theorists such as Rousseau were fully aware that the actual historical origins of the state were bloody, lawless, and violent. Rousseau was concerned with developing the philosophical fiction of the social contract in order to deduce the *legitimate* basis of our obligation to political authority. The notion of a legitimate social contract could then serve as a powerful critique of existing regimes whose rule could not lay claim to such legitimacy (which for Rousseau could only take the form of popular sovereignty). A notion of legitimacy conceived in these terms, however, is utterly irrelevant to Nietzsche's aristocratic concern with the fate of culture.

The meaning of the ascetic ideal

In the third and final essay Nietzsche poses the question: 'what is the meaning of ascetic ideals?' (Nietzsche begins by speaking of ascetic ideals but soon focuses his attention on the ascetic *ideal*). I cannot convey the full richness of his analysis here – of art, music, religion, and philosophy – but will concentrate on what he has to say about the will to truth, because it provides some vital clues to an understanding of what is entailed in the attempt to overcome morality.

Nietzsche criticises the ascetic ideal, and the power it has exerted over humanity, because, in its Christian form, it is an ideal which has been placed in the service of a devaluation of life. Asceticism denotes any practice which places self-denial at the centre of its understanding of life. An ascetic life is a self-contradiction for Nietzsche since it expresses a will which does not simply want to attain mastery over something in life, but over life's most basic and powerful conditions (III, 11). It would be mistaken to suppose that Nietzsche opposes ascetic practices completely, since the kind of greatness which he esteems requires sacrifice and self-discipline. What he is opposed to are practices of self-denial which devalue earthly, sensual life.

The meaning of the ascetic ideal is, paradoxically, that humanity has had no meaning apart from this ideal. The dominance of the ascetic ideal means that 'something was *lacking*, that man was surrounded by a fearful *void*, he did not know how to justify ... to affirm himself' (III, 28). Man could not find an answer to the great question of life: 'why do I suffer?' It is thus the meaninglessness of suffering, not the fact of suffering, which accounts for the misery mankind has experienced in its history. Christian morality has had the effect of preserving the human will in the face of a suicidal nihilism experienced at the time of the decay and corruption of the Roman Empire. In this example, the ascetic ideal arises out of the protective instincts of a degenerating and reactive will to power. This leads Nietzsche to recognising the paradoxical fact that the ascetic ideal of Christianity represented an artifice in the service of the preservation of life (III, 13). The Christian religion succeeded in altering the direction of the *ressentiment* felt by the weak and the oppressed, by placing suffering under the perspective of guilt which served to deepen it by making it 'more inward, more poisonous, more life-destructive' (the doctrine of original sin teaches that the 'self' itself is to be blamed for its suffering). Through its interpretation of the meaning of Christ's example, including his death on the Cross, Christianity succeeded in giving a meaning to suffering. The crucifixion shows that suffering can be redemptive and that death is not the end (Nietzsche contests the Church's interpretation of Christ's life and death in *AC* 32, 34, 39, 42). Christian morality was the 'great antidote against practical and theoretical nihilism' (*WP* 4). However, with the advent of nihilism, which follows in the wake of the death of God, Christianity is no longer able to provide civilisation with the cultural and ethical foundations of its existence.

The will that is concealed in the ascetic ideal hides a hatred of the senses and of beauty; it is a 'longing to get away from all appearance, change, becoming, death'. Nietzsche is opposed to the Christian practice of the ascetic ideal because it considers its goal to be a universal one, applicable to all races and all societies. It interprets everything that exists, including epochs, nations, peoples, and world-history, in accordance with the realisation of its goals (III, 23). In addition, he holds that Christianity has waged a war against aristocratic virtues and values, including the feelings of reverence and distance which are necessary for every elevation of man and advancement in culture. Out of the *ressentiment* of the masses Christianity has forged its chief weapon against everything noble and joyful on earth (*AC* 43). If nihilism is to be overcome Christian values must be exposed for what they are – the values of the weak, the world-weary, and the decadent – and a new foundation established for the creation and legislation of values.

In spite of it being a 'rebellion against the most fundamental presuppositions of life', the will of the ascetic ideal was at least a will, a secret 'will to nothingness'. Now, however, with the advent of the death of God humanity is plunged into the possibility of a crippling nihilism in which it must once again confront the wisdom of a Silenus (the wisdom which teaches that what is best is not to be born, and the second best is to die soon). It is the destiny of Zarathustra to restore health and beauty to man's senses and to teach the law of life as the law of 'self-overcoming' – life must forever create and destroy itself anew.

But how is Christianity to be overcome? Nietzsche's argument is that Christianity and morality, like all great things, *overcome themselves*. He posits 'self-overcoming' as the law of life, showing that his own thought relies on a notion of nature to legitimate his support of 'life' *contra* morality. Nietzsche argues that Christianity develops a desire (a will) for *truth*. Ultimately, this will to truth in Christianity becomes transmuted into intellectual cleanliness and eventually into probity. What has really conquered the Christian God is Christianity itself: the 'confessional subtlety of the Christian conscience translated and sublimated into scientific conscience'. It is the scientific conscience that reveals the 'truth' about Christian morality – that it is a lie which is born of lowly, immoral origins. As Nietzsche puts it in section 27:

All great things bring about their own destruction through an act of self-overcoming: thus the law of life will have it, the law of the necessity of 'self-overcoming' in the nature of life – the lawgiver himself eventually receives the demand: '*patere legem, quam ipsi tulisti* [submit to the law you yourself proposed]'. In this way Christianity as a *dogma* was destroyed by its own morality; in the same way Christianity *as morality* must now perish, too: we stand on the threshold of *this* event. After Christian truthfulness has drawn one inference after another, it must end by drawing its *most striking inference*, its inference *against* itself.

What defines the modernity of our present-day existence is that it is within us – 'we moderns' – that the will to truth, which has informed Christian-moral culture for two thousand years, becomes 'conscious of itself as a *problem*'. We now view it as 'dishonest, mendacious, feminism, weakness, and cowardice' to view nature as if it were a proof of goodness and the workings of an omnipotent God, or 'to interpret history as the glory of a divine reason, as the perpetual witness to a moral world order and moral intentions'. It is the rigour with which we pursue this logic of 'self-overcoming' which makes us 'good Europeans', the 'heirs of Europe's longest and bravest self-overcoming'. The overcoming of the will to truth is at the same time the overcoming of morality, since our drive for truth has been built on moral foundations and has been inspired by moral needs. Nietzsche closes the penultimate section of the book on a tremendously powerful and dramatic note, one which, with our consciousness of the horrors and tragedies of the twentieth century, can only make us shudder:

As the will to truth thus gains self-consciousness – there can be no doubt of that – morality will gradually *perish* now: this is the great spectacle in a hundred acts reserved for the next two centuries in Europe – the most terrible, most questionable, and perhaps also the most hopeful of all spectacles. (III, 27)

This passage is echoed in *Ecce Homo*, where Nietzsche refers to himself in uncanny terms as a posthumous fate whose name will one day be associated with 'something tremendous – a crisis without equal on earth, the most profound collision of conscience', and whose 'truth is *terrible*, for so far one has called *lies* truth'. Here Nietzsche also calls himself the 'first *decent* human being' who stands in opposition to the lies of millennia. He contradicts as no one has ever contradicted before, but is nevertheless, he informs his readers, the opposite of a nay-saying philosopher. Nietzsche is prepared to throw himself to the lions, to offer himself as the bringer of glad tidings, as someone who would rather be a buffoon than pronounced a holy man, and to sacrifice all (his sanity included) if it means that a type of man that *justifies* man could once again be possible (a type towards which we would feel awe and pride as opposed to pity and contempt) (*OGM* I, 12). Nietzsche's critique of morality culminates in a terrifying logic of destruction.

CONCLUSION

In many respects the third essay of the *Genealogy of Morals* can be read as an untimely meditation on science. Nietzsche insists that modern science is not the opposite of the ascetic ideal, but simply the latest and noblest expression of it (III, 23). Science does not believe in an ideal above itself. As a result it gives rise to an intellectual stoicism which refuses to either affirm or deny, but simply halts before the factual. Science is unable to create values and so it requires a 'value-creating power' in the service of which it can believe in itself (III, 25). The practice of science is a strange one since its discoveries, such as that of man's origins amongst the apes, encourage humanity to lose its respect for itself and to engage in 'self-contempt'. It is interesting that this is precisely the effect of Nietzsche's genealogical inquiries as well, the whole point of which is to demystify the world. Nietzsche, however, accuses science of being too serious, of lacking a capacity for self-parody. Science, he says, rests on the same foundation as the ascetic ideal: 'a certain *impoverishment of life*... the affects grown cool, the tempo of life slowed down, dialectics in place of instinct, seriousness imprinted on faces and gestures' (III, 25). Nietzsche now turns to celebrate art as the human practice which is able to overcome the seriousness of the ascetic ideal and of science. He speaks of 'Plato versus Homer' as the 'complete, genuine antagonism' (III, 25). As in his first published book, *The Birth of Tragedy*, Nietzsche once again points to the necessity of art as a corrective to science and the theoretical view of life. Only art, he says, is able to sanctify the lie and to grant 'the will to deception' a good conscience. Art is the great stimulus to life viewed as self-overcoming will to power.

In the closing sections of the book Nietzsche invites us to raise a number of critical questions: What is it in us that wants truth? Why do we wish not to be deceived? To what extent is life bearable without ideals? And must they always be ascetic in the sense that they devalue life? As one commentator has argued, Nietzsche's aim is not to abandon the will to truth, but to re-establish it on foundations that will divorce it from the values which have guided the ascetic ideal in its denigration of the sensual forces of life.[11]

The third essay is important because it contains a self-reflective gloss on the first and second essays which puts into suspension some of the more apocalyptic – I am tempted to say messianic – statements made in the text (especially in the final sections of the second essay). Nietzsche is wary of setting himself up as a new authority, a new ascetic priest who will lead humanity 'over' man. In this essay he locates the presence of the ascetic ideal in the most unlikely places or sources – in historiography as well as modern science, and in his own thinking too. Even when we think we are overcoming the ascetic ideal we discover we are deft practitioners or secret worshippers of it. The end-point of Nietzsche's investigation into the genealogy of morals is perhaps depressing for those who are looking for redemption from the death of God and the collapse of Christianity. Nietzsche's final message seems to be that there is no alternative to the ascetic ideal other than a parodic overcoming of it. What is needed now are not new prophets, but 'comedians of the Christian-moral ideal' (III, 27).

CHAPTER 7

O humanity!
Nietzsche on great politics

Humanity! Has there ever been a more hideous old
woman among old women – (unless it were 'truth': a
question for philosophers)?

Nietzsche, The Gay Science 377

I should hate to come before my fellow men in the guise of
a prophet, a monster, and a moral scarecrow.

Nietzsche, letter to Peter Gast (October 1888)

I do not challenge individuals – I challenge humanity...
However the judgement may fall, for or against me, my
name is linked up with a fatality the magnitude of which
is unutterable.

Nietzsche, letter to his sister (December 1888)

Nietzsche's response to the problem of nihilism, and the crisis of
authority it gives rise to, is a complex one. He devises the figure
of Zarathustra to represent the 'self-overcoming of morality'
and to teach the meaning of the overman. He inquires into the
origins and descent of moral values and legal notions in order to
combat a Christian and moral reading of history and man's
evolution. I would argue that there are essentially two kinds of
politics Nietzsche offers his readers. One is a less well-known
'politics of survival', which consists not in legislating new values
and law-tables for man, but in playing in parodic and ironic
fashion with the ideals of humanity. Here Nietzsche does not
foresee a simple solution or end to nihilism, but devises strategies
for its endurance. The other is the more familiar 'politics of
cruelty' associated with Nietzsche's aristocratic radicalism.
Here the aim is to gain control of the forces of history and
produce, through a conjunction of philosophical legislation and

political power ('great politics'), a new humanity. It is not possible to say which of the two Nietzsche wished to promote, or which he considered the more authentic, owing to the fragmentary and incomplete nature of his final output. In this chapter I shall concentrate on critically examining the coherence of Nietzsche's aristocratic conception of politics, since it is one which runs consistently throughout his writings. It is also the only overt or explicit politics which it is possible to associate with him.

In *Beyond Good and Evil* (1885) and elsewhere (see especially the fifth book of *The Gay Science*, 1887) Nietzsche embraces a machiavellian–inspired immoral politics, which believes it is able to justify its despotic rule through the cultivation of a higher and nobler culture, and which will redeem 'life' from the effects of two thousand years of Christian-moral culture. 'The time for petty politics is over', Nietzsche informs us, 'the next century will bring with it the fight for the dominion of the earth – the compulsion to great politics' (*BGE* 208). Great Politics is a politics which does not restrict itself to the petty politics of nationalism or of 'happiness', but concerns itself with 'the European problem', that is, 'the cultivation of a new caste that will rule Europe' (*BGE* 251). Concerning the 'immorality' of this task, Nietzsche writes, 'Expressed in a formula one might say: *every* means hitherto employed with the intention of making mankind moral has been thoroughly *immoral*' (*TI* 'The Improvers of Mankind', 5). Nietzsche's political thinking is preoccupied with the question whether the animal 'man' can undergo further development and enhancement in the age of the death of God and the advent of nihilism. The concern with 'great politics' is neither accidental nor peripheral to his overall philosophical project, but arises in a very deep sense from its most fundamental concerns.

For Nietzsche, one of the most important aspects of the attempt to think through the problem of nihilism is the need to develop an understanding of how new values can be created and fashioned through the conjunction of philosophical legislation and political power. He argues, for example, that once we recognise that the democratic movement which dominates modern politics is not only a form of the decay of political organisation, but equally a diminution of man into 'the perfect herd animal (the man of "free society")', then we will recognise that the only way forward is 'toward new philosophers', that is towards free spirits who experience tasks such as the revaluation of values as 'compulsions':

there is no choice; toward spirits strong and original enough to provide the stimuli for opposite valuations and to revalue and invert 'eternal values'; toward forerunners, toward men of the future who in the present tie the knot and constraint that forces the will of millennia upon *new* tracks. To teach man the future as his *will*, as dependent on a a human will, and prepare great ventures and over-all experiments of discipline and cultivation by way of putting an end to that gruesome dominion of nonsense and accident that has so far been called 'history'. (*BGE* 203)

We must see the revaluation of values, not in terms of some arcane academic exercise, but as crucial to the cultivation of great politics. In *Ecce Homo*, for example, Nietzsche says that for him 'the question concerning the descent of moral values' is the most fundamental of all questions since 'it is crucial for the *future* of humanity' (*EH* 'Daybreak', 2).

Throughout his writings, and especially in the writings of his mature period, Nietzsche is adamant that it is only an aristocratic society which can justify terrible but noble sacrifices and experiments, for only this kind of society is geared towards, not justice or compassion, but the continual self-overcoming of man – and of life. In a note from the time of *Beyond Good and Evil* he speaks of the cultivation of a master race which will constitute the future masters of the earth. It will form a 'new tremendous aristocracy, based on the severest self-legislation' and employ 'democratic Europe as its most pliant and supple instrument for taking control of the destinies of the earth' (*WP* 960). He looks forward to the masters of humanity in terms of a group of 'artist-tyrants' who look upon man as a sculptor works upon his stone. Although dissociating itself from the 'racial indecency now parading in Germany today' (*GS* 377), Nietzsche's great politics does rest on a rejection of the major ideologies of the modern period and their visions of 'man'. In section 377 of *The Gay*

Science Nietzsche speaks of the 'children of the future' who feel
disfavour with all ideals which might make one feel at home in
this 'fragile, broken time of transition'. He speaks of a 'we' who
'conserve' nothing and who do not want to return to past
periods. They are neither 'liberals' who work for progress, nor
socialists who dream of 'equal rights', 'a free society', and 'no
more masters and no more servants'. They are new conquerors
who love danger, war, who refuse to be reconciled to, or
compromised and castrated by the present, and who, above all,
realise that every enhancement of 'man' requires a new kind of
enslavement (*GS* 377).

Nietzsche understands his politics as being neither individualistic nor collectivistic. The former, he argues, 'does not
recognise an order of rank and would grant one the same
freedom as all', while the latter fails to generate a notion of
individual greatness. Great politics, therefore, does not 'revolve
around the degree of freedom that is granted to the one or to the
other or to all, but around the degree of *power* that the one or the
other should exercise over others or over all'. The decisive
question is to what extent 'a sacrifice of freedom, even
enslavement, provides the basis for the emergence of a *higher
type*' (*WP* 859). The question great politics asks is to what extent
could one '*sacrifice the evolution of mankind* to help a higher species
of man to come into existence?' The only legitimation which
can be given to the homogenisation of modern European man
brought about by the dominion of democratic politics in the
present age, is that it should serve a 'higher sovereign type' (*WP*
898). In opposition to the 'dwarfing and adaptation of man to
a specialised utility, a reverse movement is needed', which
consists in producing a 'synthetic, summarising, justifying
man', who requires the distance created by 'opposition of the
masses' in order to inspire his attempt at noble greatness. The
exploitation of the masses by the higher aristocracy of the
future, considered as the maximum point in the exploitation so
far, justifies itself only on account of those for whom this
'exploitation' has meaning. The political thinking Nietzsche
wishes to combat is that which is based on an 'economic
optimism', which rests on the delusion that the 'increasing

expenditure of everybody must necessarily involve the increasing welfare of everybody' (*WP* 866).

Nietzsche supports his belief in aristocratic rule by drawing on his notion of life as will to power, which he posits in terms of a law of nature. He argues, for example, that, although refraining from violence and exploitation may become good manners among individuals in appropriate conditions, if it is extended to become 'the fundamental principle of society' then it becomes 'a will to the *denial* of life, a principle of disintegration and decay' (*BGE* 259). Nietzsche's argument is that every body, if it is to be a *living* body – including the body politic – must possess 'an incarnate will to power', a will to 'grow, spread, seize, become predominant – not from any morality or immorality but because it is *living* and because life is simply will to power'. 'Exploitation', he reasons, 'does not belong to a corrupt or imperfect society: it belongs to the *essence* of what lives, as a basic organic function; it is a consequence of the will to power, which is after all the will of life'. Exploitation, therefore, should not be imagined away, but recognised as 'the primordial fact of all history' (ibid.). To a certain extent Nietzsche's political thought stands or falls with the validity of this insight, and whether or not his critique of metaphysics, which denies that we can ever have access to true knowledge about the world, permits him to make such a deduction about nature and 'reality'.

Nietzsche's mature political thinking represents an aristocratic critique of liberal democratic politics. What Nietzsche understands by liberal democracy is a society which is based, amongst other things, on a secularisation of Christian values, including a levelling equality, a cult of pity and compassion, and an emphasis on privacy and a devaluation of politics as an arena of conflict (*BGE* 202). Liberal democracy can be regarded as a social formation which places the emphasis on liberal values of privacy and individuality rather than on democratic practices and the ideal of collective autonomy. In a sense it creates a depoliticised society, since it establishes itself on the basis of formal legal relationships between abstract persons who are considered bearers of 'natural rights'. For Nietzsche the rise of liberal egalitarianism threatens to obliterate aristocratic virtues, with equality of rights turning into 'equality in violating rights', and liberalism representing 'a common war on all that is rare, strange, privileged, the higher man, the higher soul, the higher duty, the higher responsibility, and the abundance of creative power' (*BGE* 212). Of course, a similar kind of critique of liberalism was made by Hitler and the Nazis in order to promote German greatness through heroic suffering and sacrifice. However, the greatness that Nietzsche has in mind is that of culture, not of a nationalism and a militarism inspired by *ressentiment*. Nevertheless, this point may serve as a tentative answer to the question raised by Jacques Derrida of how a 'reactive' culture like Nazism could exploit the same language and rallying cries as the 'active' culture Nietzsche was seeking to promote.[1]

Nietzsche saw himself as a thinker destined to propound some 'hard truths' in a soft age. In his attack on Christianity, and his critique of liberalism, he can be seen to be reviving a 'hard', Platonic conception of freedom. This is clear, for example, in a number of passages in *Twilight of the Idols*. In section 37 of 'Expeditions of an Untimely Man', for example, he argues that every strong age is characterised by a chasm between man and man, and between class and class, which makes possible 'the multiplicity of types, the will to be oneself, to stand out'. Ours is a weak age characterised by 'equality' and the diminution of 'all organizing power... the power of separating, of opening up chasms'. In section 39 he argues that 'democracy' has always been 'the declining form of the power to organise', thus reversing his earlier positive estimation of democracy in the works of his middle period. Today, he argues, modern human beings live very fast and have an irresponsible notion of freedom: 'wherever the word "authority" is so much as heard one believes oneself in danger of a new slavery'. He defines freedom in terms of severe self-discipline: 'for what is freedom?' he asks. He replies that it is to be defined as 'the will to self-responsibility. That one preserves the distance which divides us' (ibid., 38). It is this conception of freedom which is undermined by liberalism: 'Liberalism: in plain words, *reduction to the herd animal*'. Liberal institutions 'undermine the will to power' and represent 'the levelling of mountain and valley exalted to a moral principle' (ibid.).

Despite the excessive nature of Nietzsche's critique of modern social life, and some of the alarming features of his aristocratic radicalism, he does illuminate a number of important features about politics in the modern age. Perhaps his most acute insight derives from his claim that liberalism has resulted in a weak and undisciplined notion of freedom, and that it rests on an empty relativism which severs us from the powerful traditions of the past. We are no longer sure what we believe in; we have cultivated the art of tolerance to such a fine degree that the validity of any and all beliefs is sanctioned. As a result, the order of rank among values is undermined, resulting in a lazy conception of freedom. Ours is a cynical and sceptical age; an age which has a negative conception of destruction. It is an age without direction and one which refuses to recognise that man can only possess value to the extent that he is regarded as a stone in a great edifice (*GS* 356). For Nietzsche the capacity to build a new future depends on an ability to see a fundamental continuity with the strengths of the past in the form of traditions. But it is precisely this which is lacking in modernity: 'The entire West has lost those instincts out of which institutions grow, out of which the *future* grows' (*TI* 'Expeditions', 39). The 'genius of organisation' is lacking (*GS* 356), and, as a result, we now experience a period of decay and corruption:

Again danger is there, the mother of morals, great danger, this time transposed into the individual, into the neighbour and friend, into the alley, into one's own child, into one's own heart, into the most personal and secret recesses of wish and will: and what may the moral philosophers emerging in this age have to preach now? (*BGE* 262)

It has been argued in this book that Nietzsche does not share the modern preoccupation with the question of political legitimacy. For Nietzsche this is a necessary consequence of the task of the revaluation of values and of the self-overcoming of morality. A cultivation of the tragic view of life cannot rely on notions of social justice in order to legitimate aristocratic authority and rule. But here we encounter a fundamental problem with Nietzsche's political thought: if God is dead, if political rule can no longer be based on divine sanction, *and* if he is compelled to sacrifice the modern question of legitimacy (of 'rights', of equality, liberty, justice, etc.), then by what means can Nietzsche legitimate his great politics? In fact Nietzsche does have a conception of legitimacy, but it is not the modern one which centres on a notion of social contract. Nietzsche seeks to legitimate aristocratic rule through a notion of *culture*. The legitimacy of the new artist-tyrants he speaks of, is not 'moral' but 'supra-moral' (*übermoralisch*). They do not legitimate their actions in humanist terms, but by appealing to the necessity of overcoming 'man'. But then the great problem arises, a problem faced head on by Zarathustra, of how an aristocratic politics can appeal to human beings living in a non-aristocratic age and social world, and entice them to transfigure themselves and become overhuman.

Nietzsche's critique of morality is deeply paradoxical in the sense that it appeals to our moral conscience (we must recognise the rightness of the self-overcoming of morality). Nietzsche's genealogy of morals shows us a noble past, a triumphant slave revolt in morality, and a confused, directionless present. But the way in which he envisages the overcoming of the present through the 'supra-moral' leadership of 'artist-tyrants' fails to realise the full consequences of the fact that modern human beings have been constituted as moral beings; chiefly, that two thousand years of training by Christian-moral culture cannot be simply overturned by the amoral actions of noble tyrants. I believe that the central problem of Nietzsche's conception of great politics is this problem of morality and how it can be 'overcome'.

Nietzsche's political vision of a renewed aristocratic, tragic culture is full of tensions which are never adequately dealt with in his work. His political thought does not recognise that its aristocratic principle of rulership is affected by the modern framing of the question of legitimacy. To what extent is the cultivation of an aristocratic political discipline possible without at the same time giving rise to a politics of resentment? Given that the aim is to produce greatness by rendering the majority, in Nietzsche's own words, 'incomplete human beings', it is difficult to see how Nietzsche's aristocrats could maintain their rule without recourse to highly oppressive instruments of political control and manipulation. Do not the 'majority' have a will to power which desires to express its 'freedom'? By failing to address the question of legitimacy on the level of social justice and the 'right of subjectivity', as Hegel described the right of the modern individual to self-determination, it is difficult to see how aristocratic rule as conceived by Nietzsche could be maintained except through ruthless forms of political control. It is not simply that I am being sentimental here, appealing to an innate human essence which desires freedom and that will naturally rebel against the kind of enslavement Nietzsche proposes. My aim is to question the internal coherence of Nietzsche's political thinking. It is Nietzsche himself, after all, who speaks of reducing certain individuals to '*incomplete*' human beings.[2]

The difficulties Nietzsche has in providing his conception of great politics with legitimacy can be seen in the way in which he presents his interpretation of life as will to power. Nietzsche insists at one point that an inquiry into the origin of moral values is in no way identical with a critique of these values (*WP* 254). Such an inquiry can only serve to prepare the ground for a critical attitude towards them. In answer to questions such as 'What are our moral tables really worth? What is the outcome of their rule? For whom?', Nietzsche says that the only principle which can serve as a principle of critique is life itself. However, we need 'a new, more definite, formulation of the concept "life". My formula for it is: life as will to power' (ibid.). The central weakness of Nietzsche's formulation of a critique of moral values in terms of the principle of will to power is that it rests on a deeply problematic opposition between morality and life. His argument is that morality is a negation and denial of life, that life is fundamentally amoral. The only justification which can be provided of life is that made from an aesthetic supra-moral viewpoint. In *The Anti-Christ* he writes that life must be considered in terms of an 'instinct for growth' and for 'power: where the will to power is lacking there is decline. My assertion is that this *will* is lacking in all the supreme values of mankind' (*AC* 6).

However, the historical insights gained by his genealogy of morals render such a position questionable, since one of the main discoveries of genealogical history is that the slave revolt in morality also represents a will to power. As Nietzsche himself recognises, 'in the history of morality a will to power finds expression, through which now the slaves and the oppressed, now the ill-constituted and those who suffer from themselves, attempt to make those value judgements that are favourable to them' (*WP* 400). The contrast drawn between 'morality' and 'life' is abstract in that, as genealogical analysis reveals, the slave revolt in morality is not just simply a revolt against 'life', but rather a revolt against a particular form of life, one of political oppression and religious alienation experienced, for example, by the Jewish people under the Romans.[3] The highest values that have been esteemed so far, and which at present are undergoing a process of dissolution and devaluation, are a special instance of life conceived as will to power. These values are predominantly moral and religious values which reflect the alienation of human beings from their social and political world.

In spite of its critique of man the sick animal, Nietzsche's thought remains humanist in that it places 'man', albeit in his lordly overhuman guise, at the centre of its view of the universe. Man's animal existence is insufficient, while the moral evolution of man has resulted in a tormented soul. The problem of man, as Nietzsche identifies it, is that his sickness is incurable. We cannot rid ourselves of memory, conscience, guilt, responsibility, in short, of everything which makes us *human* (if sick ones). In his most telling moments Nietzsche recognises that there can be no escape from the predicament which is the human condition. The only way out is through a reawakening of the tragic sense in which the suffering and pain of human existence is rendered intelligible. The *Übermensch* is something halfway between childish fantasy and profound extra-moral redemption. Nietzsche's aspiration for the more-than-human reflects his own innermost desires, fears, hopes, and dreams...and ours too.

It can be said in conclusion that if one finds Nietzsche's solutions deficient or inadequate to the problems of human existence, he is at least astute in showing that in believing, or in choosing to fight for, a certain way, or conception, of life it is primarily a question of values and commitments. He shows us the context – a world in which God is dead and nihilism reigns supreme – in which we must make choices today. But are there real choices in life? Or are there only afflictions and predicaments? Living in an epoch of nihilism presents human beings with the tremendous theoretical and practical challenge of how to ground and justify a common political life in the absence of the support traditionally provided by absolute, transhistorical moral and religious values. Nietzsche is not the first philosopher to articulate the problem of nihilism as the decisive problem of the modern age, but he is the first to express the dilemmas it presents in such stark and ominous terms. His is a political mode of thinking given not just to individuals but to *humanity*. His demand for a revaluation of all values requires human beings to carry out acts of supreme self-examination. He leaves us with an important challenge, the necessity of thinking through the experience of the nothing (*nihil, das Nichts*). How can nihilism be resisted? How can it be endured? Can it be overcome, or must we submit to it? And then begin anew? Perhaps the new can begin when man is displaced from the centre and we await, with due care and an attentive responsibility, the arrival of the post-man epoch. Who will send this destiny to humanity? Humanity itself?

In summary, we can say that Nietzsche's thought contains both enabling and debilitating aspects. On the 'positive' side (the progressive dimension of his thought) I would single out the following for special attention:

(i) The instructiveness of his genealogy of morals. Nietzsche is not simply concerned with a retrieval of forgotten (aristocratic) origins, but with opening up history to an art of interpretation or exegesis (*Auslegung*). In this way, 'history' is transformed from an antiquarian and nostalgic exercise into a critical and praxial one. In writing about the past we are, in effect, writing a history of the *present*. In opening up the past to

different traditions and evolutions it is Nietzsche's aim to
overcome both monologism and monotheism. In the hands of
Nietzsche morality loses its unilateral force and becomes
something complex, hybrid, and multilateral.

(ii) His noble conception of the self and the way in which he
extends this to a possible conception of social life. We tend to
associate Nietzsche almost exclusively (but legitimately, as I
have done here, for example) with a politics of domination. But
there is another dimension to his political thinking where
Nietzsche envisages the possibility of a peaceful coexistence
between different human types (say between the overhuman
and the human), in which the former pursue artistic self-
creation and self-discipline and the latter preoccupy themselves
with mundane and material pursuits. The overhuman are to
exist free of both political power and economic wealth. The
important thing for Nietzsche is that a human type is allowed
the space to cultivate greatness and experiment in human living
and acting. In the merely 'human' realm a levelling equality is
to rule; but in the overhuman realm there will be an
'enhancement' of 'antitheses and chasms'. The goal is '*not* to
conceive of the latter as masters of the former'. Rather, 'two
types...are to exist side by side' (*KSA* 10, p. 244). Similarly in
Ecce Homo Nietzsche speaks of a 'higher' self in terms of an
individual who is able to achieve an 'order of rank among
capacities', to practise 'the art of dividing without making
inimical..."reconciling" nothing; a tremendous multiplicity
which is none the less the opposite of chaos' (*EH* 'Why I Am So
Clever' 9). Unfortunately, nowhere in his published output
does Nietzsche develop at length, or even in outline, the
possibilities contained in this challenging conception of the self
and of social life.

(iii) His conception of art (and, by extension, of nature). It is
easy to misconstrue the role of art in Nietzsche's thinking and
accuse him of aestheticism. But art is not conceived in terms of
a refuge in his thinking. Art is valued by Nietzsche for two main
reasons; firstly, because it enables human beings to endure life
in the face of the terror and absurdity of existence; and
secondly, it acts as the great *stimulus* of life, encouraging human

beings not to recoil from the horror of existence, but to seek its furtherance and perpetual self-overcoming. Nietzsche does not aestheticise human existence, if we mean by that that he covers up its ugly or fearful aspects (this is precisely what morality and religion do according to Nietzsche). Neither is he an aestheticist if we mean someone who extends art to every level of human existence. In his thinking art plays a very specific role and function: to transfigure nature (*physis*) and to overcome the debilitating effects produced by looking into the abyss of human existence and acknowledging the meaningless cruelty and suffering which characterise world-history. One of the best presentations of Nietzsche's conception of art is to be found in his untimely meditation on Wagner. Human beings, he says, are placed in need of art once they recognise the principal causes of human suffering (Nietzsche mentions the following: that human beings do not share all knowledge in common; that their ultimate insights can never be fixed and made certain for all time; and that abilities are divided unequally). Put simply, for Nietzsche the importance of art consists in the fact that it enables us to carry on living. It does this by revealing to human beings the *sublimity* and significance of their struggles, their suffering, and their failures. *Without* art we would be unable to understand suffering (it would simply overwhelm us and destroy our capacity for action). Moreover, we would find it impossible to be moral without the indirect instruction art provides, because we would be unable to make sense of, and endure, the fact that a great deal of human affairs 'is determined by force, deception, and injustice' (*RWB* 4, p. 212). Art is to be understood as 'the activity of man in repose'. Although the struggles it depicts 'are simplifications of the real struggles of life', art, like dreams, enables us to comprehend and endure life by producing 'the *appearance* of a simpler world, a shorter solution to the riddle of life'. Just as a healthy human being cannot do without sleep, so the cultivated human being cannot exist without the appearance of a simpler world disclosed by art: 'Art exists *so that the bow shall not break*' (ibid., p. 213).

Nietzsche is convinced that mankind can only be 'ennobled' through an education and training in tragic art. The only guarantee for the future of humanity consists in its '*retention of the sense for the tragic*' (ibid.). This education is primarily an education of the 'individual'. It consecrates him or her to something higher than him- or herself. This, says Nietzsche, is precisely what tragedy *means*: individuals are freed of the 'terrible anxiety which death and time evoke' in them. 'At any moment', he writes, 'in the briefest atom of his life's course', the individual, through this appreciation of the tragic sense, 'may encounter something holy that outweighs all his struggle and all his distress' (ibid.). With tragic wisdom comes 'freedom'. For Nietzsche 'the free man can be good or evil but the unfree man is a disgrace to nature'. Freedom can only be attained through our own actions, it does not fall into our lap like a miraculous gift. What is required today is a humanity which '*has a genuine need of art*', a need which will restore 'the language of nature' 'in the world of man' (ibid., 11, p. 252).

Nietzsche admired the Greeks for their intellectual honesty and their creative artistry. The Greeks recognised the *reality* of violence, of envy, of strife, of obscenity, etc., in human life (what Nietzsche calls the 'general economy of the whole); their great achievement as a culture was to integrate them 'in the edifice of society and morals'. Greek social and political institutions, therefore, were not built on a rigid distinction of good and evil, of black and white: 'Nature, such as it shows itself, is not disavowed, but *integrated*, assigned to worship on special days... a release appropriate to the forces of nature was sought, not their destruction and denial' (*KSA* 8, pp. 78–9). The problem of the present, however, is that modern human beings live inauthentically, oscillating between a hypocritical Christianity and a timid revival of antiquity (*SE* 2). Nietzsche seeks to impart to his readers a sense of the tragic mood and an understanding of tragic culture. Hence his preoccupation with the Greeks: Greek culture is simply the best example we have of a people who appreciated the tragic nature of human existence and who were not overwhelmed by it.

(iv) That Nietzsche, for the most part, never allies the tasks of philosophy, or of art, with explicit political goals such as the promotion of a national culture or identity. For Nietzsche, thinking can only retain its integrity and independence through its 'untimeliness'. This means that the philosopher must not follow any particular idol or ideology. He or she must not place thought in the service of the prejudices or the fashions of their age. 'The creative artist's urge to help is too great, the horizon of his philanthropy too spacious, for his purview to be limited to the area bounded by any one nation'. Philosophical conceptions and art speak not to nations, but to individual human beings (*RWB* 10). Moreover, as he bluntly and boldly states several years later in his final testament, *Ecce Homo*: 'To think German, to feel German – I can do everything, but *that* is beyond my powers' (*EH* 'Why I Write Such Excellent Books' 2).

On the negative side, the regressive dimensions of his thought centre largely on his mature conception of politics. Whereas in his early writings Nietzsche sees philosophy as supra-political (in the sense that its tasks are quite different and its comprehension of life so much more profound) (see *SE* 4, pp. 147–8), in his final position he seeks to give politics a philosophical grounding and legitimation with a notion of 'great politics'. Through a conjunction of political power and philosophical legislation man is to be overcome and history given a new direction. The existing one thousand goals of various peoples are to be united and brought together in the positing and creation of a new *single* goal and people: the *Übermensch* (*Z* 'Of the Thousand and One Goals'). Nietzsche's thinking here is problematic for two reasons: firstly, it remains deeply metaphysical (voluntarist and idealist) – while Nietzsche is severely critical of Christian-moral culture for its teaching of redemption, he still offers a teaching which retains its focus on man and his elevation, and which requires, for its fulfilment, the sacrifice of the present for some undecided and unknowable future (the willed production of an overhumanity); and, secondly, Nietzsche's thinking fails to appreciate sufficiently that the conception of great politics lacks legitimacy in the age of moral nihilism.

Nietzsche's thinking on the *Übermensch*, the eternal return, and the ascetic ideal, points in the direction of the necessity of constituting a new will. However, while humanity may be in

need of a fundamental attitudinal and volitional transformation, Nietzsche's insights into the modern condition of nihilism
show that change cannot come about through the simple
assertion of a strong, heroic will. The 'will' has been formed and
deformed by certain moral and cultural practices, and a
revitalised will can only be created through the long-term
fashioning of new cultural practices and social institutions. In
Nietzsche the problem of politics in the modern age becomes
linked, therefore, to a notion of culture. His own thinking shows
the need for a philosophical education (*paideia*) which will
prepare the ground for the constitution of a new human type
through revaluating all values.

In its social and political aspects, Nietzsche's thinking
concerns itself with how the sentiments and passions of a noble
morality, resting on a superabundant health, can be cultivated
again in the modern age. But while in the early period of his
thought he recognises the obliqueness of philosophy's task, and
while in the texts of his middle period he recognises the
outdatedness of hierarchical social structures (the result of the
decline of traditional authority and traditional feelings of
subordination), in his 'mature' thinking he jettisons these
former insights and places his hopes for a regeneration of
humanity on a new legislation and new enslavement in which
philosophy and politics will come together to constitute an
overhumanity. Towards the end of his sane life Nietzsche writes
Ecce Homo in order to tell his readers 'who he is'. But he fails to
realise the central paradox of this final attempt to give himself
a clear and coherent identity; that the matter of his authorship
is something which lies beyond his control. He writes this final
testament in order to prevent people from doing mischief with
him. But the tragedy of Nietzsche's philosophy is that it inspired
not only the curious and the courageous, but also the indolent
and the impotent.

PART IV

The question of Nietzsche now

CHAPTER 8

Nietzsche and contemporary liberalism

> The central issue for political theory is not the constitution
> of the self but the connection of constituted selves.
>
> Michael Walzer (1990)

INTRODUCTION

In this chapter I will take a look at the work of two
contemporary philosophers who have tried to face up to
Nietzsche's challenge and sought to utilise his ideas in the
service of a redefined and radicalised liberalism. The two
examples I have chosen are, firstly, the work of Richard Rorty,
who has accepted the basic import of Nietzsche's critique of
Western metaphysics that truth is a fiction and that modern
human beings have to construct their lives without the support
of either eternal truths or absolute values, which has led him to
advocate what he calls a 'liberal ironism'; and, secondly, the
work of William Connolly who, under the influence of the work
of Michel Foucault, has argued for a 'late-modern' conception
of liberal politics based on a synthesis of Nietzschean insights
into modernity and an independent theory of justice. The
'radical liberal' describes someone who wishes to uphold the
traditional liberal values of toleration, autonomy, individuality,
and free expression, but who wishes to avoid positing a spurious
universalism by relying on an inclusive ideal of human nature.
The problem of politics for the radical liberal is that of how to
institute a society which has a shared ethical life, but which
allows for the recognition of otherness and the affirmation of
difference. This concern with otherness and difference is also

shared by feminist writers and will be examined in the next chapter. The work of these two thinkers shows how fertile Nietzsche's ideas can be for rethinking the political today. At the same time, however, the tensions evident in their appropriations also illustrate that there are serious problems in domesticating Nietzsche's thought in order to make it compatible with a liberal–humanist political vision.

THE LIBERAL IRONIST

Richard Rorty argues that the late-modern liberal must face head-on the challenge presented by Nietzsche's insights into the modern nihilistic condition, and respond by affirming the absolute contingency of liberal values.

In the introduction to his book *Contingency, Irony, and Solidarity*, Rorty argues that it is not necessary to agonise over Nietzsche's choice between culture and politics.[1] Liberal democracy is a form of association which has recognised the futility of the attempt to create a social order where everyone is both a member of a just society and engages in the labour of self-creation. At the level of theory, Rorty contends, there is simply no way to bring self-creation and justice together, since the language of the former is private and unshared, while that of the latter is necessarily public and shared. We thus need to treat the demands of self-creation and human solidarity as 'equally valid, yet forever incommensurable'. The product of this toleration of the demands of both culture and politics is the 'liberal ironist'. He or she is a liberal in that they believe that cruelty is the worst thing a human being can do, and an ironist to the extent that they are 'the sort of person who faces up to the contingency of his or her own most central beliefs and desires – someone sufficiently historicist and nominalist to have abandoned the idea that those central beliefs and desires refer back to something beyond the reach of time and chance'. To be a liberal ironist is to accept that we are what we are, and that we can give no transhistorical explanation of why we hold certain views and beliefs, but we hope that our ungroundable desires and commitments will lead to a more tolerable world in which the amount of suffering within it will significantly diminish. There can be no question of arguing in transhistorical terms for the moral superiority of liberal democracies. Instead Rorty legitimises liberalism in aesthetic terms. He believes that it is the best form of association produced to date, since it maximises the opportunities for (safe) self-creation.

What is the relevance of Nietzsche to this picture of the modern world? 'About two hundred years ago', Rorty's story goes, 'the idea that truth was made rather than found began to take hold of the imagination of Europe'.[2] Overnight the French revolutionaries show that social relations and political institutions can be changed at will, while Romantic poets such as William Blake show what happens when art is no longer thought of as an imitation of reality, but as an act of self-creation. Nietzsche is important, Rorty argues, because he is the first philosopher who explicitly suggests that we drop the whole notion of 'knowing the truth' about the world. The idea of representing 'reality' by means of language, which would enable us to find a single context for all human lives, needs to be jettisoned. Nietzsche proposes the novel idea that 'self-knowledge' is 'self-creation': 'The process of coming to know oneself, confronting one's contingency...is identical with the process of inventing a new language – that is, of thinking up some new metaphors'.[3] There can be no literal account of either the self or the world, for we can only describe both through the medium of metaphorical language. The process by which human beings do this is a creative and artistic one which is best seen in the way in which poets construct language. Thus, what Rorty wishes to celebrate about Nietzsche is the way in which he supposedly constructed his life in terms of a work of art:

The drama of an individual life, or of the history of humanity as a whole, is not one in which a preexistent goal is triumphantly reached or tragically not reached. Neither a constant external reality nor an unfailing interior source of inspiration forms a background for such dramas. Instead, to see one's life, or the life of one's community, as a dramatic narrative is to see it as a process of Nietzschean self-overcoming. The paradigm of such a narrative is the life of the genius who can say of the relevant portion of the past, 'Thus I willed it', because she has found a way to describe that past never knew, and thereby found a self to be which her precursors never knew was possible.[4]

Rorty's use of Nietzsche to promote a post-modern liberalism is mediated by a reading of Freud. Rorty uses Freud to show that we do not have to choose between a universalist morality and an amoral aestheticism, say between, for example, Kant's universalist ethic of the categorical imperative and Nietzsche's ethic of the unique and incomparable *Übermensch*. Rorty argues that the significance of Freud as a moral philosopher is that he provides us with a way of looking at human beings which helps us avoid making such a choice. Freud eschews the idea of there being a paradigmatic human being. As such, 'he lets us see both Nietzsche's superman and Kant's common moral consciousness as exemplifying two out of many forms of adaptation, two out of many strategies for coping with the contingencies of one's upbringing'.[5] Freud recognised that each persona has its advantages and disadvantages. The poet is an inspiration, but often infantile, while the moral man is mature, but quite often boring. However, Freud does not ask us to make a choice between them, but to recognise that there is no such thing as a dull unconscious. Thus, what 'makes Freud more useful and more plausible than Nietzsche is that he does not relegate the vast majority of humanity to the status of dying animals'.[6] Rorty quotes Philip Rieff's assessment of Freud that he 'democratized genius by giving everyone a creative unconscious'.[7]

Rorty speaks of a culture of 'liberalism' in its ideal form as one which would be enlightened and secular through and through. 'It would be one', he writes, 'in which no trace of divinity remained, either in the form of a divinized world or a divinized self... The process of de-divinization... would, ideally, culminate in our no longer being able to see any use for the notion that finite, mortal, contingently existing human beings might derive the meanings of their lives from anything except other finite, mortal, contingently existing human beings.'[8] What is needed to support this culture is not a theory of human nature (this is the kind of metaphysics which we, as good, gentle Nietzscheans, must reject), but a 'rhetoric of liberalism'. Rorty explains:

> This would mean giving up the idea that liberalism could be justified, and Nazi or Marxist enemies refuted, by driving the latter up against an argumentative wall – forcing them to admit that liberal freedom has a 'moral privilege' which their own values lacked. From the point of view I have been commending, any attempt to drive one's opponent up against a wall in this way fails when the wall against which he is driven comes to be seen as one more vocabulary, one more way of describing things. The wall turns out to be a painted backdrop, one more work of man, one more bit of cultural stage-setting.[9]

In other words, both Nazism and Marxism are ways of describing the world, and there exists no good reason why a person should not choose to be a Nazi or a Marxist. The way we make our choices should not be seen in accordance with rational, transhistorical criteria (there are none), but analogous to the way in which we choose friends or heroes.[10] There exists no deep moral essence within us that we can tap into, and which would allow us to step outside or beyond the historical contingencies and accidents of socialisation. What Rorty objects to about the Nazi or the Marxist (the linking of the two is his not mine), is that they are not *ironic* about their beliefs and values, but actually take them seriously and adhere to them dogmatically and fervently.

Rorty's advocacy of a rhetoric of liberalism does result in the endorsement of a particular set of political arrangements. In particular, he argues against the positive view of liberty (found in Rousseau, Hegel, and Marx) which construes society as playing a key role in providing citizens with opportunities for the expression of self-determination, and enabling the attainment of autonomy through the mediation of social institutions, and in favour of the negative view of liberty which seeks to privatise desires for self-expression and self-creation.[11] Rorty expresses his political creed as follows – a little dogmatically, it should be noted, for someone who defines himself as a liberal ironist:

The sort of autonomy which self-creating ironists like Nietzsche...seek is not the sort of thing that *could* ever be embodied in social institutions. Autonomy is not something which all human beings have within them and which society can release by ceasing to repress them. It is something which certain particular human beings hope to attain by self-creation, and which a few actually do... The compromise advocated in this book amounts to saying: *Privatize* the Nietzschean–Sartrean–Foucauldian attempt at authenticity and purity, in order to prevent yourself from slipping into a political attitude which will lead you to think that there is some social goal more important than avoiding cruelty.[12]

Rorty's reading of Nietzsche, and the modern intellectual tradition is an imaginative, if unconvincing, attempt to render the aristocratic value of self-creation compatible with a liberal polity (it is important to note that, as the above passage makes clear, Rorty does not wish to democratise this ideal). Missing from this, however, is any recognition of the anxiety which informed Nietzsche's choice of art *contra* politics. It would be too easy to say that the reason for this is because Rorty has conclusively shown that the terms of Nietzsche's opposition are false because they rest on metaphysical foundations about human nature which 'we' no longer believe in. Unlike Rorty, Nietzsche does not conceal his elitism, but admits that in making a choice in favour of an aristocratic polity he is condemning the vast majority to an impoverished life. This is necessary for Nietzsche if we wish to produce greatness in culture, which can only be enjoyed by a few human beings. However, through their cultivation of greatness and pursuit of the adventurous and experimental, the inhuman and the superhuman, these choice human beings will justify the very existence of the human race. Rorty seems fairly sanguine about the fact that, in a secular age, there can be no appeal to objective, transhistorical criteria (no appeal to criteria at all) in giving legitimacy to one's most cherished ideals and deeply held beliefs.

The danger Rorty faces, but never discusses, is that of expounding a philosophy of solipsism. His emphasis on self-creation as a private affair is one which encourages a retreat from the social world into the world of private fantasy. In fact, Rorty's privatisation of the self falls back on the illusion of classical liberalism, which posited a pre-political self in full possession of human faculties, such as free will and conscience, independent of cultural processes of socialisation. The same myth of the self is found in Rorty in spite of his celebration of the idea that self is made not given. He never makes clear where our liberal and human commitments come from. Who is this liberal ironist that Rorty talks about, and whose prime motivation in human action is the desire to avoid being cruel to others? Rorty wants us to be 'bourgeois nihilists', that is, people who recognise that 'nothing is true, everything is permitted', but who, at the same time, hold that 'cruelty is the *worst* we do' and so we need to be kinder and gentler towards another. But this injunction not to be cruel has the status of an inexplicable and unknowable command in Rorty. As a result, his ethical nihilism culminates in a debilitating irrationalism: why should we be motivated by an ethic whose source we can neither know nor understand?

For Nietzsche the degeneration of political and cultural life in modern Europe could be partly explained by the absence of a vibrant and vigorous public life. In the absence of strong customs and traditions society is in danger of either turning into an anarchic state in which anything goes, or being overtaken by a herd morality and a timid conformity. Both lead to the dissolution of culture. For Nietzsche, heroic self-creation is not governed by society (it is the creation of individuals living experimentally), but its effects impact upon society. In this respect, Nietzsche's conception of heroic action is much closer to that of Hannah Arendt than of Rorty. Nietzsche and Arendt, in fact, would both argue that Rorty's emphasis on self-creation as a private act represents a retreat from the social world, and is symptomatic of the degeneration of creative action which characterises the modern period.

Rorty's liberal ironism rests on a problematic separation of private self-creation and public justice. In making this separation Rorty neutralises the effects of critical thinking as theory is stripped of any social and political implications. Because of the emphasis on self-creation as a private act, Rorty is unable to see that an aesthetic liberalism possesses radical and positive possibilities for a reconstitution and reconstruction of the public sphere. We have to turn to the work of another contemporary liberal to see what these possibilities might be.

THE RADICAL LIBERAL

In his book *Political Theory and Modernity* (1988) William Connolly has argued in favour of privileging a 'Nietzschean perspective' in order to interrogate the assumptions of modernity.[13] The advent of the reign of nihilism in the West allows us to recognise the illusions and myths which have sustained the project of modern political theory: the desire for self and social transparency, and the wish to see ourselves reflected in a world we have made by mastering everything which comes under our control. Things which escape our control are defined and delimited as 'forms of otherness' in need of normalisation: madness, irrationality, perversity, chaos, and disorder. Thus, the 'Rousseauian' desire, inherited by Marxism, for an ethico-political community based on the values of equality and liberty, in which all are united in a general will, has to be seen as little more than the desire for a perfectly transparent world in which the self has realised its supposed 'true' nature. This radical project of modernity, Connolly argues, offers a depoliticised ideal of modern life in which politics becomes reduced to a mere technical means for achieving the common good. 'The Rousseauian vision collapses', he writes

not because it is impossible for some to have faith in it, but because its faith is not generalizable in the modern age in which it is offered. Its eloquence can only speak to some; its vision is a nightmare to many.[14]

Contemporary thought allows faith no place to hide. Nietzsche is to be regarded as the key thinker of our times, for he 'insists upon thinking dangerously during a time of danger'.[15]

Connolly's reading of the tradition of modern political thought, and of Nietzsche's place within it, is influenced and inspired by the work of Michel Foucault. The significance of

Nietzsche, according to Foucault's original and radical interpretation of his work, is that he is the first to think about power outside of the confines of political theory.[16] What Foucault means by this is that in his understanding of power, Nietzsche does not rely on traditional notions of sovereignty and law, which would mean that power is viewed as something essentially negative and prohibitive. Nietzsche, Foucault contends, sees power everywhere, and views life itself in terms of a permanent contest between different forces of power. Power is now viewed in 'positive' terms, that is, as something which is not simply a reflection of human subjects who are oppressed by power, but which is productive of them. 'Power' for Foucault only exists in its exercise; it is not to be seen as the metaphysical property which a human subject has or possesses. Power, says Foucault, is neither a structure nor an institution, but rather, 'the name one attributes to a complex strategical situation in a particular society'.[17]

Foucault's re-thinking of power leads him to claim that the tradition of modern political thought is implicated in the dominant 'disciplinary' forms of power. He argues that we need to understand the exercise of power not in terms of 'right', but in terms of technique, not in terms of 'law' but in terms of normalisation, and not in terms of 'abuse' but in terms of punishment and control. Our modern political rationality has developed alongside a new political technology of power which has produced the 'individual' as a subject of the state enjoying rights and owing obligations. Modern political thought, Foucault contends, is inadequate to the task of thinking critically about the new forms of power, since it bases its understanding of power on a belief in the existence of a rational, ahistorical subject. Modern political thought poses the questions of political philosophy as a question of right/law, such as: What are the limits of power? How can power be given limits to restrict its use and abuse? But these questions simply take for granted the existence of a rational human subject which is deemed to exist in some pre-power or pre-political realm and which is then 'exploited' or 'oppressed' by power and in need of 'rights' to protect it. The radical, and challenging, point Foucault wishes to make, is that forms of power constitute, through disciplinary practices, types of human subjects. In constructing a discourse of legitimacy, which centres on notions of law and sovereignty, Foucault contends that political theory conceals or effaces the domination which is intrinsic to power.[18] By speaking of the 'rights' of the sovereign and the obligations of 'subjects' as if these were neutral descriptions of the properties of fully constituted rational individuals, modern political thought has concealed from our view the fact that discourses of right and legitimacy are not simply ways of protecting individuals from the existence of power, but also disciplinary practices which constitute human subjects in *new* relationships of power.

It is these claims about power which inform Foucault's critique of liberalism as a political ideology. For Foucault, liberalism is flawed in that it posits an abstract and ahistorical notion of the human individual or subject. Any critique of society which liberalism can offer is, according to Foucault, of limited value, since it singularly fails to appreciate that modern institutions are based on disciplinary practices of power and forms of knowledge whose prime objective is not simply to grant individuals private spaces of freedom, but to 'normalise' them. In rejecting *tout court* a notion of the autonomous subject, Foucault runs the risk of depriving himself of any substantive basis from which to criticise the present system of power, which would enable him to envisage a positive overcoming of forms of domination.[19]

William Connolly follows Foucault in holding that the entire modern project of freedom and emancipation (reflected in different ways in the ideologies of liberalism and socialism) is caught up in an imperialistic discourse of mastery and domination which is blind to its own uncritical assumptions about the self and the world. Inspired by Foucault's analysis of the major discourses of modernity (on madness, on discipline and punishment, on sexuality, etc.), Connolly argues that any set of norms or standards that becomes endowed with authority and legitimacy represents an ambiguous achievement, since it will establish its hegemony by excluding and denigrating forms of otherness which do not fit into its confines. In place of tolerating ambiguity, modernity prefers the discipline of social harmony and the ideal of a self-inclusive community. Connolly states the dilemma in the following terms:

Human life is paradoxical at its core, while modern reason, penetrating into new corners of life, strives to eliminate every paradox it encounters. This is a dangerous combination, with repressive potentialities. It is dangerous to deny the paradox, either by ignoring the urge to unity or by pretending that it can be realized in life. The denial, often expressed in liberal theories of the 'open society', overlooks ways in which the urge finds expression in the life of the present, and the pretense, expressed in communitarian protests against the *anomie* of liberal life, hides the political character of actual or ideal settlements behind a smokescreen of transcendental imperatives. Both responses go well with a sublimated politics of inclusivity, a politics in which the world is treated as a place susceptible to human mastery or communal realization and everyone is organized to fit into these complimentary projects.[20]

As a way out of this impasse Connolly turns to Nietzsche, widely regarded as an unlikely source, as he admits himself, for those in need of enlightenment about the plight of liberal democracies today. However, Connolly maintains that Nietzsche's thought is conducive to our present self-understanding, since it eschews all transcendental and teleological justifications of the present and confronts history in all its contingency. Moreover, Nietzsche's thought, Connolly contends, does not contain within it a single theory of politics, but 'a diverse set of ethical and political possibilities'.[21] Nietzsche is important because he recognises that we moderns no longer feel at home in the world, and because his thought seeks to overcome the feeling of homesickness by refusing to posit a total view of the world. To support his reading of Nietzsche, Connolly offers an unorthodox interpretation of the doctrine of will to power. This doctrine does not simply posit a will to domination and mastery. It also contains a counter-ontology which challenges the anthropomorphic view that the world is susceptible to human mastery. However, Connolly does recognise the inadequacy of Nietzsche's own thinking on the fate of politics in the modern world. The demand for justice is not simply the disguised expression of a weak and resentful will, as Nietzsche argues, but arises out of a political system based on economic exploitation and political oppression.

Connolly argues that we need today a 'post-Nietzschean' political theory made up of Nietzsche's counter-ontology of otherness and an independent reflection into the nature of late modernity. A notion of justice will play a central role in this synthesis, where it refers not just to one virtue amongst many, but to the structure of society itself (the organisation and distribution of society's resources and goods – including the value or good of self-creation).[22] As Connolly points out, a human being's resentment towards life comes from two main sources: from rage against a meaningless human condition where the pain and suffering of life are without significance or purpose, and from the arrangement of social and political institutions which impose injury and exploitation on others for the benefit of a few. He argues that a late-modern political perspective

would appreciate the reach of Nietzschean thought as well as its sensitivity to the complex relations between resentment and the production of otherness, but it would turn the genealogist of resentment on his head by exploring democratic politics as a medium through which to expose resentment and to encourage the struggle against it.[23]

Connolly does not wish to completely jettison liberal political philosophy, but calls for a 'reconstituted, radicalized liberalism'. This is a liberalism which would be able to tolerate the competing demands of individuality and community within modernity, and which could cope with the tension between the need for a common life and the inevitable points of subjugation in any set of common norms. A 'liberal radicalism' is sensitive 'to the rights of difference against the weight of mastery and normality'.[24] A 'brave ethic' of 'letting be' is needed to replace the discredited discourse of political modernity, which has sought to satisfy the need for self-realisation through the dream of a self-inclusive community, and in which continued economic expansion is seen as a precondition of liberty. Nietzsche's relevance to this task is that he offers a model of the self which does not resent its own mode of organisation and the contingent conditions of temporal existence. Connolly locates this mode of a non-resentful self in Nietzsche's idea of the self, which is able to give style to its character by transforming everything it is, including the good and the bad, the noble and the ugly, into a controlled and dynamic whole. One could also locate it in his teaching of eternal return, which invites us to assume responsibility for who we are, and to achieve contentment with ourselves (as Nietzsche pointed out, those who do not feel content with their lives are the ones most likely to express resentment towards others).

The Foucaultian challenge is particularly instructive in showing the inadequacy of traditional liberal humanism for thinking about politics and power in the modern period. Although not without its own problems, it does succeed in showing that any account of the human subject has to take the form of a 'genealogy of morals' (a history of how the self has become what it is, which abandons both humanist metaphysics and moralism). In addition, it shows us that it is necessary to have an attitude of suspicion towards 'liberal' claims that modern subjects are 'free' ones, since what we might take to be 'freedom' could, in reality, be new forms of control and discipline. As a result, any clear-cut distinction between 'private' and 'public' realms is rendered problematic. This point will be developed further in the next chapter.

Since Plato, political philosophers have envisaged the polity as a means of disciplining and controlling the self. This is the process which Nietzsche refers to in the second essay of the *Genealogy* as the cultivation (*Züchtung*) of an animal – the human being – which is capable of making promises. Once you can make promises, in Nietzsche's schema, you are a 'political animal' who can exercise responsibility, relate to others in terms of a notion of trust, and make judgements. You have become an animal with consciousness/conscience. A Nietzschean perspective on the political shows that the attainment of autonomy by the human subject is an ambiguous achievement. The cost of civilising the human animal, in terms of the repression and control of the drives and energies, was also the theme of Freud's study into the discontent, or the discomfort, (*Unbehagen*) which 'civilised' social and political life produces in individuals. It is necessary to recognise the *impossibility* of political life, that is, the fact that social existence always produces an excess, a surplus, and an otherness which it is unable to control and master, but which constantly threatens to undermine its civility. The question a radical Nietzscheanism has to pose is this: is it possible to channel and cultivate this excess and otherness in a way which leads to the creation of a new, healthy, post-*ressentiment* human type? And, if so, what role would 'politics' play in this process of cultivation?

There is something risible about the attempt to enlist Nietzsche's thinking to the cause of a post-modern liberalism. Is Nietzsche not the great decodifier who resists all attempts to rigidify life and so prevent the flow of self-overcoming, whether through Christian ethics or bourgeois politics? This is how Gilles Deleuze conceives of Nietzsche's significance in his remarkable essay on 'Nomad Thought'.[25] For Deleuze Western philosophy, from Plato to Hegel, has sought to justify the power of law and the authority of social institutions over and against the passion of nomadic life. From the earliest despotic states to modern liberal democracies the history of sedentary peoples has been constituted by a discourse of sovereignty. Philosophic discourse has thus been closely allied with contracts, institutions, and the administration of law. If Nietzsche does not 'belong' to philosophy it is because he is one of the first to conceive of a nomadic discourse which represents a 'counter-philosophy'. Nietzsche's aim is not to become another bureaucrat of reason or a calculator of 'man', but to announce the advent of a new style of politics and the formation of a new 'we'.

We 'conserve' nothing; neither do we want to return to any past periods; we are not by any means 'liberal'; we do not work for 'progress'... We simply do not consider it desirable that a realm of justice and concord should be established on earth... we are delighted with all who love, as we do, danger, war, and adventures, who refuse to compromise, to be captured, reconciled, and castrated... Is it not clear that with all this we are bound to feel ill at ease in an age that likes to claim the distinction of being the most humane, the mildest, and the most righteous age that the sun has ever seen? It is bad enough that precisely when we hear these beautiful words we have the ugliest suspicions. What we find in them is merely an expression – and a masquerade – of a profound weakening, of weariness, of old age, of declining energies. What can it matter to us what tinsel the sick may use to cover up their weakness? Let them parade it as their *virtue*; after all, there is no doubt that weakness makes one mild, oh so mild, so righteous, so inoffensive, so 'human'! (*GS* 377).

CHAPTER 9

Nietzsche and feminism

The basic error and the most elementary human blindness is not a refusal to acknowledge death, but a refusal to remember birth, that one was born.

Peter Sloterdijk, 'Eurotaoism' (1988)

INTRODUCTION

If Nietzsche seems an unlikely source for a radicalised liberalism, then he must be regarded as an even unlikelier source for a radicalised feminism. Nevertheless, this is how his work has been interpreted in recent years in some quarters. I will examine how certain feminist writers have responded to the challenge of Nietzsche's work and dealt with its tensions. The consensus which seems to be emerging is that the most fertile aspect of his writings for the formulation of a feminist philosophy lies not in their overt pronouncements on women, but in their 'style(s)', in their attempt to communicate a philosophy of the body, in their disclosure of the metaphoricity of philosophical discourse, and in the exemplary way in which they are seen to deconstruct the 'phallogocentric' bias of Western thought and reason.[1] It is perhaps no coincidence that the deployment of Nietzsche – *the* philosopher of difference, according to Gilles Deleuze[2] – by feminist writers is taking place at the same time that radical political theorists, including feminists, are seeking to articulate a philosophy of otherness and difference. A number of feminists have argued that it is necessary to go beyond the impasse of equality, in which women gain equality only by assuming the identity of men and hence effacing sexual difference. They have suggested that a new mode of thought is required, which is able to affirm difference and celebrate otherness, without positing either a totalitarian politics based on a spurious universalism or a hierarchical politics in which masculine or feminine values are neatly differentiated and one considered superior to the other. It is this search for a new ethics and politics within feminism which makes the reception of Nietzsche potentially so fertile and challenging. Again, his attack on liberal humanism is seen to have possible positive benefits for a radicalised liberalism. As in Foucaultian thought, we find in radical feminism a critique of the rational, ahistorical human subject posited within liberal political thought. The aim is not to abandon liberal ideals of autonomy and individuality, but to rethink and reground them.

A number of questions need to be asked about this appropriation of Nietzsche: how useful is Nietzsche's thought for a feminist politics of difference, given his commitment to an aristocratic polity and his affirmation of a masculine, Napoleonic virility? Is it sufficient for feminism, and radical political thought in general, simply to engage with Nietzsche solely in terms of the question of style? Or must they also engage with the substance of his saying? My aim in this chapter is to be neither systematic nor exhaustive, but to give a sense of the main debates and the key issues which are at stake.

NIETZSCHE AND EUROPEAN FEMINISM

The views on women we find expressed in Nietzsche's texts are both varied and complex. They do not add up to a coherent 'philosophy of woman'. They reveal contradictory tendencies and prejudices in which Nietzsche both celebrates female sexuality as something powerful and subversive, but fears it when it becomes disassociated from the social functions of child-rearing and motherhood.

Nietzsche wrote as a critic of European 'liberal' feminism, speaking out against what he saw as the emasculation of social life and the rise of a sentimental politics based on altruistic values. He attacked the idea that women would be emancipated once they had secured equal rights. Certain passages in his work show quite unequivocally that he regarded the whole question of women's emancipation to be a misguided one. For Nietzsche, modern ideas about society and politics have led to a degeneration in our thinking about the social roles and functions of men and women. Modern women are being encouraged to struggle for 'equal rights', but this struggle, if successful, will lead to a gradual erosion of women's influence and power. In a fragment from 1870–1 on the theme of 'The Greek Woman' Nietzsche considers Plato's view that women should enjoy a full, equal share in 'rights, knowledge, and duties' (*GW* p. 21; *KSA* 7, p. 170).[3] But, in advocating the abolition of an order of rank between men and women, where the former are active in the realm of 'culture' and the latter restricted to the realm of 'nature', Plato had simply allowed himself to be seduced by the most powerful women of antiquity, women who themselves did not realise that they remain most powerful when they restrict themselves to the domain of motherhood. In Greek society, Nietzsche argues, women, as mothers and child-rearers, held that position 'which the highest will of the State [*höchste Staatswille*] assigned to them' (ibid., p. 24; p. 172).[4] Women were esteemed in Greek antiquity as never since. Women gained importance by sacrificing themselves to the 'obscure' realm of a private life and devoting their lives to bearing and rearing great sons. Nietzsche writes: 'The Hellenic woman as *mother* had to live in obscurity [*Dunkel*], because the political instinct [*politische Trieb*] together with its highest aim demanded it' (ibid., p. 23; p. 172).

This view finds expression several years later in *Human, All Too Human*. In section 259 of this work Nietzsche speaks of classical Greek culture as a 'masculine culture' (*Cultur der Männer*, literally a 'culture of men') in which the most important relationships are the homoerotic ones between adult males and young boys. What dominated male–female relationships was 'child-begetting and sensual pleasure'. There was no encouragement of 'spiritual commerce' or 'love-affairs' between men and women since, in Nietzsche's eyes, this would have undermined the basis on which Greek culture was produced. He adds that if women such as Electra and Antigone were presented as major figures on the stage of tragedy, this was only '*endurable* in art: one would not want it in life'. He concludes this passage by stating that:

The women had no other task than to bring forth handsome, powerful bodies in which the character of the father lived on as uninterruptedly as possible and therefore to counteract the nervous over-excitation that was gaining the upper hand in so highly developed a culture. It was this that kept Greek culture young for so relatively long a time; for in the Greek mothers the Greek genius again and again returned to nature. (*HAH* 259)

Nietzsche opposes himself to the modern European feminist movement because he regards it as subversive of the production of culture. He thus labels women who seek economic independence and political rights 'abortive females' who resent those women who have turned out well (namely, the ones capable of giving birth) (*EH* 'Why I Write Such Good Books', 5). The problem with Nietzsche is that, while he recognises the power of women's sexuality, speaking in favour of women's enjoyment of sex and arguing against chastity in marriage, he nevertheless assigns to women pregnancy and child-rearing as necessary tasks which complete and fulfil their nature, without which they become rancorous individuals.

As Nietzsche saw it, one of the great dangers of the women's movement in attempting to enlighten women about womanhood is that it teaches women to unlearn their fear of man. When this happens, he argues, woman – 'the weaker sex' – abandons her most womanly instincts (*BGE* 239). Why, Nietzsche asks, should women wish to become like men when woman's 'prudence and art' consists in grace, play, and lightness? Why should they want to pursue the 'truth' about woman when her great art is the lie and her highest concern 'appearance and beauty'? (ibid., 232). In opposition to 'modern ideas' on man and woman, Nietzsche argues that real instruction on the relationship of the sexes is to be found in Oriental cultures.[5] He suggests that a man of depth, 'including that depth of benevolence which is capable of severity and hardness', needs to think of woman 'as a possession [*Besitz*], as property [*Eigenthum*] that can be locked, as something predestined for service and achieving her perfection in that' (ibid.,

238). Nietzsche detects a 'masculine stupidity' in the women's movement, which can lead only to a degeneration of 'woman'. No 'social contract' can put right the inequality of men and women, and the necessary injustice in their relationship (*GS* 363). The problem, he suggests, like problems associated with other 'modern ideas', goes back to the French Revolution and its ideals of equality. In order to combat this process of degeneration, the sexes must learn that what men respect in woman is her '*nature*... the tiger's claw under the glove, the *naïveté* of her egoism, her uneducability and her inner wildness' (*BGE* 239). He idealises Napoleon as the figure who triumphed over the plebeian ideals of the revolution and once again established 'man' as 'master over the businessman, the philistine, and over "woman" who has been pampered by Christianity and the enthusiastic spirit of the eighteenth century, and even more by "modern ideas"' (*GS* 362).

Nietzsche is capable of real insight into male–female identities, as when he recognises, in section 131 of *Beyond Good and Evil*, that both men and women deceive themselves about each other because what they honour and esteem are their own ideals. Thus, men like women to be peaceful and obedient when women are '*essentially* unpeaceful' and 'wild'. Nietzsche also positively challenges Christianity for the way in which its resentment against the foundations of life has made something impure and dirty of sexuality (*TI* 'What I Owe to the Ancients', 4). However, in spite of some positive aspects to his thinking on women, what prevails in his thought is the conviction that women's lives are fundamentally connected to motherhood and child-rearing, and that, through fulfilling the tasks of their social functions, they are destined to play a '*secondary* role' (*BGE* 145). Any woman who aspires to be something which is not connected to child-rearing – such as a scholar, for example – is described as sexually 'sterile' (*BGE* 144).

NIETZSCHE, THE SELF, STYLE, AND WOMAN

It is difficult to believe that a philosopher who stated that a real friend of women is someone who tells them that 'woman should be silent about woman' (*BGE* 232), and who, as we have seen, speaks disparagingly of 'emancipated women' as 'abortive females', could be of any use to feminism. Recent readings of Nietzsche by a number of women philosophers and political theorists, however, have advanced positive and powerful ways in which his ideas and texts can be opened up and moved in the direction of a feminist textual and political practice. Rosalyn Diprose, for example, has argued that Nietzsche's critique of the humanist self found in Christianity and liberalism, of the idea that lying behind all action there is to be found a constant, stable, fixed ego, describes a 'positive mode of resistance to social domination and normalization' which is especially pertinent to the concerns of feminists and their attempts to struggle against essentialism.[6] Nietzsche's thinking on the self contains an emphasis on ambiguity, on plural identity, on the affirmation of the constructed self in terms of an artistic task in which one freely gives 'style' to one's character, all of which can be useful for articulating a kind of feminist mode of thought which seeks to subvert an essentialising of human identity, whether female or male, which would simplify and efface 'difference'. The mythical subject that needs to be attacked and deconstructed in this fashion is the male subject of bourgeois society and bourgeois history:

For Nietzsche, the 'other' placed most at risk, by an ethics of equality is not woman but the sometimes cruel, sometimes enigmatic, always exceptional Noble spirit. The way Nietzsche appears to single out a sole aristocratic victim is somewhat surprising to a contemporary reader and has drawn criticism from some commentators. However, that Nietzsche appears to seek to save an elite and somewhat frightening figure from the workings of the democratic state is, in part, a product of historic necessity. It was the noble man, embellished by a memory of Greek nobility, who, more than any other, symbolized what was thrown into relief by the rise of the liberal individual in the nineteenth century. But this is no longer the case: a century of 'equality' has created its own hierarchy of value and hence, its own order of differences to be marginalized and effaced. All the same, on the question of Nietzsche's explicit exclusion of women from the possibility of self-creation, the excuses run out.[7]

A great deal of the 'reactive' nature of Nietzsche's aristocratic radicalism can be seen to stem from the *ressentiment* of the noble man who feels that his privileges are under threat, and the value he places on difference and distance about to be rendered extinct. Diprose suggests that Nietzsche's anti-feminism 'is not so much inconsistent but symptomatic of his own *ressentiment*'.[8] As Diprose acknowledges, there is an important aspect to Nietzsche's critique of nineteenth-century egalitarianism from which feminism can learn; his point has become a matter of increasing concern to feminists themselves with the maturity of the feminist movement. In the attempt to seek and establish equality – primarily, that of equality before the law – oppressed groups often make the mistake of clothing themselves in the attire of their oppressors or masters. They seek, quite understandably, a portion of the power which the masters have and which they wield. But, in the satisfaction of this very human desire, these groups fail to realise that 'the law' which will make them equal is the law as defined and legislated by those in power: for women living under patriarchy, for example, the law is the law of 'man'.

In his essay on Nietzsche and woman called *Spurs*, the French philosopher Jacques Derrida suggests that Nietzsche's radicalness lies in the way in which his thinking is characterised by a plurality of styles, and by a practice of writing which eschews adopting stable identities or positing fixed essences. When, in the preface to *Beyond Good and Evil*, Nietzsche claims that all (male) philosophers have been dogmatic in their assumptions about truth, and compares this to their inexpertise with women, he is saying that just as there is no single, unitary 'Truth' about life or reality to be discovered, so there is no such 'truth' about woman to be found, for, like 'truth', she does not exist. The provocative suggestion contained in Derrida's reading is that Nietzsche's objections to classical feminism can be seen to contain the 'post-feminist' message that women's attempts to define 'woman as such' commit the same essentialist fallacies as the masculinist tradition of Western philosophy. He writes: 'Feminism is nothing but the operation of a woman who aspires to be like a man ... It wants a castrated woman. Gone the style.'[9]

Perhaps the most important contention in *Spurs* is the claim that 'truth' understood as a 'feminine' operation cannot be defined in philosophy's attempt to master reality. The 'feminine' is not to be mistaken for woman's 'femininity' or for female sexuality, that is, for any 'of those essentializing fetishes which might still tantalize the dogmatic philosopher, the impotent artist or the inexperienced seducer who has not yet escaped his foolish hopes of capture'.[10] Derrida contends that we can locate three figures of woman in Nietzsche. The triadic scheme which governs Nietzsche's writing is as follows:

> He was, He dreaded this castrated woman.
> He was, He dreaded this castrating woman.
> He was, he loved this affirming woman.[11]

Kelly Oliver has defined this typology of woman in Nietzsche as corresponding to three types of will: the will to truth, the will to illusion, and the will to power. The castrated woman refers to 'the feminist who negates woman in order to affirm herself as man'.[12] Instead of creating truth and a plural identity, the castrated woman claims to discover truth, to discover woman as she is 'in and for herself'. In striving for 'objective truth' about woman, she denies the freedom which resides in affirming the ambiguity and multiplicity of meaning. As such, the type of feminism which pursues objectivity is hostile to the flux of life, to life as will to power.[13] The 'castrating woman' is the artist who plays with truth in order to disguise herself and resist the metaphysician's attempt to pin her down and fix her meaning. However, this kind of woman can be easily seduced by her own illusion when she clings fanatically to her ideals and forgets that she herself created them: 'She is the actor as the hysterical little woman. She mistakes the means, her illusion, for an end. The castrating woman becomes another version of the castrated woman.'[14] The 'affirming woman' signifies the self-overcoming of the will to truth and the will to illusion; she is the Dionysian force which abandons all foundations and certainties, 'the original mother, the unexhausted procreative will of life which is the will to power'.[15] Moreover:

She is hollow like a womb. She is the space, the womb, from which everything originates. This space is distance: the affirming woman is not an object in the distance: rather she is distance. Her power is distance. As distance, as space – pure womb – she does not exist. Just as there is no woman, there is no truth.[16]

Derrida enlists Nietzsche's attempt to write with style(s) (conceived as a feminine operation) to support the cause of deconstruction and its critique of what he calls 'the metaphysics of presence', where being or self-consciousness is seen to be always 'present' to itself. The question of style becomes a question of *strategy* in which the possibility of a 'radically deferred, indeterminate style of writing' is explored 'in order to avoid all essentialisms and stable categories'.[17] As Derrida puts it:

Reading is freed from the horizon of the meaning or truth of being, liberated from the values of the product's production or the present's presence. Whereupon the question of style is immediately unloosed as a question of writing.[18]

In spite of its suggestive brilliance, Derrida's reading of Nietzsche is a troubling one. It seems to me to be important, largely for practical political reasons and objectives, that the question of woman is not reduced to a mere figure or metaphor, possessing only the status of a rhetorical trope. To claim, as Derrida does, that Nietzsche writes with the hand of woman, is to run the risk of adding insult to injury by furthering philosophy's insidious silencing of women. If male philosophers such as Nietzsche or Derrida can write with the hand of woman, what is the role and purpose of female philosophers?[19] As Rosi Braidotti has written: 'Isn't it strange that it is precisely at the time in history when women have made their voices heard socially, politically, and theoretically that philosophical discourse – a male domain *par excellence* – takes over "the feminine" for itself?'[20] Is it not Derrida who castrates woman by turning the issue of woman's emancipation from a question of politics (of power) into one of style? Not once in *Spurs* does he engage with either the history or the theoretical and practical struggles of feminism. Derrida simply refuses to take seriously the fact that Nietzsche meant what he said and that he believed that women should have neither political power nor social influences. As one commentator has pointed out, Derrida's exploration of the question of woman in Nietzsche as a question of style 'removes the social issue of woman from the cultural context'.[21] It is a strategy which results in an idealised man and an idealised woman, as well as an idealised notion of style. While the reader of Nietzsche knows what she is getting and is able to take up a critical stance against it, if she so wishes, the reader of Derrida is denied any accessibility to the issue of gender either in Nietzsche or in the tradition of Western philosophy as a whole. Derrida's position is characterised by its sheer vagueness and remoteness.[22] The danger of adopting Derrida's 'playful' approach is that it runs the risk of turning gender – the very question of woman it raises – into a non-issue, or an issue of only dubious interest to dogmatic philosophers who have no real knowledge or familiarity with the charms and graces of women.

NIETZSCHE AND THE 'FEMININE': KOFMAN AND IRIGARAY

Nietzsche's critique of metaphysics is a critique of its dualistic nature. For example, he challenges the way in which it has established reason as superior to, and over, emotion or passion. As such, it can be seen to offer a form, or a style, of critique which seeks to reinstate the 'feminine' in philosophy, and to do so in a way which ultimately challenges any hierarchical opposition of 'masculine' and 'feminine'. If we read Nietzsche's texts carefully we discover, not simply that they are littered with misogynistic remarks, but that they also deconstruct their own phallocentric pretensions, largely through a celebration of woman as a metaphor representing the creative forces of life (life and woman conceived as the force of difference).

Nietzsche's critique of the tradition of philosophy from Plato to Kant rests on the insight that it has misunderstood the body.

From Plato onwards, philosophers have castrated their reflections on life from the body of experience which underlies them. Their fundamental world-views rest on a metaphysics of resentment: resentment towards sensual life, towards desire, towards the body. For Nietzsche, philosophy is maternal in that it rests on the unity of body and soul. The task is not, as it is in Plato, to liberate the soul from the prison house of the body, but to recognise that the 'soul is only a word for something in the body' (*Z* 'Of the Despisers of the Body'). The true philosopher is one who recognises that her thoughts are born out of the pain of experience which, like the experience of childbirth, should be endowed with 'blood, heart, fire, pleasure, passion, and agony, conscience, fate, and catastrophe' (*GS* Preface 3). It is only the experience of great pain which affords us the deepest insights into the human lot. Nietzsche makes the important point that the experience of such pain does not make us 'better' human beings, but only more 'profound' ones. The aim of such 'dangerous exercises in self-mastery' should not be 'self-forgetting', but rather to emerge from them a 'changed' and 'different' person. We are still capable of loving life, he says, but the kind of love we have for it can be compared to that of our love for someone (in his case a woman) who now causes doubt in us (ibid.).

Sarah Kofman has warned against rushing headlong into pronouncing Nietzsche to be a straightforward misogynistic philosopher. She argues that it is highly significant that Nietzsche should, in the preface to the second edition of *The Gay Science* (1887), use the Greek female demon Baubô as a symbol for 'truth', since it is Baubô who is subversively connected to notions of female fertility and fecundity. The figure of Baubô appears in the Eleusinian mysteries, where she is portrayed as a dry nurse connected to Demeter, the goddess of fecundity who, through a loss, has been comforting herself like a sterile woman. Baubô makes her laugh by pulling up her skirt and showing her belly on which a figure has been drawn. The gesture of the lifting of the skirt is meant to shock Demeter into fecundity. Kofman, in her highly imaginative reading of Nietzsche, connects female fecundity with the idea of the productivity of truth. What is necessary, Nietzsche writes in the section where he speaks of this obscene female demon, Baubô, is to stop courageously at the surface, at the fold, the skin, to adore appearance, and in this way one achieves superficiality 'out of profundity'. Kofman links the legend of Baubô with Nietzsche's conceptions of philosophy and truth:

The figure of Baubô indicates that a simple logic could never understand that life is neither depth nor surface, that behind the veil, there is another veil... It signifies also that appearance should cause us neither pessimism nor skepticism, but rather the affirming laugh of a living being who knows that despite death life can come back indefinitely.[23]

By identifying the wisdom of life with Baubô, Nietzsche is identifying 'truth' with the female reproductive organs which symbolise the eternal fecundity and creativity of life, its cycle of creation and decay, the circle that is a will to power, a will to innocence, and a will to self-overcoming through reproduction. Kofman notes, 'in the Eleusinian mysteries, the female sexual organ is exalted as the symbol of fertility and a guarantee of regeneration and eternal return of all things'.[24] However, what Kofman neglects in her original construal of Nietzsche is that, although he deploys a notion of female fertility and productivity in a very positive way, he does not permit women to become philosophers themselves (if they have such an aspiration they are labelled 'sterile scholars'). The extent, therefore, to which Nietzsche's conceptions of truth and philosophy are of positive value for a 'feminine writing' must be seriously questioned.

Ultimately, I believe it is necessary to locate a real ambiguity at the heart of Nietzsche's thinking; which is that it often finds itself caught in a tension between two quite different kinds of libidinal economy. On the one hand, it manifests an 'economy of the proper' (denoting notions of property, possession, self-aggrandisement, etc.), and, on the other hand, it expresses an 'economy of the gift', in which the emphasis is not on 'possession' or 'acquisition', but on 'squandering' and 'letting go'. This might explain why, for example, the doctrine of 'will to power' assumes in his writings two quite different, and incompatible, forms: a will to mastery and domination and a will to let go and to let be (*Gelassenheit*). However, having located such a distinction in his work, it is also necessary to appreciate that even in its 'gift-giving' form, the will to power in Nietzsche can still be read as a distinctly 'masculine' notion, since it conceives of the will in terms of a self-originating, independent, autonomous force which rests on the negation of heteronomous forces (notably woman as the 'other') (see especially, *Z* 'Of the Gift-Giving Virtue' section 1).

Amongst contemporary French theorists, Luce Irigaray has arguably done the most to articulate the 'feminine' in philosophy, however problematic a task it might be. Although often accused of subscribing to a self-defeating biological essentialism, it can be argued, in defence, that Irigaray's much misunderstood work attempts to articulate a complex, non-hierarchical experience of the world in which the female voice, which has been excluded from the discourse of philosophy, is uttered and received for the first time.[25] Irigaray instructively locates the source of her own difficulties, and of any attempt to speak the voice of the other:

> Woman has no gaze, no discourse... that would allow her to identify with herself... Hence, woman does not take an active part in the development of history, for she is never anything but the still undifferentiated opaqueness of sensible matter, the store (of) substance for the sublation of self, or being as what is, or what she is (or was), here and now.[26]

Irigaray's attempt to 'write the body', by evoking the female genitals to describe a libidinal economy centred on touch, feeling, flow, and perpetual play, challenges the phallocentric prejudices and assumptions of male reason and rationality which persist in governing the discourse of philosophy, as well as the institutions of our political life.

In her amorous engagement with Nietzsche, Irigaray interrogates his pretensions as a philosopher of maternity and of the body. Her reading serves as a challenge to those put forward by Kofman. She questions his fears, his anxieties, and his dreams and nightmares about woman, and locates in his thinking a fundamental *ressentiment*:

A man who really loves does not spare the one he loves, you claim. And that just shows how little you feel when you refuse to fight with – your woman. Keeping for the night your envy and your hate.

But I want to interpret your midnight dreams, and unmask that phenomenon: your night. And make you admit that I will dwell in it as your most fearsome adversity. So that you can finally realize what your greatest *ressentiment* is. And so that with you I can fight to make the earth my own, and stop allowing myself to be a slave to your nature. And so that you finally stop wanting to be the only god.[27]

Nietzsche affirms woman as the source of life only by denying to woman her own independent reality and experience of the world. Her mediation of the world through a man always assumes the form of an inferior position, one of natural servitude and obligation. And so his affirmation of woman contains a negation of her autonomous being: he will not let woman be, will not let her speak for herself. On Nietzsche's exclusion of woman Irigaray writes:

If from her you want confirmation for your being, why don't you let her explore its labyrinths? Why don't you give her leave to speak? From the place where she sings the end of your becoming, let her be able to tell you: no.[28]

In his desire to achieve the impossible, *to give birth to himself* as a self-made philosopher, Nietzsche expresses a fundamental resentment towards that which he feels ardour for and most esteems – maternal creativity. This resentment is comparable to the resentment he detects in the will's desire to will backwards, that is, to will the past and what has been. As Irigaray writes on this complex but crucial point:

To overcome the impossible of your desire – that is surely your last hour's desire. Giving birth to such and such a production, or such and such a child is a summary of your history. But to give birth to your desire itself, that is your final thought. To be incapable of doing it, that is your highest *ressentiment*. For you either make works that fit your desire, or you make desire itself into your work. But how will you find the material to produce such a child?

With extraordinary insight Irigaray examines the nature of Nietzsche's masculine resentment towards life and towards woman:

And, going back to the source of all your children, you want to bring yourself back into the world. As a father? or a child? And isn't being two at a time the point where you come unstuck?

Because, to be a father, you have to produce, procreate, your seed has to escape and fall from you. You have to engender suns, dawns, and twilights other than your own.

But in fact isn't it your will, in the here and now, to pull everything back inside you and to be and to have only one sun? And to fasten up time, for you alone? And suspend the ascending and descending movement of genealogy? And to join up in one perfect place, one perfect circle, the origin and end of all things?[29]

Nietzsche wants to attain the impossible and to will backwards so as to give birth to himself. To achieve this he must devalue woman by construing her existence as dependent on man for its fulfilment (when, in reality, every male that exists is dependent on a woman for his coming into the world, for his gift of life). Nietzsche's resentment of the creative independence of women is surely evident in his description of the emancipated woman as an abortive female. But note, there is nothing particularly unique about Nietzsche's resentment: it is typical of patriarchy. As Peter Sloterdijk has argued, Nietzsche's conception of autonomy, of self-creation through self-birth, is a 'masculine' one in the sense that the subject posited is one which must stand its own ground, independent and proud, and suppress what it regards as the horror and ugliness of its own birth: a birth in which it was in a relationship of dependency. Nietzsche speaks of the necessity of ridding oneself of the nauseous view presented to us by the miscarried, the stunted, and the poisoned.[30] Sloterdijk raises the crucial question when he asks: is not 'this self-birthing...only the exertion of the original evasion of an unbearable origin?'[31] Nietzsche's evasion of his – and our – human, all too human origin, results in a hatred of the mediocre, the handicapped, the feminine, and the natural.

In *Thus Spoke Zarathustra* Nietzsche construes male–female relationships in accordance with his aristocratic prejudices. For example, in the discourse on 'Of Old and Young Women', man is conceived in terms of 'depth' and woman in terms of 'surface'. A strict apartheid is to govern their relationship. The man is simply a means for the woman (the end is the child: 'everything about woman has one solution: it is called pregnancy'); for the man, the woman is both danger and play: 'Man should be trained for war and woman for the recreation of the warrior: all else is folly.' Moreover, 'The man's happiness is: I will. The woman's happiness is: He will.' Nietzsche's presumptions here are sexist because he conceives of woman's 'shallowness' not, as Derrida claims, because she is a 'mystery' and an 'ambiguity', but because she is a 'lack': woman needs a man to give her existence depth and significance.

Irigaray's reading shows that Nietzsche's deployment of a notion of female creativity is deeply problematic. It is necessary to be aware of the way in which, in patriarchal culture, the sanctification of motherhood has served as a useful tool for keeping women in subordinate, 'secondary' positions (the home, the private realm, etc.). However, an affirmation of female fecundity and procreativity does not have to reduce women to a maternal role. The problem with the notion of a 'feminine' creativity is that it has been appropriated by male philosophers who have denigrated women and, on the whole, favoured their exclusion from the discourse of philosophy and from the institutions of public life. Women have been denied creative speech: have been rendered *silent*. Or, in the odd exception where they have been allowed to participate, it is on condition that they speak like men.

CONCLUSION

Nietzsche, I would argue, can only become important for radical thinking about the nature of men and women when the question of style is transformed into a question affecting politics and history. To begin with, the question of the 'feminine' and the 'masculine' has to be linked up with the history of women's oppression and of patriarchy. These are not two separate issues: the exclusion of women from philosophy corresponds to the exclusion of women from the public realm and the supremacy of 'masculine' values over 'feminine' ones in political life. Even when a philosopher, such as Plato for example, seems to go against the grain and to grant equality to women, women are required to subdue their female qualities (emotion, passion, intuition, etc.), and acquire male characteristics. As Diana Coole notes, 'Emancipated women are consequently those who approximate the male norm: they are rational, repressed, self-disciplined, autonomous, competitive, and so on.'[32]

The discourse of political philosophy has been established on the basis of a series of oppositions (male/female, reason/desire, public/private), which presuppose the validity of the historical construction of the self as a juridical subject. This self is not neutral, but 'male', replete with 'masculine' virtues and values. As feminists repeatedly emphasise, what we are is not 'nature' but 'history'. Recent feminist thought poses a tremendous challenge to the liberal humanist conception of human identity. In liberal political thought the existence of the human subject is simply taken for granted and its rationality and autonomy assumed. But it is clear that our identities as political and legal subjects have been constructed on the basis of a negation of 'woman' and the 'feminine' as forms of otherness. Thus, a post-modern (as in 'post-man') politics must place at the top of its agenda the issue of sexual difference.

The issue is no doubt much more complex than I am presenting it here in terms of an exclusion of the feminine and an affirmation of the masculine. It could be argued, for example, that the 'feminine' has *not* been excluded from Western philosophy and art, but has simply been appropriated by men (like Nietzsche, for example), and that, while male philosophers and artists have been celebrated for their display of 'feminine' aspects and attributes, women artists (and not only artists) who articulate or reveal 'masculine' values and facets are seen as 'unwomanly' and as grotesque deformations of nature. Thus, while men are able to play with their identities in terms of masculine and feminine attributes, women are not allowed this freedom, but are assigned fixed roles and restricted identities in patriarchal culture. Here I am not identifying the 'feminine' with passive ('slave') qualities such as meekness, humility, patience, and so on. As the story of Baubô shows, the 'female' has the power to shock and disturb common conceptions of womanhood, revealing a subversive lewdness and obscenity.

One writer who has challenged the assignation of fixed sexual identities for both women and men is Hélène Cixous. Like Irigaray she has had to face the charge of biological essentialism in her effort to articulate a 'feminine writing'. One of the difficulties surrounding a radical sexual politics stems from the fact that otherness has never been tolerated in history, but has been perpetually subjected to reappropriation and assimilation. Cixous urges us to speak with caution on the question of sexual difference, suggesting that the oppositions of 'man/masculine' and 'woman/feminine' should be used with qualification in order to recognise that not all men repress their femininity, while some women inscribe only their masculinity (and vice versa). Thus, 'Difference is not distributed...on the basis of socially determined "sexes".'[33] She argues this precisely to warn against the dangers of lapsing into an essentialist interpretation:

It is impossible to predict what will become of sexual difference – in another time (in two or three hundred years?) But we must make no mistake: men and women are caught up in a web of age-old cultural determinations that are almost unanalyzable in their complexity. One can no more speak of 'woman' than of 'man' without being trapped within an ideological theater where the proliferation of representations, images, reflections, myths, identifications, transform, deform, constantly change everyone's Imaginary and invalidate in advance any conceptualization.[34]

What is to be imagined? Cixous invites us to conceive of a radical transformation of behaviour, roles, mentalities, and of politics, the effects of which are unthinkable from the narrow horizon of present perspectives. She singles out three things needed for radical reform: firstly, a general change in the structures of training and education (effecting the production and reproduction of meaning, myth, and representation); secondly, a liberation of sexuality aimed at transforming each person's relationship to his or her body in the direction of an affirmation of bisexuality so as to approximate 'the vast, material, organic, sensuous, universe that we are'; and, thirdly, political transformations of social institutions and structures, as there can be no change in libidinal economy without a change in political economy. The result of all this, as she points out, would be that what we interpret as 'masculine' and 'feminine' today would no longer remain, and neither would the common logic of difference be contained within the dominant opposition of a phallocentric mode of reasoning and a masculine form of politics.

What is required to realise this task is the coming into being, the birth, of what Nietzsche named the overhuman, new human beings who have gone beyond man the sick animal. 'We', Nietzsche taught, 'must *become* those that we *are*'; in the words of Cixous: men and women who are 'complex, mobile, open'. In becoming those that they 'are', the overhuman will become men and women whose identities surpass anything even Nietzsche could have imagined in his wildest dreams.

CHAPTER 10

The perfect nihilist
(or the case of Nietzsche)

Animals as critics. – I fear that animals consider man as a being like themselves that has lost in a most dangerous way its sound animal common sense; they consider him the insane animal, the laughing animal, the weeping animal, the miserable animal.

Nietzsche, The Gay Science 224

The fairest virtue of the great thinker is the magnanimity with which, as a man of knowledge, he intrepidly, often with embarassment, often with sublime mockery and smiling – offers himself and his life as a sacrifice.

Nietzsche, Daybreak 459

I conclude this reading of Nietzsche as political thinker with some suggestions on how best we can understand and appropriate his thought today. The key issue, I believe, is that of how we are to construe the meaning and significance of Nietzsche's description of himself as 'the first perfect nihilist'. Nietzsche believes that his experience as the first perfect nihilist has an exemplificatory status. His experience of nihilism is to serve as an example, not to be imitated, which would be folly, but as something to learn from and from which new life can grow. He is offering himself to us as a sacrifice: a *free offering*. He considers himself to be the teacher of our age *par excellence*, since his thinking reveals both signs of descent (of the decadence of life) and ascent (of the growth and abundance of life), and therefore represents both an end and a new beginning. The meaning of his thinking is fundamentally ambiguous or double-natured (*zweideutig*).

Nietzsche's analysis of the phenomenon of nihilism is

important because it shows that the roots of the spiritual and ethico-political crises of the West lie deep within its historical and philosophical culture. Nietzsche argues that it is important not to mistake the symptoms of nihilism, such as social distress and moral decay, for its causes. He insists that it is the end of the 'Christian-moral' interpretation of the world which has brought about the experience of nihilism. This once-hegemonic interpretation of the world has lost its sanction in the present age, resulting in an experience of dislocation and disorientation, in which human beings are no longer certain of the 'place' they inhabit as beings in the world and are unsure as to the direction in which their existence is moving. Humanity has a sense of impending catastrophe, but also an intimation and anticipation of new dawns, new suns, and new seas.

When Nietzsche speaks of the advent of nihilism in terms of the arrival of the uncanniest of all guests, he claims that he is describing what is coming and what can no longer come differently. 'This history can be related even now, for necessity is itself at work here', he writes (*WP* Preface 2). Nietzsche sees necessity at work in the modern experience of nihilism because he thinks that the history of the West has been built on nihilistic foundations. In constructing forms of knowledge and ideals and truth, for example, Western metaphysics and religion have denied, or denigrated, the sensual, bodily aspects of finite human existence. However, with the development of the 'will to truth' the foundations on which humanity's ideals and values have been constructed become subjected to critical self-reflection and self-examination, resulting in their destruction through a process he calls 'self-overcoming'.[1] The advent of nihilism has become necessary for our time because it represents 'the ultimate logical conclusion of our great values and ideals', and this means that we have to experience nihilism before we can find out what values these 'values' really had. At some point in the future there will be time for the creation of new values (ibid., 4). For the time being, however, we have 'to pay' for having been Christians for two thousand years.

Nihilism must assume the character of fate for modern human beings, therefore, because it lies deep within their historical formation and deformation. Its experience must form an essential part of our becoming what 'we' are (this partly explains why, for Nietzsche, a 'revaluation of all values' has to take the form of a *genealogy* of morals: but who are 'we'?). The categories of metaphysical thinking, of reason as such, categories like 'aim', 'unity', and 'truth', have been deployed from an anthropocentric perspective to satisfy the human need for an intelligible, calculable, and controllable universe. Thus Nietzsche is able to claim that it is faith in the categories of reason which is the 'cause' of nihilism since it is this faith which has encouraged human beings to measure the value of the world 'according to categories which refer to a purely fictitious world' (*WP* 12B). The values by which mankind has so far attempted to render the world estimable, but which are now undergoing a process of *devaluation*, are the results of certain utilitarian perspectives which have been 'designed to maintain and increase human constructs of domination (*menschlicher Herrschafts-Gebilde*)'. What we find here, says Nietzsche, is 'the *hyperbolic naiveté* of man, positing himself as the meaning and measure of the value of things' (ibid.; *KSA* 13, p. 49).

As we have seen, Nietzsche believes that all great things, including morality, Christianity, and truth itself, bring about their own destruction through an act of self-overcoming. Thus the 'self-overcoming of morality,' by which Nietzsche means that morality comes to question itself ('what is morality?') and to recognise its other ('immorality') at its foundation, comes about through Christianity's own cultivation of a will to truth (for example, the importance placed on confession and getting to the root of things: *original* sin). Eventually the Christian will to truth leads to the development of modern science and the formation of an intellectual conscience in which 'truth' outgrows the roots from which it has grown and matured. 'After Christian truthfulness has drawn one conclusion after another, it will finally draw the *strongest* conclusion, that *against* itself' (*OGM* III, 27). Modern culture finds itself undergoing a fundamental disorientation when it discovers that its faith in science rests on *metaphysical* foundations: 'that Christian faith which was also the faith of Plato, that God is the truth, that truth is divine. But what if... God himself should prove to be our most enduring lie?' (*GS* 344).

Man, says Nietzsche, is 'the reverent animal' (*verehrendes Thier*) who esteems that which he creates. His problem is that he has now become mistrustful – philosophical one might say – and views the world as ungodly, immoral, and inhuman. He now experiences a deep pessimism concerning the value of the world, seeing it as utterly valueless and feeling contempt towards his former reverence. Modern humanity thus finds itself caught in a difficult bind in which, if it chooses to abolish its reverence, it will, at the same time, be forced to abolish itself. This, says Nietzsche, is the 'question mark' (*Fragezeichen*) of modern nihilism:

> Have we not exposed ourselves to the suspicion of an opposition – an opposition between the world in which we were at home up to now with our reverences that perhaps made it possible for us to *endure* life, and another world *which is we ourselves* – an inexorable, fundamental, and deepest suspicion about ourselves that is more and more gaining worse and worse control of us Europeans and that could easily confront coming generations with a terrifying Either/Or; 'Either abolish your reverences or – *yourselves!*' (*GS* 346)

As Nietzsche points out, the latter would amount to nihilism; but would not also the former? This is the question which removes us from the domain of choice and shows us our existence in terms of a fateful predicament.

Nietzsche had a fear of nihilism because he knew that its realisation would result in universal moral decay and spiritual corruption. In his early untimely meditation on history, for example, he writes presciently about the fate of modernity and the part his own mature ideas (will to power, perspectivism, etc.) are destined to play in that fate:

> To what end the 'world' exists, to what end 'mankind' exists, ought not to concern us at all... except as objects of humour: for the presumptuousness of the little human worm is the funniest thing at present on the world's stage; on the other hand, do you ask yourself why you, the individual, exist?... I know of no better aim of life than that of perishing *animae magnae prodigus*, in pursuit of the great and the impossible. If, on the other hand, the doctrines of sovereign becoming,

of the fluidity of all concepts, types, and species, of the lack of any cardinal distinction between man and animal – doctrines which I consider true but deadly – are thrust upon the people for another generation with the rage for instruction that has by now become normal, no one should be surprised if the people perishes of petty egoism, ossification and greed, falls apart and ceases to be a people; in its place systems of individualist egoism, brotherhoods for the rapacious exploitation of the non-brothers, and similar creations of utilitarian vulgarity may perhaps appear in the arena of the future. (*HL* 9)

In the course of his intellectual development, however, Nietzsche came to learn that the experience of nihilism was one which could not be avoided and which had to be confronted. On one, deep level nihilism is something primordial which lies at the origins of the human experience of existence, in the sense that it denotes our recognition that our being-there rests on the possibility of our *not* being-there. This is the experience of the *nihil* (*das Nichts*) which Nietzsche saw as lying at the heart of the tragic culture of the ancient Greeks. As a people the Greeks were faced with overcoming the wisdom of Silenus, which taught that the best thing was not to be born, not to be, to be *nothing* (*nichts zu sein*), and the second best thing was to die as soon as possible (*BT* 3).

Nihilism is both an existential experience and a historical phenomenon for Nietzsche. On one level, the contemporary experience of nihilism shares the same primordial roots as the Greek experience. But it is also specific to a late-modern occidental consciousness which is experiencing the collapse of its cultural horizon (Christian-moral culture). Once the will to truth gains self-consciousness – in which we ask questions such as, why pursue truth? Why not be deceived? Why not value illusion? Is truth but an illusion? Does truth arise out of error, and morality out of immorality? – nihilism will develop in terms of an inexorable logic and its challenge will need to be faced head-on, even if it results, at least initially, in a debilitating epistemological and axiological nihilism. The obligation is upon modern human beings, however, to recognise both the danger and the promise of their predicament. For Nietzsche it is

insufficient simply to appeal to the wisdom of our dear
moral(istic) philosophers:

> The dangerous and uncanny point has been reached where the
> greater, more manifold, more comprehensive life transcends and *lives
> beyond* the old morality ... All sorts of new what-fors and wherewithals;
> no shared formulations any longer; misunderstanding allied with
> disrespect; decay, corruption, and the highest desires gruesomly
> entangled; the genius of the race overflowing from all cornucopias
> good and bad; a calamitous simultaneity of spring and fall, full of new
> charms and veils that characterize young, still unexhausted, still
> unwearied corruption. Again danger is there, the mother of morals,
> great danger, this time transposed into the individual, into the
> neighbour and friend, into the alley, into one's own child, into one's
> own heart, into the most personal and secret recesses of wish and will:
> what may the moral philosophers emerging in this age have to preach
> now? (*BGE* 262)

It is in this crucial passage that we encounter what is perhaps
Nietzsche's greatest problem as a self-proclaimed 'philosopher
of the future'. If nihilism denotes a crisis of authority (of values
and beliefs), resulting in a situation in which it is 'irrational and
trivial to impose the demands of morality upon mankind' (*D*
108), since a universally recognised goal for humanity is lacking
at present, then what will *Nietzsche* preach now? Nietzsche seeks
not only to recollect the past and to show us our origins and
formation in a new light, but also to create new values and to
declare a new future for man. But with what authority does he,
as a philosopher-legislator, speak in the epoch of nihilism in
which 'nothing' is held to be true in a universally binding sense,
and in which 'everything' is permitted? (*OGM* III, 24)

Nietzsche's response is to write for all and none and to
postpone, or defer, the moment of the historical actualisation of
his teaching, projecting it into the dimension of an unknown
and uncertain future. To a certain extent, Nietzsche subscribes
to Marx's dictum that philosophers have a responsibility not
only to interpret the world, but also to change it. The
philosopher, says Nietzsche, is the human being 'of the most
comprehensive responsibility who has the conscience for the
overall development of mankind' (*BGE* 61). However, in the

epoch of nihilism it is impossible for philosophy simply to command and to tell noble lies. What Nietzsche seeks to do as a thinker, I believe, is to *prepare* us for change. He shows that humanity has a history, that it has been (de-)formed in a particular way, and that the end of the Christian-moral interpretation of the world offers the possibility of another beginning. It becomes possible to navigate new seas since the *horizon* is now 'free' again (*GS* 343).

In his most self-reflexive moments Nietzsche calls into question his own pretensions as a philosopher-legislator, and, ironically, becomes the most democratic of philosophers, since he allows his readers the freedom of interpretation. Nietzsche views the reception of his teaching in terms of a fate. It is his destiny, he tells us, to be one of those who are born posthumously. It will be a posthumous birth which of necessity will be associated with a 'crisis without equal on earth', with 'the most profound collision of conscience'. At the same time that he discloses his identity as a destiny, however, as a thinker whose writings will divide humanity into those who come *before* and those who come *after*, he warns his readers that this little piece of dynamite who goes by the name of 'Friedrich Nietzsche' may also be a buffoon. In this respect Nietzsche calls our attention to his priestly aspirations and warns us to treat his teachings of redemption with suspicion.[2] In coming to terms with his work we find ourselves forced to ask, and Nietzsche encourages us to ask, questions such as: was he so clever? Was he so wise? Did he write such brilliant books? Is he a destiny? The aim of Nietzsche's thinking is not to create a new religion, but a new autonomy. What I would like to call 'an ethics of reading' lies at the centre of his pedagogy. Whenever we ask the question of Nietzsche's identity – who is Nietzsche? What does he *mean* for us? – we are also asking after our own identity. It is in this sense that the first perfect nihilist can truly instruct and provoke us. Through an encounter with his philosophy we can come to a comprehension of the signs – of descent and ascent, of sickness and health – of our age. In this way is it possible to 'go over' (*übergehen*) Nietzsche, as we must.[3]

In accordance with his deepest thinking, Nietzsche wants his readers to receive him beyond good and evil. This does not mean that we are prohibited from criticising, or even rejecting, his ideas. It does mean, however, that a reception of his work must transcend the level of a simple 'yes' or 'no'. We must engage his work and confront its challenge, which is nothing less than the challenge of thought and a challenge to think. I can think of no better way of ending this particular encounter with Nietzsche than citing the following words from a draft he wrote for the preface to his planned, but never completed, *magnum opus*:

THE WILL TO POWER

A book for *thinking*, nothing else. It belongs to those for whom thinking is a *delight*, nothing else. −
That it is written in German is untimely, to say the least: I wish I had written it in French so that it might not appear to be a confirmation of the German *Reich*.
The Germans of today are not thinkers any longer: something else delights and impresses them...
It is precisely among the Germans today that people think less than anywhere else. But who knows? In two generations one might no longer require the sacrifice involved in any nationalistic squandering of power and in becoming stupid.[4]

Notes

1 A QUESTION OF STYLE? AN INTRODUCTION TO READING NIETZSCHE

1 It has recently been argued by one interpreter that, not only is a notion of truth indispensable to Nietzsche's concerns, but that he does hold that true knowledge about an objective reality is both possible and desirable. See Maudemarie Clark, *Nietzsche on Truth and Philosophy* (Cambridge: Cambridge University Press, 1990).
2 See Erich Heller, *The Importance of Nietzsche: Ten Essays* (Chicago: University of Chicago Press, 1988), p. 17.

2 NIETZSCHE'S LEGACY

1 Golo Mann, *The History of Germany Since 1789* (Middlesex: Penguin, 1985), pp. 328–9.
2 My account draws heavily on material provided by Peter Bergmann in his informative study, *Nietzsche. The 'Last Anti-Political German'* (Bloomington: Indiana University Press, 1987), especially pp. 19–59. J. G. Herder studied in Königsberg under Kant, but was as much affected in his thinking by the pietistic and anti-rationalistic J. G. Hamann, as he was by Kant and the German enlightenment. After two years of travel, during which time he had several meetings with Goethe, Herder became the head of the Lutheran Church in Weimar. Truth for him was not the product of reason, but of the whole creative power of the individual, expressed in language, myth, religion, and poetry. For further detail see H. Holborn, *A History of Modern Germany 1648–1840* (London 1965), pp. 325–8.
3 P. Bergmann, *Nietzsche. 'The Last Anti-Political German'*, p. 29.
4 Quoted in ibid., p. 46.
5 Ibid., p. 47.
6 G. Mann, *The History of Germany Since 1789*, p. 396.
7 On this point see R. Hinton-Thomas, *Nietzsche in German Politics*

and Society 1890–1918 (Manchester: Manchester University Press, 1983), p. 122.

8 For an eye-opening analysis of Nietzsche's influence on the left after his mental collapse see the study by R. Hinton-Thomas (n. 7) above.

9 See Ernst Nolte, *Nietzsche und der Nietzscheanismus* (Frankfurt: Propylaen, 1990), p. 268. See also his study, *Der Faschismus in seiner Epoche* (Munich: R. Piper Verlag, 1979, fifth edition), pp. 529–35.

10 For further details on the mishandling of Nietzsche's work by his sister see Walter Kaufmann, *Nietzsche. Philosopher, Psychologist, and Antichrist* (New Jersey: Princeton University Press, 1974, fourth edition), pp. 4–8, 15–18, 442–5; H. F. Peters, *Zarathustra's Sister. The Case of Elisabeth Förster-Nietzsche* (New York 1977); and the recent study by Ben MacIntyre, *Forgotten Fatherland: The Search for Elisabeth Förster-Nietzsche* (London: Macmillan, 1992).

11 See the documentation provided by R. E. Kuenzli, 'The Nazi Appropriation of Nietzsche', *Nietzsche-Studien*, 12 (1983), 428–35.

12 See 'Nietzsche and the Fascists' in G. Bataille, *Visions of Excess: Selected Writings 1927–1939* (Manchester: Manchester University Press, 1989), pp. 183–4.

13 Kuenzli, 'The Nazi Appropriation of Nietzsche', p. 435.

14 See J. P. Stern, *Nietzsche* (Glasgow: Collins, 1978), p. 79.

15 See Howard Williams, 'Nietzsche and Fascism', *History of European Ideas*, 11 (1989), 897–8. See also Margaret Canovan, 'On Being Economical with the Truth: Some Liberal Reflections', *Political Studies*, 38 (March 1990), 5–20, who views Nietzsche, in his preference for natural hierarchy over natural equality, as the 'spiritual father of fascism' and a 'source of so much proto-fascist thinking', p. 17.

16 The Oxford English Dictionary defines 'machiavellian' as deceitful, perfidious, and cunning action. In the history of Western thought 'machiavellism' has come to signify the principle of *realpolitik* – that expediency is always preferable to morality in statecraft. Part of Machiavelli's modernity consists in his separation of politics from both morality and religion. For further insight see J. Leonard, 'Public versus Private Claims: Machiavellism from Another Perspective', *Political Theory*, 12 (November 1984), pp. 491–506. See also Bernard Crick's introduction to N. Machiavelli, *Discourses* trans. L. Walker (Middlesex: Penguin, 1970).

17 See Georges Bataille, *On Nietzsche*, trans. B. Boone (London: Athlone Press, 1992), Appendix I, 'Nietzsche and National Socialism', p. 171.

18 John Gunnell, *Political Philosophy and Time* (Connecticut: Wesleyan University Press, 1968), p. 8.

19 For further insight into this characterisation of nihilism see the original study by Mark Warren, *Nietzsche and Political Thought* (Cambridge, Massachusetts: MIT Press, 1988), especially pp. 15–17.

20 A thought-provoking reading of the political implications of nihilism along these lines was given by R. J. Hollingdale in a paper delivered to an undergraduate seminar in the Department of Political Studies at Queen Mary and Westfield College in March 1992, entitled 'Nietzsche and Politics' (unpublished).

21 On the noble lie or myth see Plato, *The Republic*, trans. H. D. P. Lee (Middlesex, Penguin, 1970), pp. 156–61. The myth tells of the fashioning of the three main classes of society (the rulers or guardians, the auxiliaries, and the workers) in terms of their cultivation in the depths of the earth. In the formation of each class there was added an element: gold in the rulers, silver in the auxiliaries, and bronze in the farmers and workers. The story is designed to give a mythical basis to Plato's theory of justice, which holds that being just is about minding one's own business and performing the function one has been allotted in society. Lee translates Plato's foundation myth as 'magnificent myth' and argues that the conventional translation of 'noble lie' is a bad one since it suggests that Plato saw the myth simply as a means of political propaganda. The 'myth' is rather to be seen as replacing the national traditions of a community and as expressing its ideals.

22 See Carole Pateman, *The Problem of Political Obligation. A Critique of Liberal Theory* (Oxford: Polity Press, 1985).

23 See T. Hobbes, *Leviathan* (Harmondsworth: Penguin, 1990), chapter thirteen.

24 See J. Locke, *Two Treatises of Government* (Cambridge, Cambridge University Press, 1988), book two, chapter two.

25 See J. J. Rousseau, *The Social Contract*, trans. G. D. H. Cole (London: Dent 1973), book one, chapter six: 'The problem is to find a form of association which will defend and protect with the whole common force the person and goods of each associate, and in which each, while uniting himself with all, may still obey himself alone, and remain as free as before'.

26 See Stephen K. White, 'Heidegger and the Difficulties of a Postmodern Ethics and Politics', *Political Theory* 18: 1 (February 1990), 80–103, at 87–8.

27 Affinities between Arendt and Nietzsche have been noted by Shiraz Dossa in his engaging study, *The Public Realm and the Public*

Self. The Political Theory of Hannah Arendt (Waterloo, Ontario: Wilfred Laurier University Press, 1989), pp. 61 and 68. For a more detailed exploration of the connection see Dana R. Villa, 'Beyond Good and Evil: Arendt, Nietzsche, and the Aestheticization of Political Action', *Political Theory* 20: 2 (May 1992), 274–308.

28 Nietzsche's scepticism towards the practice of Athenian democracy is not without historical basis. As John Gunnell notes in his *Political Philosophy and Time*, p. 123, the original aristocratic spirit of the *agon*, when translated into the democracy of Athens, resulted in a subversion of the meaning of *polis* life with 'individual striving and the permanence of the state' becoming incompatible and 'political man' being replaced by 'economic man'. For further insight on this point see Tracy B. Strong, *Friedrich Nietzsche and the Politics of Transfiguration* (Berkeley: University of California Press, 1975), pp. 192–202.

29 See N. Machiavelli, *The Prince*, tr. G. Bull (Middlesex: Penguin, 1961), especially chapter 18.

30 See S. Dossa, *The Public Realm and the Public Self*, p. 93. Arendt, like Machiavelli, makes a distinction between 'normal human behaviour' which has to be judged in terms of the motives and consequences of action, and action in the political realm in which citizens are not burdened by the mundane considerations of everyday life and in which activity is judged, not by the moral standards of ordinary life, whether intentions or consequences, but by the excellence of words and deeds. See Dossa, p. 94.

The basis of Nietzsche's critique of Kant's moral philosophy can also be found in this point. Kant argues that the way in which we can judge the moral worth of an action is by deciding whether it is motivated by a 'good will'. We can do this by subjecting action to the test of the 'categorical imperative', which asks of any proposed action: can you turn the maxim of this action into a universal principle of conduct applicable to all rational beings? See I. Kant, *Groundwork of the Metaphysic of Morals*, trans. H. J. Paton (New York: Harper and Row, 1964), pp. 69–71, and 88–91. Nietzsche views Kant's categorical imperative as a 'Moloch of abstraction' which amounts, in effect, to a slave type of morality in which, on account of the principle of universalisability, great, noble individual action cannot be undertaken. In *Twilight of the Idols* 'Expeditions of an Untimely Man', number 29, he describes Kant's moral philosophy as providing the best formula of the civil servant: 'the civil servant as thing in itself set as judge over the civil servant as appearance'. See also chapter six of the present study.

31 See Bhikhu Parekh, *Hannah Arendt and the Search for a New Political Philosophy* (London: Macmillan, 1981), p. 182.

32 My interpretation of this passage is taken from Lou Salomé, *Friedrich Nietzsche. The Man in his Works* (Connecticut: Black Swan Books, 1988), p. 137.

33 See R. J. Hollingdale, introduction to Schopenhauer, *Essays and Aphorisms* (Middlesex: Penguin, 1970), pp. 20–2, and Schopenhauer 'On Affirmation and Denial of the Will to Life', in *Essays and Aphorisms*, pp. 61–6.

34 See Hobbes, *Leviathan*, chapter 10. In chapter 11 Hobbes writes: 'I put for a generall inclination of all mankind, a perpetuall and restlesse desire of Power after and power, that ceaseth only in Death'.

35 See Paul Patton, 'Politics and the Concept of Power in Hobbes and Nietzsche', in P. Patton (ed.), *Nietzsche, Feminism, and Political Theory* (London: Routledge, 1993).

36 Salomé, *Friedrich Nietzsche*, pp. 121–3.

37 For a moral (and moralistic) response to Nietzsche's provocation and challenge see Philippa Foot, 'Nietzsche's Immoralism', *New York Review of Books* (13 June 1991), 18–22.

38 Thomas Mann, *Nietzsche's Philosophy in the Light of Contemporary Events* (Washington: Library of Congress, 1947), p. 3.

39 Ibid., p. 17.

40 Ibid., p. 36.

41 Albert Camus, *The Rebel* (1951), trans. A. Bower (Middlesex: Penguin, 1971), p. 57.

42 Ibid., p. 58.

43 Ibid., p. 64.

44 Ibid., p. 69.

3 NIETZSCHE AND THE GREEKS: CULTURE VERSUS POLITICS

1 New translations of both of these essays by Carol Diethe are forthcoming in the new Cambridge University Press edition and translation of *On the Genealogy of Morality*.

2 Tracy Strong points out, correctly in my view, that Apollo and Dionysus are not to be construed in terms of an oppositional, dialectical 'duality' but as a 'twoness'. With this distinction Nietzsche is not positing a simple opposition between instinct or intuition and reason. See his essay, 'Aesthetic Authority and the Tradition: the Greeks and Nietzsche', *History of European Ideas*, 11 (1989), pp. 989–1007. See also the careful and incisive reading offered by John Sallis in his book, *Crossings, Nietzsche and the Space of Tragedy* (Chicago: University of Chicago Press, 1991).

3 In 'The Problem of Socrates' in *Twilight of the Idols*, Nietzsche speaks of Socrates' origins amongst the 'lowest orders', and argues

that Socrates' irony is the expression of 'the *ressentiment* of the rabble'. However, this is a somewhat idiosyncratic view. Socrates was the son of a craftsman. According to I. F. Stone, *The Trial of Socrates* (London: Johnathan Cape, 1988), pp. 117–21, he was, in origins, background, and training, a typical 'middle-class snob'. According to Ellen Meiksins Wood and Neal Wood, his politics were those of a typical aristocrat who opposed the levelling tide of democracy which had swept across Athens. He opposed what he saw as the political degeneration brought about by democracy, including the tyranny of the majority and the rise of a vulgar commercialism. He saw the 'people' as an ignorant mass motivated by self-interest and envious of the noble and the wealthy. They argue that Socrates sought to defend the interests of the traditional landed aristocracy and their distinctive class culture, comprising a proud independence, a disdain for labour, polished manners, and a devotion to sport, music and dancing. His aim, they argue, was to replace Athenian democracy 'by the rule of an aristocratic–oligarchic elite'. See their study, *Class Ideology and Ancient Political Theory: Socrates, Plato, and Aristotle in Social Context* (Oxford: Basil Blackwell, 1978), p. 97. It is certainly true that the people influenced by Socrates, such as Alcibiades in the revolution of 411 and Critias in the successful revolution of 404, set out to subvert Athenian democracy.

Elsewhere, Wood and Wood have argued that a *polis* that is aristocratic in substance (ruled by the good or the best) must be oligarchic in form (ruled by the rich). Their view that oligarchy is a necessary if not sufficient condition of aristocracy, is certainly one shared by Nietzsche and is clearly stated by him in his essay on the Greek state. Compare *On the Genealogy of Morals*, essay one, section 5, where Nietzsche notes the correspondence between Greek words for 'good' and 'noble' and 'wealthy' and 'powerful'. See Wood and Wood, 'Socrates and Democracy', *Political Theory* 14:1 (February 1986), 55–82, note 3. For another view of the relationship between Socrates and democracy see Richard Kraut, *Socrates and the State* (New Jersey: Princeton University Press, 1984), especially pp. 194–245. For insight into the historical context of the condemnation of Socrates by the Athenian democrats see Ernest Barker, *Greek Political Theory. Plato and His Predecessors* (1918) (London: Methuen, 1977), pp. 108.

For an extensive treatment of Nietzsche on Socrates see Werner J. Dannhauser, *Nietzsche's View of Socrates* (Ithaca: Cornell University Press, 1974).

4 Peter Bergmann, *Nietzsche. The 'Last anti-Political German'* (Bloomington: Indiana University Press, 1987), p. 50. For Nietzsche's

later rejection of Schopenhauer see *Twilight of the Idols* 'Expeditions of an Untimely Man', number 21, where he argues that, far from representing an overturning or overcoming of the Christian-moral world-view, Schopenhauer's philosophy is, in fact, the heir to it, offering no more than a 'nihilistic total devaluation of life'. Schopenhauer himself conceded the point when he wrote revealingly: 'my doctrine could be called the true Christian philosophy, however paradoxical this may seem to those who refuse to penetrate to the heart of the matter but prefer its superficialities', in A. Schopenhauer, *Essays and Aphorisms*, trans. R. J. Hollingdale (Middlesex: Penguin, 1970), p. 63. Schopenhauer regarded Christianity as containing the same 'truth' as Brahmanism and Buddhism, namely, the need to seek salvation from a suffering existence through a denial of the will. See A. Schopenhauer, *The World as Will and Representation*, trans. E. F. J. Payne (New York: Dover Publications, 1958), II, p. 628.

5 Ibid., p. 51. R. J. Hollingdale, in the introduction to his translation of *Essays and Aphorisms*, p. 36, explains the delay in Schopenhauer's recognition (*The World as Will and Representation* was published in 1819) in terms of the fact that it was not until the German rush into industrialisation in the 1860s, 1870s, and 1880s, that a German audience was created which was receptive to his work. As he points out, Schopenhauer's pessimism appealed to those who saw that nineteenth-century progress would not inevitably lead to the millennium, and that the miserable human condition persisted in the face of social improvement and technological achievement.

6 An example of such a reading can be found in J. P. Stern's *Nietzsche* (Glasgow: Collins, 1978). See also Alasdair MacIntyre, *After Virtue. A Study in Moral Theory* (London: Duckworth Press, 1981), pp. 107–8.

7 On Rousseau see Arthur M. Melzer, *The Natural Goodness of Man: On the System of Rousseau's Thought* (Chicago: University of Chicago Press, 1990). On Hegel, see Charles Taylor, *Hegel and Modern Society* (Cambridge: Cambridge University Press, 1979).

8 R. Tuck, *Hobbes* (Oxford: Oxford University Press, 1989), pp. 72–3.

9 For an examination of the Nietzsche–Plato relationship see Catherine Zuckert, 'Nietzsche's Re-reading of Plato', *Political Theory*, 13:3 (May 1985), pp. 213–39; and Alex McIntyre, '"Virtuosos of Contempt": An Investigation of Nietzsche's Political Philosophy Through Certain Platonic Political Ideas', *Nietzsche-Studien*, 21 (1992), pp. 184–210. On the point of Plato's artistry, John Gunnell has argued that Plato is as much a poet as his predecessors in his setting forth of the nature of the virtuous soul

and the cosmic polity. See Gunnell, *Political Philosophy and Time*, p. 135.

10 See Henry Staten, *Nietzsche's Voice* (New York: Cornell University Press, 1990), pp. 83–5.

11 See K. Marx, 'Economic and Philosophical Manuscripts of 1844', in *The Early Writings*, trans. R. Livingstone (Middlesex: Penguin, 1975), pp. 279–401.

12 The 'romantic anti-capitalist' defines someone who opposes the capitalist order, but who is unable to locate the social and economic determinants of the modern crisis of culture or propose a progressive and radical transformation of society. For further insight see M. Löwy, *Georg Lukács. From Romanticism to Bolshevism* (London: New Left Books, 1979).

13 See Wood and Wood, *Class Ideology and Ancient Political Theory*, p. 26.

14 The best expositor and advocate of the ideals of democracy writing today has to be Cornelius Castoriadis. For an introduction to his thought see the collection of essays, *Philosophy, Politics, Autonomy: Essays in Political Philosophy* (Oxford: Oxford University Press, 1991).

4　NIETZSCHE ON MODERN POLITICS

1 Compare Marx on this point, 'On the Jewish Question', in *The Early Writings*, trans. R. Livingstone (Middlesex: Penguin, 1975), pp. 225–6. For Marx democracy translates the Christian notion of man as a 'sovereign being' into a secular maxim. He argues that the 'perfected Christian state' is the 'atheist state', the 'democratic state', p. 222.

2 T. Hobbes, *Leviathan* (Cambridge, Cambridge University Press, 1990), chapter 13.

3 See G. W. F. Hegel, *Philosophy of Right*, trans. T. M. Knox (Oxford: Oxford University Press, 1967), paras. 142–8.

4 See J. J. Rousseau, *The Social Contract and Discourses*, trans. G. D. H. Cole (London: Dent, 1973), book two, chapter seven.
　　The term 'possessive individual' is taken from C. B. Mac-Pherson and refers to the individual of modern liberal acquisitive society which views its life primarily in terms of material possessions. In modern liberal thought the self is viewed as a possession which owns its internal essence and the externalization of this essence in the form of private property. See MacPherson, *The Political Theory of Possessive Individualism* (Oxford: Oxford University Press, 1962), pp. 263–4.

5 For this characterisation of Nietzsche's philosophy see George

Brandes, *Friedrich Nietzsche* (London: Heinemann, 1914). Brandes made this characterisation known to Nietzsche when he received a copy of the *Genealogy of Morals* from him. Nietzsche replied by calling it 'the shrewdest comment on me I have so far read'. See Ronald Hayman, *Nietzsche: A Critical Life* (London: Quartet Books, 1980), p. 314.

Although my concern has not been to trace any specific influences on the formation of Nietzsche's political thought, it can be noted that his aristocratic taste was also that of his great mentor too. Schopenhauer wrote: 'If you want Utopian plans, I would say: the only solution to the problem is the despotism of the wise and noble members of a genuine aristocracy, a genuine nobility, achieved by mating the most magnanimous men with the cleverest and most gifted women. This proposal constitutes *My Utopia* and my Platonic Republic', *Essays and Aphorisms*, trans. R. J. Hollingdale (Middlesex: London 1970), p. 154. Schopenhauer's political thinking draws most heavily on the theories of Plato and Hobbes. The existence of the state, law, and justice, are a result of the inadequacy of relying upon pure morality. The state is constructed not simply to put an end to egoism, but to counter the injurious consequences resulting from a plurality of egoistic individuals. See A. Schopenhauer, *The World as Will and Representation*, trans. E. F. J. Payne (New York: Dover Publications, 1969), I, chapter 62, especially pp. 343–50.

6 On the topic of 'Rousseau and revolution' see Arthur M. Melzer, *The Natural Goodness of Man: On the System of Rousseau's Thought* (Chicago: University of Chicago Press, 1990), pp. 261–5.

5 ZARATHUSTRA'S TEACHING OF THE OVERMAN

1 On this point see Hannah Arendt's essay, 'What is Authority?' in Arendt, *Between Past and Future. Eight Exercises in Political Theory* (1961) (Middlesex: Penguin, 1983), pp. 91–141.

2 On Nietzsche as a proponent of local rebellions (as opposed to global revolution) see Daniel W. Conway, 'Overcoming the *Übermensch*: Nietzsche's Revaluation of Values', *Journal of the British Society for Phenomenology*, 20 (October 1989), 211–24.

3 See Walter Kaufmann, *Nietzsche, Philosopher, Psychologist, and Antichrist* (New Jersey: Princeton University Press, 1974), p. 308.

4 See Nietzsche, *Twilight of the Idols* 'The Four Great Errors', section 8:

What alone can our teaching be? That no one *gives* a human being their qualities: not God, not society, not parents or ancestors... *No one* is accountable for existing at all, for being constituted as they are, or for living in the circumstances and surroundings in which they find themselves. The fatality of their nature cannot be disentangled from the fatality of all that which has been and will be... One is necessary, one is a piece of fate, one belongs to the whole, one *is* in the whole – there exists nothing which could judge, measure, compare, condemn our being, for that would be to judge, measure, compare, condemn the whole... *But nothing exists apart from the whole!...this alone is the great liberation* – thus alone is the *innocence* of becoming restored.

5 Joan Stambaugh's study, *Nietzsche's Thought of Eternal Return* (Baltimore: Johns Hopkins University Press, 1972) offers a highly informative reading of the eternal return. As she points out, pp. 29–30, although Nietzsche uses the expressions 'return' (*Wiederkunft*) and 'recurrence' (*Wiederkehr*) interchangeably, their meaning is quite different. 'Return' implies a going back and completion of a movement; while 'recurrence' implies another occurrence or beginning of a movement. The German prefix *Wieder* means both 'back' and 'again'. On the same (*das Gleiche*), Stambaugh argues (pp. 31–2) that this is not to be understood, as one might readily think, in terms of a content, but rather as a process since, for Nietzsche, there is no static content, no substance ('what is x?') in the traditional sense which can return. As she points out, *das Gleiche* does not, strictly speaking, mean the 'same', but lies somewhere between the 'same' and the 'similar'.

6 For an incisive interpretation of the relationship between the overman and eternal return see chapter six of Wolfgang Müller-Lauter's study, *Nietzsche. Seine Philosophie der Gegensätze und die Gegensätze seiner Philosophie* (Berlin and New York: Walter de Gruyter, 1971), 'Der Weg zum Übermenschen', pp. 116–34.

7 The classic refutation of the doctrine of eternal return in terms of a cosmological hypothesis can be found in Georg Simmel's study of 1907, *Schopenhauer and Nietzsche* (Amherst: University of Massachusetts Press, 1986), trans. H. Loiskandl et al., pp. 170–9. In the last decade or so a number of leading commentators, including Bernd Magnus and Alexander Nehamas, have argued that the existential import of the doctrine can stand and hold weight independently of its cosmological truth-claim – it could be argued that Nietzsche's efforts to give scientific credibility to the doctrine works against its real significance, which is existential and ethical. See B. Magnus, 'Nietzsche's Eternalistic Counter-Myth', *Review of Metaphysics*, 26 (1973), 604–16; and A. Nehamas, 'The Eternal Recurrence', *Philosophical Review*, 99 (1980), 331–56.

8 A. C. Danto, *Nietzsche as Philosopher* (New York: Macmillan, 1965), p. 211. See also Martin Heidegger, 'Who is Nietzsche's

Zarathustra?', in David B. Allison, (ed.), *The New Nietzsche* (Cambridge, Massachusetts: MIT Press, 1985), pp. 64–80.

9 J. Stambaugh, *Nietzsche's Thought of Eternal Return*, p. 107.

10 G. Deleuze, *Nietzsche and Philosophy* (London: Athlone Press, 1983), p. 71.

11 See Ronald Bogue, *Deleuze and Guattari* (London: Routledge, 1989), p. 31.

12 Ibid., p. 33.

13 In her *Nietzsche on Truth and Philosophy* (Cambridge: Cambridge University Press, 1990), pp. 285–6, Maudemarie Clark has argued that an affirmation of the thought of eternal return excludes moral condemnation/judgement since it requires us to affirm much that we might find abominable and abhorrent in the past, such as the Holocaust. Any evaluation of the eternal return must, therefore, she argues, involve deciding between the moral point of view and Nietzsche's standpoint beyond good and evil. However, I have argued that the doctrine can only make sense for a being who is 'moral' (in the autonomous sense, such as the 'sovereign individual' which Nietzsche discusses in the *Genealogy of Morals*). It is important to understand precisely in what way the teaching is to be understood as an ethical imperative. Like Kant's categorical imperative, the thought of eternal return has a universal form, but, unlike the categorical imperative, it does not posit a universal content (although Kant's imperative is formal it does presuppose that any action subjected to its test can be universalised so as to apply to all rational beings). Eternal return provides the form of universality only in the act of returning, whereas what is willed to return (the actual content) cannot be universalisable in Nietzsche's thinking beyond good and evil, since there can be no good and evil which is universally valid for all. *Contra* Kant, Nietzsche insists that each one of us must invent our own virtue and devise our own categorical imperative (*AC* 11). 'Judgement' then, for Nietzsche, is *invention*.

14 G. Simmel, *Schopenhauer and Nietzsche*, p. 174.

15 E. Heller, *The Importance of Nietzsche. Ten Essays* (Chicago: University of Chicago Press, 1988), p. 12.

16 Clark, *Nietzsche on Truth and Philosophy*, p. 275.

17 Ibid., p. 272.

18 L. Lampert, *Nietzsche's Teaching* (New Haven: Yale University Press, 1987), p. 258.

19 D. W. Conway, 'Overcoming the *Übermensch*', p. 212.

6 A GENEALOGY OF MORALS

1 See Paul Cantor, 'Friedrich Nietzsche: the Use and Abuse of Metaphor', in D. S. Miall (ed.), *Metaphor: Problems and Perspectives* (Brighton: Harvester Press, 1982), pp. 71–89, at p. 74. On p. 84 Cantor suggests that one of the reasons why Nietzsche exposed his work to the possibility of gross misinterpretations is that he left unclear the metaphoric status of his expressions, thus making it 'easy for his readers to take the "wrong" metaphors in his prose literally'.

2 On this point see Michel Foucault's now classic essay, 'Nietzsche, Genealogy, and History', in Paul Rabinow (ed.), *A Foucault Reader* (Middlesex: Penguin, 1984), pp. 76–101. Despite some astute points, Foucault's essay strikes me as perverse in a number of ways. It perhaps tells us more about Foucault's conception of history than it does Nietzsche's. See my *Nietzsche contra Rousseau* (Cambridge: Cambridge University Press, 1991), pp. 119–25.

3 This point should serve to show that the attempt to identify Nietzsche's thinking with that of Callicles is quite superficial. For Callicles it is the weak – 'the majority' – who manufacture laws and devise conventions of what is just and unjust. See Plato, *Gorgias*, trans. W. C. Hembold (Indianapolis: Bobbs-Merrill Co., 1979), p. 51. In section 26 of *Daybreak* Nietzsche argues that the origins of morality lie in the social needs (security, etc.) of the human animal: 'The beginnings of justice, as of prudence, moderation, bravery – in short, of all we designate as the *Socratic virtues*, are *animal*: a consequence of that drive which teaches us to seek food and elude enemies. If we consider that even the highest human being has only become more elevated and subtle in the nature of his food and in his conception of what is inimical to him, it is not improper to describe all moral phenomena as animal.'

4 The best example of a philosophy which identifies the moral worth of an action in terms of the intentions behind its performance is that of Kant. A great deal of Nietzsche's thinking on morals can be seen in terms of a critique of Kant. For further insight see my essay 'Nietzsche on Autonomy and Morality: the Challenge to Political Theory', *Political Studies*, 34 (June 1991), pp. 270–86.

5 Sophocles, 'King Oedipus' in *The Theban Plays*, trans. E. F. Watling (Middlesex: Penguin, 1974), pp. 25–69.

6 See E. R. Dodds, 'On Misunderstanding *Oedipus Rex*', in M. J. O'Brien (ed.), *Twentieth Century Interpretations of Oedipus Rex* (New Jersey: Prentice-Hall, 1968), pp. 17–30, at p. 28.

7 See R. P. Winnington-Ingram, 'The *Oedipus Tyrannus* and Greek Archaic Thought', in ibid., pp. 81–90, at p. 86.

One of the reasons, of course, why Nietzsche so esteemed Greek tragedy is because of the manner in which it revealed the human character. As John Gunnell points out in his *Political Philosophy and Time* (Connecticut: Wesleyan University Press, 1968), pp. 103–10, classical tragedy is not the study of the subjectivity of the tragic hero as depicted in modern tragedy from Shakespeare onwards. It is not concerned to present the personality of the hero in the sense of an autonomous self emerging as the centre of decision and anxiety; rather the hero is 'a paradigmatic self constituted by its action, not a progressive revelation of a unique personality', p. 104. See also Hegel on Oedipus in *The Philosophy of Right*, trans. T. M. Knox (Oxford: Oxford University Press, 1967), para. 118.

8 It is on this point concerning a 'sovereign' individual that Hannah Arendt departs from Nietzsche in her thinking. For Arendt freedom is 'given under the condition of nonsovereignty', *The Human Condition* (New York: Doubleday, 1959), p. 220. What Arendt means is that free action is spontaneous and creative, it is not the kind of action in which one is in control (or 'sovereign').

9 Compare S. Freud, *Civilization and Its Discontents*, volume 12 of the Pelican Freud Library, ed. A. Dickson (Middlesex: Penguin, 1985), p. 286, where Freud writes: 'it is impossible to overlook the extent to which civilization is built up upon a renunciation of instinct'. His view of the origins and nature of conscience is remarkably similar to that provided by Nietzsche in the *Genealogy*. See Freud, pp. 315–26.

10 T. Hobbes, *Leviathan* (Cambridge: Cambridge University Press, 1990), chapter 13. Hobbes writes that in the absence of a common power there can be no 'notions of Right and Wrong, Justice and Injustice have there no place'.

11 See M. Clark, *Nietzsche on Truth and Philosophy*, pp. 197–203.

7 O HUMANITY! NIETZSCHE ON GREAT POLITICS

1 See J. Derrida, 'Otobiographies: Nietzsche and the Politics of the Proper Name', in H. Bloom (ed.), *Friedrich Nietzsche* (New York: Chelsea House Publishers, 1987), p. 126.

2 Nietzsche overlooks, and seems blind to, the motivation behind a politics of equality. As Michael Walzer points out in his book *Spheres of Justice. A Defence of Pluralism and Equality* (Oxford: Basil Blackwell, 1983), pp. xii–xiii, although the root meaning of equality is negative, in that it seeks to abolish particular sets of differences in different times and places, an egalitarian politics cannot simply be reduced to a politics of envy and resentment (this, in fact, is what Marx called 'crude communism'). He writes:

'envy and resentment are uncomfortable passions; no one enjoys them; and I think it is accurate to say that egalitarianism is not so much their acting out as it is a conscious attempt to escape the condition that produces them'. Egalitarian politics are a practical response to the experience of subordination and exclusion, not the expression of a natural envy or resentment. As Walzer points out, what gives rise to egalitarian politics is not the fact that there are rich and poor, but that the rich 'grind the faces of the poor' and impose their poverty upon them through force and domination. Needless to say, Nietzsche was fully aware of the realities of aristocratic–oligarchic rule; more than that, he saw positive aspects to the exploitation and domination of the poor (the 'weak') by the rich (the 'strong').

3 I owe this insight to Robert B. Pippin, 'Nietzsche and the Origins of Modernism', *Inquiry*, 26 (1983), 151–80, at 162.

8 NIETZSCHE AND CONTEMPORARY LIBERALISM

1 R. Rorty, *Contingency, Irony, and Solidarity* (Cambridge: Cambridge University Press, 1989), Introduction.
2 Ibid., p. 3.
3 Ibid., p. 27.
4 Ibid., p. 29.
5 Ibid., p. 35.
6 Ibid.
7 See P. Rieff, *Freud. The Mind of the Moralist* (London: Methuen, 1965).
8 Rorty, *Contingency, Irony, and Solidarity*, p. 45.
9 Ibid., p. 53.
10 Ibid., p. 54.
11 For further exploration of this distinction see the classic essay by Isaiah Berlin, 'Two Concepts of Liberty' in A. Quinton (ed.), *Political Philosophy* (Oxford: Oxford University Press, 1967), pp. 141–53.
12 Rorty, *Contingency, Irony, and Solidarity*, p. 65.
13 William E. Connolly, *Political Theory and Modernity* (Oxford: Basil Blackwell, 1988).
14 Ibid., p. 66.
15 Ibid., p. 136.
16 See M. Foucault, *Power/Knowledge: Selected Interviews and Other Writings 1972–77*, ed. C. Gordon (Brighton: Harvester Press, 1980), p. 53.
17 M. Foucault, *The History of Sexuality: Volume One*, trans. R. Hurley (Middlesex: Penguin, 1979), p. 93.

18 M. Foucault, *Power/Knowledge*, p. 95.
19 See M. Walzer, 'The Communitarian Critique of Liberalism', *Political Theory*, 18:1 (February 1990), 6–23, at 21. Walzer has also defended the modern tradition against Foucault, arguing that it provides a kind of knowledge, in the form of political philosophy and philosophical jurisprudence, which 'regulates disciplinary arrangements across our society', thus offering a 'critical perspective' on all networks of constraint. See M. Walzer, 'The Politics of Michel Foucault', in D. C. Hoy (ed.), *Foucault. A Critical Reader* (Oxford: Basil Blackwell, 1986), pp. 51–69, at p. 66.
20 Connolly, *Political Theory and Modernity*, p. 139.
21 Ibid., p. 140.
22 See J. Rawls, *A Theory of Justice* (Oxford: Oxford University Press, 1972). For a 'Nietzschean' critique of Rawls see Allan Bloom, *The American Political Science Review*, 69 (1975), 648–62. Bloom calls Rawls' theory 'A First Philosophy for the Last Man'.
23 Connolly, *Political Theory and Modernity*, p. 175.
24 Ibid., p. 174.
25 G. Deleuze, 'Nomad Thought', in D. B. Allison (ed.), *The New Nietzsche* (Cambridge, Massachusetts: MIT Press, 1985), pp. 148–9.

9 NIETZSCHE AND FEMINISM

1 See James A. Winders, *Gender, Theory, and the Canon* (Madison: University of Wisconsin Press, 1991), pp. 120–3.
2 Gilles Deleuze, *Nietzsche and Philosophy* (1962), trans. H. Tomlinson (London: Athlone Press, 1983).
3 The English translation of this fragment in volume two of the Oscar Levy edition of *The Complete Works of Friedrich Nietzsche* (London, T. N. Foulis, 1911), is incomplete. The complete fragment can be found in volume seven of G. Colli's and M. Montinari's *Kritische Studienausgabe* (Munich, Berlin/New York, Deutscher Taschenbuch Verlag, Walter de Gruyter, 1988), 7 [122], pp. 170–6. The fragment originally formed chapter 13 of an early version of *The Birth of Tragedy*. See *KSA* 7, p. 135 for the original plan.
4 It is important to appreciate that when Nietzsche talks of the 'Greek State' he is not thinking of the 'State' in terms of 'nation' or 'race'. Thus, for example, in a *Nachlass* note of 1870–1 he argues that the 'nationality principle (*Nationalitätenprincip*) is a barbaric crudity compared to the city-state (*Stadt-Staat*)'. See *KSA* 7, 7 [37], p. 147.
The point Nietzsche is making here finds an echo in a piece

written by Neal Ascherson in the *Independent on Sunday*, 31 January
1993, reflecting on the troubles and conflicts in the former
Yugoslavia: 'we do not have the words to describe the roots of this
crisis, but repeat the legends of dead emperors and the exploded
myths of racial ethnicity. An Athenian from the fifth century BC
would be baffled. For him, the city-state or *polis* was a structure,
not a blood relationship... Above all, he would be baffled by our
inability to describe nations in terms which are rational, not
blurred by superstition and pseudo-science. For the New World
Disorder is also, and above all, in our heads.'

5 Nietzsche's hostility towards the modern European conception of
'woman' is, in part, derived from Schopenhauer, who writes:

Woman in the Occident, that is to say, the 'lady', finds herself in a false
position: for woman is by no means fitted to be the object of our
veneration, to hold her head higher than the man or to enjoy equal rights
with him... The European lady is a creature which ought not to exist at
all: what there ought to be is housewives and girls who hope to become
housewives and who are therefore educated, not in arrogant haughtiness,
but in domesticity and submissiveness. It is precisely because there are
ladies that European women of a lower status, which is to say the great
majority of the sex, are much more unhappy than they are in the Orient.
(From *Essays and Aphorisms*, trans. R. J. Hollingdale (Middlesex: Penguin,
1970), p. 87.)

6 Rosalyn Diprose, 'Nietzsche, Ethics, and Sexual Difference',
   Radical Philosophy, 52 (Summer 1989), pp. 27–33, p. 31.
7 Ibid.
8 Ibid., p. 32.
9 Jacques Derrida, *Spurs. Nietzsche's Styles*, trans. B. Harlow (Chicago: University of Chicago Press, 1979), p. 65.
10 Ibid., p. 55.
11 Ibid., p. 101.
12 Kelly Oliver, 'Woman as Truth in Nietzsche's Writing', *Social
   Theory and Practice*, 10:2 (1984), 185–99, at 187.
13 Ibid., p. 188.
14 Ibid., p. 193.
15 Ibid., p. 195.
16 Ibid., p. 196.
17 Winders, *Gender, Theory, and the Canon*, p. 121.
18 Derrida, *Spurs*, p. 107.
19 Kelly Oliver, 'Nietzsche's Woman: The Poststructuralist Attempt
   to do away with Women', *Radical Philosophy*, 48 (Spring 1988),
   25–9.

20 Rosi Braidotti, 'The Ethics of Sexual Difference: the Case of Foucault and Irigaray', *Australian Feminist Studies*, 3 (1986), 1–13, at 2.

21 Adrian Del Caro, 'The Pseudoman in Nietzsche, or the Threat of the Neuter', *New German Critique*, 50 (Spring/Summer 1990), 133–56, at 145.

22 Ibid., p. 156.

23 Sarah Kofman, 'Baubô: Theological Perversion and Fetishism', trans. T. B. Strong, in T. B. Strong and M. A. Gillespie (eds.), *Nietzsche's New Seas* (Chicago: University of Chicago Press, 1988), pp. 175–202, at p. 197.

24 Ibid.

25 See Toril Moi, *Sexual/Textual Politics* (London: Routledge, 1988), pp. 127–50 for such a critique of Irigaray.

26 Luce Irigaray, *Speculum of the Other Woman* (1974), trans. G. C. Gill (New York: Columbia University Press, 1985), p. 224.

27 Luce Irigaray, *Marine Lover of Friedrich Nietzsche*, trans. G. C. Gill (New York: Columbia University Press, 1991), p. 25.

28 Ibid., p. 23.

29 Ibid., p. 34.

30 See Peter Sloterdijk, 'Eurotaoism', in Tom Darby et al. (eds.), *Nietzsche and the Rhetoric of Nihilism* (Ottowa, Ontario: Carleton University Press, 1988), pp. 99–116, at 110–11.

31 Ibid., p. 110.

32 Diana Coole, *Women and Political Theory* (Brighton: Harvester Press, 1988), p. 3.

33 Hélène Cixous and Catherine Clément, *The Newly Born Woman*, trans. B. Wing (Minneapolis: University of Minnesota Press, 1986), p. 81.

34 Ibid., p. 83.

10   THE PERFECT NIHILIST

1 In section 27 of the third essay of the *Genealogy of Morals* Nietzsche uses two terms interchangeably, speaking of '*Selbstaufhebung*' as the 'law of life' (*Gesetz des Lebens*) and of the law of the necessary '*Selbstüberwindung*' in the 'essence of life' (*Wesen des Lebens*). See Nietzsche, *KSA*, 5, 411; trans. *OGM* III, 27. Nietzsche construes the 'self-overcoming of morality', in terms both of a 'self-dissolution' and a 'self-conquest' or 'self-surmounting'.

2 A good example of this is the transition from essays two to three of the *Genealogy of Morals*. Nietzsche ends the second essay on a highly redemptive note, referring to 'the one', namely Zarathustra, 'who

must come one day, this victor over God and nothingness'. However, he begins the third essay, an inquiry into the meaning of ascetic ideals (including Nietzsche's ideals) by citing a passage from the discourse on 'Reading and Writing' in *Zarathustra*, drawing, albeit obliquely, the reader's attention to the need for an 'art of interpretation' when reading the text and deciphering its precise meaning.

3 A precedent for my reading of Nietzsche, in which I am proposing that his thinking be appropriated and taken up as a kind of fate beyond good and evil, can be found in Nietzsche's own reception of Wagner. In the preface to his *Case of Wagner*, for example, Nietzsche speaks of Wagner as one of his sicknesses, and writes, instructively:

> When in this essay I assert the proposition that Wagner is harmful, I wish no less to assert for whom he is nevertheless indispensable – for the philosopher... the philosopher is not free to do without Wagner. He has to be the bad conscience of his time: for that he needs to understand it best. Confronted with the labyrinth of the modern soul, where could he find a guide more initiated...? Through Wagner modernity speaks most intimately concealing neither its good nor its evil – having forgotten all sense of shame. And conversely: one has almost completed an account of the value of what is modern once one has gained clarity about what is good and evil in Wagner.

> Just as Nietzsche did in the cases of Schopenhauer and Wagner, therefore, it is possible for modern human beings to educate themselves about their age through a confrontation with his writings. But to do this effectively it is necessary that one resist the temptation of adopting a position which is simply 'for' or 'against' Nietzsche. For me this practice of reading 'beyond good and evil' – *in order to comprehend what is good and evil* – almost constitutes a definition of a philosophical education.

4 This draft preface appears in Walter Kaufmann's introduction to the Kaufmann and Hollingdale translation of *The Will To Power*.

Bibliography

The following bibliography includes all the works cited in the notes, as well as several books and essays I have consulted while researching the book.

PRIMARY SOURCES

Arendt, H., *The Human Condition*, New York, Doubleday, 1959.
   Between Past and Future. Eight Exercises in Political Theory, Middlesex, Penguin, 1983.
Aristotle, *Politics*, Cambridge, Cambridge University Press, 1988.
Berlin, I., 'Two Concepts of Liberty', in A. Quinton (ed.), *Political Philosophy*, Oxford, Oxford University Press, 1967.
Cixous, H., and Clément, C., *The Newly Born Woman*, trans. B. Wing, Minneapolis, University of Minnesota Press, 1986.
Foucault, M., *The History of Sexuality. Volume One*, Middlesex, Penguin, 1979.
   Power/Knowledge. Selected Interviews and Other Writings 1972–77, ed. C. Gordon, Brighton, Harvester Press, 1980.
Freud, S., *Civilisation and Its Discontents*, Middlesex, Penguin, 1985.
Hegel, G. W. F., *Philosophy of Right*, Oxford, Oxford University Press, 1967.
Hobbes, T., *Leviathan*, Cambridge, Cambridge University Press, 1990.
Irigaray, L., *Speculum of the Other Woman*, trans. G. C. Gill, New York, Columbia University Press, 1985.
Kant, I., *Groundwork of the Metaphysics of Morals*, New York, Harper and Row, 1964.
Locke, J., *Two Treatises on Government*, Cambridge, Cambridge University Press, 1988.
Machiavelli, N., *The Prince*, Cambridge, Cambridge University Press, 1988.
   Discourses, Middlesex, Penguin, 1983.

Marx, K., *The Early Writings*, trans. R. Livingstone, Middlesex, Penguin, 1975.

Marx, K. and Engels, F., *The German Ideology*, London, Lawrence and Wishart, 1977.

Mill, J. S., *On Liberty*, Cambridge, Cambridge University Press, 1989.

Plato, *The Republic*, Middlesex, Penguin, 1970.

   Gorgias, Indianapolis, Bobbs-Merrill Co., 1979.

Rawls, J., *A Theory of Justice*, Oxford, Oxford University Press, 1972.

Rousseau, J. J., *The Social Contract and Discourses*, trans. G. D. H. Cole, London, Dent, 1973.

Schopenhauer, A., *The World as Will and Representation* (two volumes), trans. E. F. J. Payne, New York, Dover, 1958.

   Essays and Aphorisms, trans. R. J. Hollingdale, Middlesex, Penguin, 1970.

Sophocles, *Theban Plays*, Middlesex, Penguin, 1974.

Turgenev, I., *Fathers and Sons*, Middlesex, Penguin, 1975.

Walzer, M., *Spheres of Justice. A Defence of Pluralism and Equality*, Oxford, Basil Blackwell, 1983.

SECONDARY SOURCES

Ansell-Pearson, K., *Nietzsche contra Rousseau*, Cambridge, Cambridge University Press, 1991.

   'Nietzsche on Autonomy and Morality: the Challenge to Political Theory', *Political Studies*, 34 (June 1991), 270–86.

Barker, E., *Greek Political Theory. Plato and His Predecessors*, London, Methuen, 1977.

Bataille, G., 'Nietzsche and the Fascists', in *Visions of Excess: Selected Writings 1927–39*, Manchester, Manchester University Press, 1989.

   On Nietzsche, trans. B. Boone (London: Athlone Press, 1992).

Bergmann, P., *Nietzsche. The 'Last Anti-Political German'*, Bloomington, Indiana University Press, 1987.

Bernstein, R. J., 'One Step Forward, Two Steps Backward: Richard Rorty on Liberal Democracy and Philosophy', *Political Theory*, 15 (November 1987), 538–63.

Bloom, A., 'Justice: John Rawls Vs. The Tradition of Political Philosophy', *American Political Science Review*, 69 (1975), 648–62.

Bogue, R., *Deleuze and Guattari*, London, Routledge, 1989.

Braidotti, R., 'The Ethics of Sexual Difference: The Case of Foucault and Irigaray', *Australian Feminist Studies*, 3 (1986), 1–13.

Brandes, G., *Friedrich Nietzsche*, London, Heinemann, 1914.

Camus, A., *The Rebel*, Middlesex, Penguin, 1971.

Canovan, M., 'On Being Economical with the Truth: Some Liberal Reflections', *Political Studies*, 38 (March 1990), 5–20.

Cantor, P., 'Friedrich Nietzsche: the Use and Abuse of Metaphor', in D. S. Miall (ed.), *Metaphor. Problems and Perspectives*, Brighton, Harvester Press, 1982, pp. 71–89.

Castoriadis, C., *Philosophy, Politics, Autonomy: Essays in Political Philosophy*, Oxford, Oxford University Press, 1991.

Clark, M., *Nietzsche on Truth and Philosophy*, Cambridge, Cambridge University Press, 1990.

Connolly, W. E., *Political Theory and Modernity*, Oxford, Basil Blackwell, 1988.

Conway, D. W., 'Overcoming the *Übermensch*: Nietzsche's Revaluation of Values', *Journal of the British Society for Phenomenology*, 20 (October 1989), 211–24.

'Thus Spoke Rorty: The Perils of Narrative Self-Creation', *Philosophy and Literature*, 15 (1991), 103–10.

Coole, D., *Women and Political Theory*, Brighton, Harvester Press, 1988.

Dannhauser, W. J., *Nietzsche's View of Socrates*, Ithaca, Cornell University Press, 1974.

'Friedrich Nietzsche', in J. Cropsey and L. Strauss (eds.), *History of Political Philosophy*, Chicago, University of Chicago Press, 1987, pp. 829–51.

Danto, A. C., *Nietzsche as Philosopher*, New York, Macmillan, 1965.

Del Caro, A., 'The Pseudoman in Nietzsche, or the Threat of the Neuter', *New German Critique*, 50 (Spring/Summer 1990), 133–56.

Deleuze, G., *Nietzsche and Philosophy*, trans. H. Tomlinson, London, Athlone Press, 1983.

'Nomad Thought', in D. B. Allison (ed.), *The New Nietzsche*, Cambridge, Massachusetts: MIT Press, 1985, pp. 142–50.

Derrida, J., *Spurs. Nietzsche's Styles*, trans. B. Harlow (Chicago: University of Chicago Press, 1979).

'Otobiographies: Nietzsche and the Politics of the Proper Name', in H. Bloom (ed.), *Friedrich Nietzsche*, New York, Chelsea House Publishers, 1987, pp. 105–34.

'Interpreting Signatures (Nietzsche/Heidegger): Two Questions', in L. Rickels (ed.), *Looking After Nietzsche*, Albany, State University of New York Press, 1990, pp. 1–19.

Detwiler, B., *Nietzsche and the Politics of Aristocratic Radicalism*, Chicago, University of Chicago Press, 1990.

Diethe, C., 'Nietzsche and the Other Woman' (unpublished).

Diprose, R., 'Nietzsche, Ethics, and Sexual Difference', *Radical Philosophy*, 52 (1989), 27–33.

Dodds, E. R., 'On Misunderstanding *Oedipus Rex*', in M. J. O'Brien (ed.), *Twentieth Century Interpretations of Oedipus Rex*, New Jersey, Prentice-Hall, 1968, pp. 17–30.

Dossa, S., *The Public Realm and the Public Self. The Political Theory of Hannah Arendt*, Waterloo, Ontario, Wilfred Laurier University Press, 1989.

Fischer, K. R., 'Nazism as a Nietzschean Experiment', *Nietzsche Studien*, 6 (1977), 116–22.

Foot, P., 'Nietzsche: The Revaluation of All Values', in P. Foot, *Virtues and Vices*, Oxford, Oxford University Press, 1978, pp. 81–96.

'Nietzsche's Immoralism', *New York Review of Books* (13 June 1991), 18–22.

Foucault, M., 'Nietzsche, Genealogy, and History', in P. Rabinow (ed.), *The Foucault Reader*, Middlesex, Penguin, 1984.

Gunnell, J., *Political Philosophy and Time*, Connecticut, Wesleyan University Press, 1968.

Habermas, J., 'The Entwinement of Myth and Enlightenment: Rereading *Dialectic of Enlightenment*', *New German Critique*, 26 (1983), 13–30.

Harris, E. E., 'Time and Eternity', Review of Metaphysics, 29:3 (March 1976), 464–83.

Hayman, R., *Nietzsche. A Crucial Life*, London, Quartet Books, 1980.

Heidegger, M., 'The Word of Nietzsche: "God is Dead"', in M. Heidegger, *The Question Concerning Technology and Other Essays*, trans. W. Lovitt, New York, Harper and Row, 1977, pp. 53–115.

'Who is Nietzsche's Zarathustra?' in D. B. Allison (ed.), *The New Nietzsche*, Cambridge, Massachusetts, MIT Press, 1985, pp. 64–80.

Heller, E., *The Importance of Nietzsche. Ten Essays*, Chicago, University of Chicago Press, 1988.

Higgins, K. and Solomon, R. C. (eds.), *Reading Nietzsche*, Oxford, Oxford University Press, 1988.

Hinton-Thomas, R., *Nietzsche in German Politics and Society 1890–1918*, Manchester, Manchester University Press, 1983.

Holborn, H., *A History of Modern Germany 1648–1840*, London, 1965.

Hollingdale, R. J., 'Nietzsche and Politics' (unpublished paper, 1992).

Irigaray, L., *Marine Lover of Friedrich Nietzsche*, trans. G. C. Gill, New York, Columbia University Press, 1991.

Kaufmann, W., *Nietzsche. Philosopher, Psychologist, and Antichrist*, New Jersey, Princeton University Press, 1974.

Kennedy, E., 'Women as *Übermensch*', in E. Kennedy and S. Mendus (eds.), *Women in Western Political Philosophy*, Brighton, Wheatsheaf, 1987, pp. 179–201.

Kofman, S., 'Baubô: Theological Perversion and Fetishism', trans. T. B. Strong, in M. A. Gillespie and T. B. Strong (eds.), *Nietzsche's New Seas*, Chicago, University of Chicago Press, 1988, pp. 175–202.

Kraut, R., *Socrates and the State*, New Jersey, Princeton University Press, 1984.

Kuenzli, R. E., 'The Nazi Appropriation of Nietzsche', *Nietzsche Studien*, 12 (1983), 428–35.

Lacoue-Labarthe, P., 'History and Mimesis', in L. Rickels (ed.), *Looking after Nietzsche*, Albany, State University of New York Press, 1990, pp. 209–33.

Lampert, L., *Nietzsche's Teaching*, New Haven, Yale University Press, 1987.

Leonard, J., 'Public versus Private Claims: Machiavellianism from Another Perspective', *Political Theory* 12 (November 1984), 491–506.

Love, N. S., *Marx, Nietzsche, and Modernity*, New York, Columbia University Press, 1986.

Löwy, M., *Georg Lukács: From Romanticism to Bolshevism*, London, New Left Books, 1979.

MacIntyre, A., *After Virtue. A Study in Moral Theory*, London, Duckworth, 1981.

MacIntyre, B., *Forgotten Fatherland. The Search for Elisabeth Förster-Nietzsche*, London, Macmillan, 1992.

MacPherson, C. B., *The Political Theory of Possessive Individualism*, Oxford, Oxford University Press, 1962.

Magnus, B., 'Nietzsche's Eternalistic Counter-Myth', *Review of Metaphysics*, 26 (1973), 604–16.

Nietzsche's Existential Imperative, Bloomington, Indiana University Press, 1978.

'Perfectibility and Attitude in Nietzsche's *Übermensch*', *Review of Metaphysics*, 36 (March 1983), 633–59.

'Nietzsche's Philosophy in 1888: *The Will To Power* and the *Übermensch*', *Journal of the History of Philosophy*, 24 (1986), 79–98.

Mann, G., *The History of Germany Since 1789*, Middlesex, Penguin, 1985.

Mann, T., *Nietzsche's Philosophy in the Light of Contemporary Events*, Washington, Library of Congress, 1947.

McIntyre, A., '"Virtuosos of Contempt": An Investigation of Nietzsche's Political Philosophy through Certain Platonic Political Ideas', *Nietzsche-Studien*, 21 (1992), 184–210.

Melzer, A. M., *The Natural Goodness of Man. On the System of Rousseau's Thought*, Chicago: University of Chicago Press, 1990.

Miller, D. (ed.), *The Blackwell Encyclopaedia of Political Thought*, Oxford, Basil Blackwell, 1987.

Moi, T., Sexual/Textual Politics, London, Routledge, 1988.

Müller-Lauter, W., *Nietzsche. Seine Philosophie der Gegensätze und die Gegensätze seiner Philosophie*, Berlin and New York, Walter de Gruyter, 1971.

Nehamas, A., 'The Eternal Recurrence', *Philosophical Review*, 99 (1980), 331–56.

Nietzsche. Life as Literature, Cambridge, Massachusetts, Harvard University Press, 1985.

Nolte, E., *Der Faschismus in seiner Epoche*, Munich, R. Piper Verlag, 1979, fifth edition.

Nietzsche und der Nietzscheanismus Frankfurt: Propylaen, 1990.

Oliver, K., 'Woman as Truth in Nietzsche's Writing', *Social Theory and Practice*, 10:2 (1984), 185–99.

'Nietzsche's Woman: The Poststructuralist Attempt to do away with Women', *Radical Philosophy*, 48 (Spring 1988), 25–9.

Parekh, B., *Hannah Arendt and the Search for a New Political Philosophy*, London, Macmillan, 1981.

Pateman, C., *The Problem of Political Obligation. A Critique of Liberal Theory*, Oxford, Polity Press, 1985.

Patton, P., 'Politics and the Concept of Power in Hobbes and Nietzsche', in P. Patton (ed.), *Nietzsche, Feminism, and Political Theory*, London, Routledge, 1993.

Peters, H. F., *Zarathustra's Sister. The Case of Elisabeth Förster-Nietzsche*, New York, 1977.

Pippin, R. B., 'Nietzsche and the Origins of Modernism', *Inquiry*, 26 (1983), 151–80.

Rieff, P., *Freud. The Mind of the Moralist*, London, Methuen, 1965.

Rorty, R., *Contingency, Irony, and Solidarity*, Cambridge, Cambridge University Press, 1989.

'Thugs and Theorists. A Reply to Bernstein', *Political Theory*, 15 (November 1987), 564–80.

Rosen, S., 'Nietzsche's Revolution', in S. Rosen, *The Ancients and Moderns*, New Haven, Yale University Press, 1989.

Sallis, J., *Crossings. Nietzsche and the Space of Tragedy*, Chicago, University of Chicago Press, 1991.

Salomé, L. A., *Friedrich Nietzsche. The Man in his Works*, Connecticut, Black Swan Books, 1988.

Scheler, M., '*Ressentiment*', in R. C. Solomon (ed.), *Nietzsche. A Collection of Critical Essays*, New York, Macmillan, 1973, pp. 243–58.

Schutte, O., *Beyond Nihilism. Nietzsche Without Masks*, Chicago, University of Chicago Press, 1984.

Shapiro, G., 'Nietzschean Aphorism as Art and Act', *Man and World* 17 (1984), 399–429.

Nietzschean Narratives, Bloomington, Indiana University Press, 1987.

Alcyone. Nietzsche on Gifts, Noise, and Women, Albany, State University of New York Press, 1991.

Simmel, G., *Schopenhauer and Nietzsche*, Amherst, University of Massachusetts Press, 1986.

Sloterdijk, P., 'Eurotaoism', in T. Darby et al. (eds.), *Nietzsche and the Rhetoric of Nihilism*, Ottawa, Ontario, Carleton University Press, 1988, pp. 99–116.

Solomon, R. C., (ed.), *Nietzsche. A Collection of Critical Essays*, New York, Doubleday, 1973.

'A More Severe Morality: Nietzsche's Affirmative Ethics', *Journal of the British Society for Phenomenology*, 16 (1985), 250–67.

Stambaugh, J., *Nietzsche's Thought of Eternal Return*, Baltimore, Johns Hopkins University Press, 1972.

Staten, H., *Nietzsche's Voice*, New York, Cornell University Press, 1990.

Stern, J. P. *Nietzsche*, Glasgow, Collins, 1978.

Stone, I. F., *The Trial of Socrates*, London, Jonathan Cape Ltd., 1988.

Strauss, L., 'Three Waves of Modernity', in L. Strauss, *Political Philosophy. Six Essays*, Indianapolis, Bobbs-Merrill, 1975, pp. 81–98.

Strong, T. B., *Friedrich Nietzsche and the Politics of Transfiguration*, Berkeley, University of California Press, 1975.

'Nietzsche's Political Aesthetics', in T. B. Strong and M. A. Gillespie (eds.), *Nietzsche's New Seas*, Chicago, University of Chicago Press, 1988, pp. 153–74.

'Aesthetic Authority and the Tradition: The Greeks and Nietzsche', *History of European Ideas*, 11 (1989), 989–1007.

Sugarman, R. I., *Rancor Against Time. The Phenomenology of 'Ressentiment'*, Hamburg, Felix Meiner Verlag, 1983.

Taylor, C., *Hegel and Modern Society*, Cambridge, Cambridge University Press, 1979.

Tuck, R., *Hobbes*, Oxford, Oxford University Press, 1989.

Villa, D. R., 'Beyond Good and Evil: Arendt, Nietzsche, and the Aestheticization of Political Action', *Political Theory* 20 (May 1992), 274–308.

Walzer, M., *Spheres of Justice. A Defence of Pluralism and Equality*, Oxford, Basil Blackwell, 1983.

'The Politics of Michel Foucault', in D. C. Hoy (ed.), *Foucault: A Critical Reader*, Oxford, Basil Blackwell, 1986, pp. 51–69.

'The Communitarian Critique of Liberalism', *Political Theory*, 18 (February 1990), 6–23.

Warren, M., *Nietzsche and Political Thought*, Cambridge, Massachusetts, MIT Press, 1988.

White, S. K., 'Heidegger and the Difficulties of a Postmodern Ethics and Politics', *Political Theory* 18 (February 1990), 80–103.

Williams, H., 'Nietzsche and Fascism', *History of European Ideas*, 11 (1989), 893–9.

Winders, J. A., *Gender, Theory, and the Canon*, Madison, University of Wisconsin Press, 1991.

Winnington-Ingram, R. P., 'The *Oedipus Tyrannus* and Greek Archaic Thought', in M. J. O'Brien (ed.), *Twentieth Century Interpretations of Oedipus Rex*, New Jersey, Prentice-Hall, 1968, pp. 81–90.

Wood, E. M., and Wood, N., *Class Ideology and Ancient Political Theory: Socrates, Plato, and Aristotle in Social Context*, Oxford, Basil Blackwell, 1978.

'Socrates and Democracy', *Political Theory* 14 (February 1986), 55–82.

Zuckert, C., 'Nietzsche's Re-reading of Plato', *Political Theory*, 13 (May 1985), 213–38.

A guide to further reading

BIOGRAPHIES AND INTRODUCTIONS

An excellent introduction to Nietzsche's life and thought is R. J. Hollingdale's, *Nietzsche. The Man and His Philosophy*, London, Routledge and Kegan Paul, 1965. For an empathetic life Ronald Hayman's *Nietzsche. A Critical Life*, London, Quartet Books, 1980, can be strongly recommended. In German the definitive biography of Nietzsche is that by C. P. Janz, *Friedrich Nietzsche: Biographie* (in three volumes), Munich, Carl Hanser Verlag, 1978, and to be published in an English translation by Cambridge University Press. A challenging and unusual introduction to Nietzsche's life and thought can be found in Sebastian Barker's poem *The Dream of Intelligence*, Littlewood Arc 1992. On Nietzsche's relationship with Lou Salomé, see Rudolf Binion, *Frau Lou: Nietzsche's Wayward Disciple*, New Jersey, Princeton University Press, 1968. A seriously under-estimated introduction to Nietzsche's life and thought is that by Lou Salomé herself, first published in 1894, *Friedrich Nietzsche. The Man in his Works*, Connecticut, Black Swan Books, 1988 (first English translation by Siegfried Mandel). On Nietzsche and Wagner see Roger Hollingrake, *Nietzsche, Wagner and the Philosophy of Pessimism*, London, Allen and Unwin, 1982. For a biography which is especially pertinent to an understanding of Nietzsche as political thinker see Peter Bergmann, *Nietzsche. The 'Last Anti-Political German'*, Bloomington, Indiana University Press, 1987. Walter Kaufmann's classic study, Nietzsche. *Philosopher, Psychologist, Antichrist* (first published 1950), fourth edition by Princeton University Press, 1974, remains a highly useful introduction to Nietzsche's thought. Kaufmann's book succeeded in rehabilitating Nietzsche after the abuse his principal ideas suffered under the hands of the Nazis, but is perhaps guilty of interpreting Nietzsche too much as a humanist. Other introductions which can be recommended include: Robert Ackermann, *Nietzsche. A Frenzied Look*, Amherst, University of Massachusetts Press, 1990; G. A. Morgan, *What Nietzsche Means* (first published 1941), New York, Harper Torchbooks, 1965; J. P. Stern, *A Study of Nietzsche*, Cambridge University Press, 1979; Alan White, *Within Nietzsche's Labyrinth*, London, Routledge, 1991. A highly useful collection of essays is that edited by R. C. Solomon and K. Higgins, *Reading Nietzsche*, Oxford University Press, 1988, which contains essays on every one of Nietzsche's major books. For the immediate post-war reception of Nietzsche see Thomas Mann, *Nietzsche's Philosophy in the Light of Contemporary Events*, Washington, Library of Congress, 1948, and Albert Camus, *The Rebel* (first published 1951), Penguin, 1971.

NIETZSCHE'S 'NACHLASS'

An interesting collection of some of Nietzsche's early unpublished notes can be found in *Truth and Philosophy: Selections from Nietzsche's Notebooks of the Early 1870s*, edited by Daniel Breazeale, New York, Humanities Press, 1979. A selection of Nietzsche's *Nachlass* (posthumously published material) of the 1880s can be found in *The Will To Power* trans. Hollingdale and Kaufmann, Random House, 1967. The volume plays an increasingly controversial role in the estimation of Nietzsche's philosophy. For an introduction to the debate see the essay by Bernd Magnus, 'Nietzsche's Philosophy in 1888: *The Will To Power* and the *Übermensch*', *Journal of the History of Philosophy*, 24:1 (1986), 79–98. A revised version of this essay appears under the title of 'The Use and Abuse of *The Will To Power*' in Robert C. Solomon and Kathleen Higgins (eds.), *Reading Nietzsche*, Oxford, Oxford University Press, 1988, pp. 218–37.

NIETZSCHE AND PHILOSOPHY

Over the past few decades there have appeared several major studies on Nietzsche as a key figure in the tradition of Western philosophy. The following are the most important ones to date published in English: Arthur C. Danto, *Nietzsche as Philosopher*, New York, Macmillan, 1965; John T. Wilcox, *Truth and Value in Nietzsche: A Study of his Metaethics and Epistemology*, Ann Arbor, University of Michigan Press, 1974; Richard Schacht, *Nietzsche*, London, Routledge, 1983; Maudemarie Clark, *Nietzsche. Philosophy and Truth*, Cambridge University Press, 1990. A useful collection of essays, which seeks to understand Nietzsche's philosophical significance by placing his work in the context of Kant's critical turn in philosophy, is Keith Ansell-Pearson's, *Nietzsche and Modern German Thought*, London, Routledge, 1991. See Karl Jaspers, *Nietzsche. An Introduction to the Understanding of his Philosophical Activity*, Tucson, University of Arizona Press, 1965, for an introduction to Nietzsche by one of the leading existentialist philosophers of this century.

THE NEW NIETZSCHE

Some of the most challenging (and contentious) interpretations of Nietzsche in the past few decades have been those inspired by the readings of his work offered by contemporary French thinking. Those available in English include the seminal study by Gilles Deleuze, *Nietzsche and Philosophy* (first published 1962), trans. Hugh Tomlinson, London, Athlone Press, 1983; Jacques Derrida, *Spurs. Nietzsche's Styles*, trans. Barbara Harlow, Chicago, University of Chicago Press, 1979; and Michel Foucault, 'Nietzsche, Genealogy, and History', in Paul Rabinow (ed.), *A Foucault Reader*, Middlesex, Penguin, 1984. In addition, the following can be signalled out for critical attention: Eric Blondel, *Nietzsche: The Body and Culture. Philosophy/Philological Genealogy*, trans. Sean Hand, Athlone Press, 1991; Pierre Klossowksi, *Nietzsche and the Vicious Circle* (1969), London, Athlone Press (forthcoming); and Sarah Kofman, *Nietzsche and Metaphor* (1972), London, Athlone Press, 1993. Important

collections which bear the influence of the French reading of
Nietzsche are D. B. Allison (ed.), *The New Nietzsche* (first
published 1977), Cambridge, Massachusetts, MIT Press, 1985;
M. A. Gillespie and T. B. Strong (eds.), *Nietzsche's New Seas:
Explorations in Philosophy, Aesthetics, and Politics*, University of
Chicago Press, 1988; and L. Rickels (ed.), *Looking After Nietz-
sche*, Albany, State University of New York Press, 1990. See also
Keith Ansell-Pearson and Howard Caygill (eds.), *The Fate of the
New Nietzsche*, Avebury Press, 1993. A challenging reading of
Nietzsche, inspired by the work of Freud and Derrida, is that
offered by Henry Staten in his *Nietzsche's Voice*, New York,
Cornell University Press, 1990. See also the influential study by
Alexander Nehamas, *Nietzsche. Life as Literature*, Cambridge,
Massachusetts, Harvard University Press, 1985. Informing
almost all of the 'New Nietzsche' readings is Martin Heidegger's
monumental engagement with Nietzsche (delivered in the form
of lectures in the 1930s and 1940s, first published in German in
1961, and translated into English in four volumes 1978–87,
under the editorship of David Farrell Krell). For a good
introduction to Heidegger and Derrida's readings of Nietzsche
see Alan D. Schrift, *Nietzsche and the Question of Interpretation*,
London, Routledge, 1991. For a 'confrontation' with Nietzsche
on the question of man and woman see the remarkable and
unique study by Luce Irigaray, *Marine Lover of Friedrich
Nietzsche*, trans. G. C. Gill, New York, Columbia University
Press, 1991.

NIETZSCHE AND POLITICAL THOUGHT

Recent years have seen the emergence of a serious interest in
Nietzsche's work amongst social and political theorists. The
ground was first broken by Tracy B. Strong in his *Friedrich
Nietzsche and the Politics of Transfiguration*, Berkeley, University of
California Press, 1975 (second edition 1988). Other important
studies include, Ofelia Schutte, *Beyond Nihilism. Nietzsche Without
Masks*, Chicago, University of Chicago Press, 1984; Nancy S.
Love, *Marx, Nietzsche, and Modernity*, New York, Columbia
University Press, 1986; Mark Warren, *Nietzsche and Political*

Thought, Cambridge, Massachusetts, MIT Press, 1988: William E. Connolly, *Political Theory and Modernity*, Oxford, Basil Blackwell, 1988; Bruce Detwiler, *Nietzsche and the Politics of Aristocratic Radicalism*, University of Chicago Press, 1990; Lester H. Hunt, *Nietzsche and the Origin of Virtue*, London, Routledge, 1990; Leslie Paul Thiele, *Nietzsche and the Politics of the Soul. A Study of Heroic Individualism*, New Jersey, Princeton University Press, 1990; Keith Ansell-Pearson, *Nietzsche contra Rousseau*, Cambridge University Press, 1991; David Owen, *Maturity and Modernity: Nietzsche, Weber, and Foucault*, London, Routledge, 1994. A highly critical reading can be found in John Andrew Bernstein, *Nietzsche's Moral Philosophy*, Associated University Presses, 1987. For the most recent appraisal of Nietzsche's status as a political thinker, which includes essays on his significance for feminism, see the collection edited by Paul Patton, *Nietzsche, Feminism, and Political Theory*, London, Routledge, 1993.

ARTICLES AND CHAPTERS

The following is a small selection of articles which, in one way or another, illuminate various aspects of the political dimension of Nietzsche's thought:

Ansell-Pearson, K., 'Nietzsche on Autonomy and Morality: the Challenge to Political Theory', *Political Studies*, 34:2 (June 1991), 270–86.
'Nietzsche, the Will, and the Problem of Modernity', in Ansell-Pearson (ed.), *Nietzsche and Modern German Thought*, London, Routledge, 1991, pp. 165–92.
'The Significance of Michel Foucault's Reading of Nietzsche: Power, the Subject, and Political Theory', *Nietzsche-Studien*, 20 (1991), 267–84.
Bergoffen, D. B., 'Why A Genealogy of Morals?', *Man and World*, 16 (1983), 129–38.
Blitz, M., 'Nietzsche and Political Science: The Problem of Politics', *Symposium*, 28:1 (1974), 74–86.
Cartwright, D. E., 'Kant, Schopenhauer, and Nietzsche on the Morality of Pity', *Journal of the History of Ideas* 45 (January–March 1985), 83–98.
Conway, D. W., 'Solving the Problem of Socrates: Nietzsche's

Zarathustra as Political Irony', *Political Theory* 16:2 (1988), 257–80.

'Nietzsche's Art of This-Worldly Comfort: Self-Reference and Strategic Self-Parody', *History of Philosophical Quarterly*, 9 (July 1992), 343–57.

'Comedians of the Ascetic Ideal: The Performance of Genealogy', in D. W. Conway and J. E. Seery (eds.), *The Politics of Irony*, New York, St Martin's Press, 1992.

Duffy, M. F., and Mittelman, W., 'Nietzsche's Attitude Toward the Jews', *Journal of the History of Ideas* 49 (April–June 1988), 301–17.

Eden, R., 'To what extent has the world of concern to contemporary Man been created by Nietzschean Politics?', in S. Bauschinger et al. (eds.), *Nietzsche heute*, Bern and Stuttgart, Francke Verlag, 1988, pp. 211–27.

Forbes, I., 'Marx and Nietzsche: the Individual in History', in K. Ansell-Pearson, *Nietzsche and Modern German Thought*, London, Routledge, 1991, pp. 143–65.

Golomb, J., 'Nietzsche on Authenticity', *Philosophy Today* (Fall 1990), 243–58.

Kennedy, E., 'Nietzsche: woman as *Untermensch*', in E. Kennedy and S. Mendus (eds.), *Women in Western Political Philosophy*, Brighton, Wheatsheaf, 1987, pp. 179–201.

Miller, J., 'Some Implications of Nietzsche's Thought for Marxism'. *Telos*, 37 (Fall 1978), 22–41.

Newman, M., 'Reading the Future of Genealogy: Kant, Nietzsche, and Plato', in K. Ansell-Pearson (ed.), *Nietzsche and Modern German Thought*, London, Routledge, 1991, 257–82.

Pangle, T. L., 'The Roots of Contemporary Nihilism and its Political Consequences', *Review of Politics*, 45 (1983), 45–70.

Parens, E., 'From Philosophy to Politics: On Nietzsche's ironic Metaphysics of Will to Power', *Man and World*, 24 (1991), 169–80.

Read, J. H., 'Power as Oppression', *Praxis International* 9 (April–July 1989), 72–87.

Rosen, S., 'Nietzsche's Revolution', in S. Rosen, *The Ancients and the Moderns*, New Haven, Yale University Press, 1989.

Schrift, A. D., 'Genealogy and/as Deconstruction: Nietzsche, Derrida, and Foucault on Philosophy as Critique', in Hugh J. Silverman (ed.), *Postmodernism and Continental Philosophy*, State University of New York Press, 1988, pp. 193–213.

Strong, T. B., 'Nietzsche's Political Aesthetics', in M. A. Gillespie and T. B. Strong (eds.), *Nietzsche's New Seas*, Chicago, University of Chicago Press, 1988, pp. 153–74.

Thiele, L. P., 'Nietzsche's Politics', *Interpretation* 17 (Winter 1989–90), 275–90.

Turner, B. S., 'Nietzsche, Weber, and the Devaluation of Politics', *Sociological Review*, 30 (1981), 367–91.

Veyne, P., 'Ideology According to Marx and According to Nietzsche', *Diogenes*, 99 (1977), 80–102.

Voegelin, E., 'Nietzsche, the Crisis, and the War', *Journal of Politics* 6 (1944), 177–211.

Waite, G., 'Zarathustra, or the Modern Prince: The Problem of Political Philosophy', in S. Bauschinger et al. (eds.), *Nietzsche Heute*, Bern and Stuttgart, Francke Verlag, 1988, pp. 227–51.

Warren, M., 'The Politics of Nietzsche's Philosophy of Power: Nihilism, Culture, Power', *Political Studies*, 33:3 (September 1985), 418–38.

White, R., 'The Return of the Master: An Interpretation of Nietzsche's "Genealogy of Morals"', *Philosophy and Phenomenological Research*, 48 (June 1988), 683–96.

Zuckert, C., 'Nietzsche on the Origins and Development of the Distinctively Human', *Polity*, (Fall 1983), 48–71.

Index of Names

Nietzsche is not included in this index as his name appears throughout the book.

240

Index of Subjects